After the war ends, Hatsutaro declares cheerfully that the age of *rakugo* has come. With his unshakable self-confidence, he becomes a rising star among the *futatsume*, and changes his stage name to Sukeroku. Meanwhile, Kikuhiko, yet to discover a *rakugo* style of his own, finds comfort in the arms of a geisha named Miyokichi.

When Kikuhiko plays Benten *kozo* in a *shika-shibai* play, the audience is transfixed. In the heat of that moment, he realizes what his art is for: To allow him to be himself. Now both Sukeroku and Kikuhiko have found their stride, and before long they are promoted to *shin'uchi* together. Kikuhiko decides to devote his life to *rakugo*, and breaks things off with Miyokichi.

Meanwhile, Sukeroku follows his *rakugo* where it takes him until, in an argument with his shisho, he learns that Kikuhiko will inherit the Yakumo name instead of him. Enraged, his dream shattered, he raises his hand against his teacher and is expelled from the Yurakutei lineage.

What does fate hold in store for these two young men caught in *rakugo's* spell?

And will the bond between Kikuhiko, Sukeroku, and Miyokichi survive it?

Cast of Characters

Miyokichi
Future mother of
Konatsu. Works as a
geisha.

Yakumo Yurakutei VII
Kikuhiko and
Sukeroku's shisho
(master).

Sukeroku
Changed his stage name from
Hatsutaro. Still a *futatsume*, but
already a popular draw at the *yose*
(*rakugo* hall).

DESCENDING STORIES

SHOWA
GENROKU
RAKUGO
SHINJU

Contents

Yakumo and Sukeroku

VI..5
VII..51
VIII..97

DESCENDING STORIES

SHOWA GENROKU RAKUGO SHINJU

YAKUMO & SUKEROKU: 6

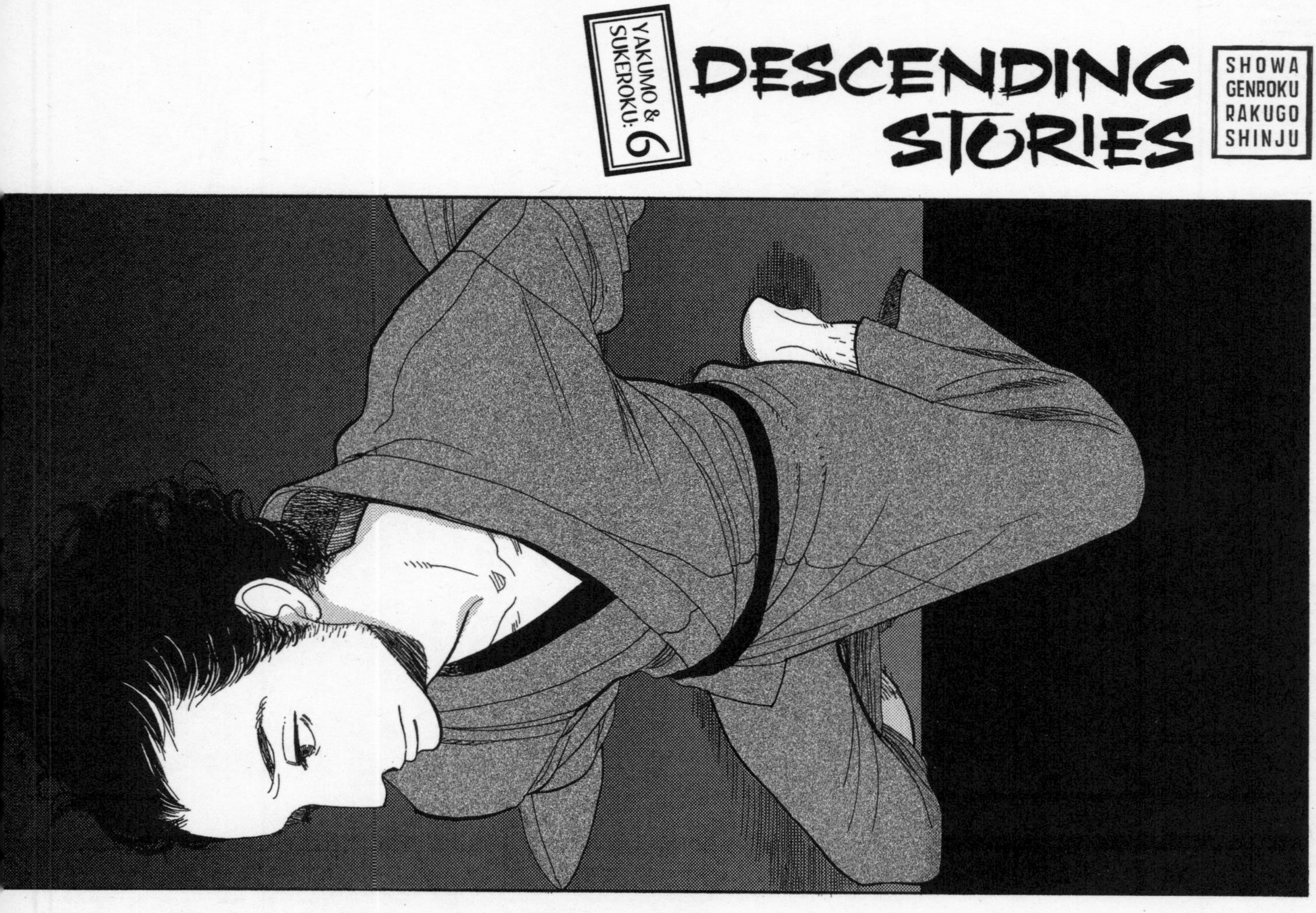

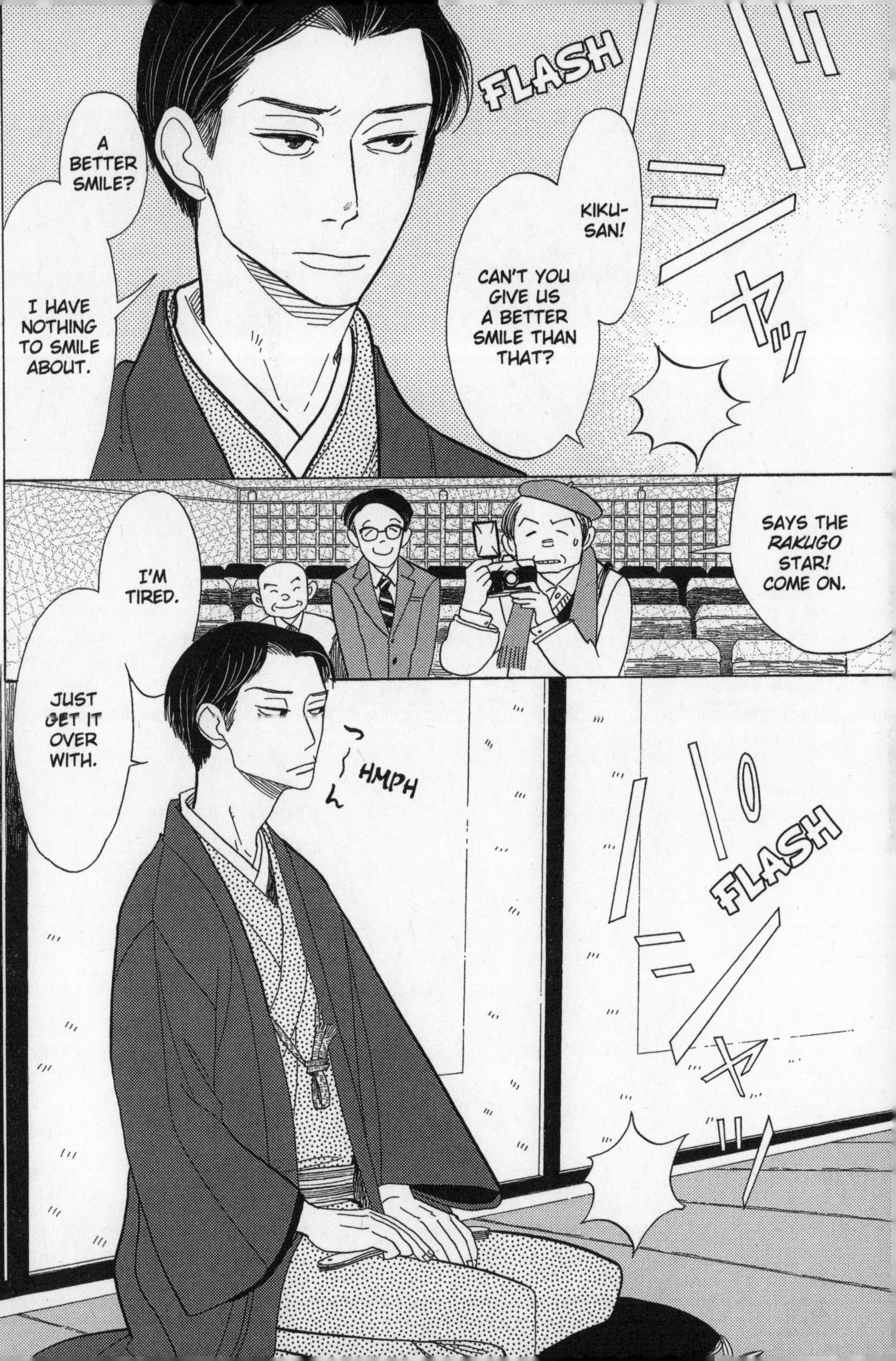
FLASH
KIKU-SAN!
CAN'T YOU GIVE US A BETTER SMILE THAN THAT?
A BETTER SMILE?
I HAVE NOTHING TO SMILE ABOUT.
SAYS THE RAKUGO STAR! COME ON.
I'M TIRED.
JUST GET IT OVER WITH.
FLASH
HMPH

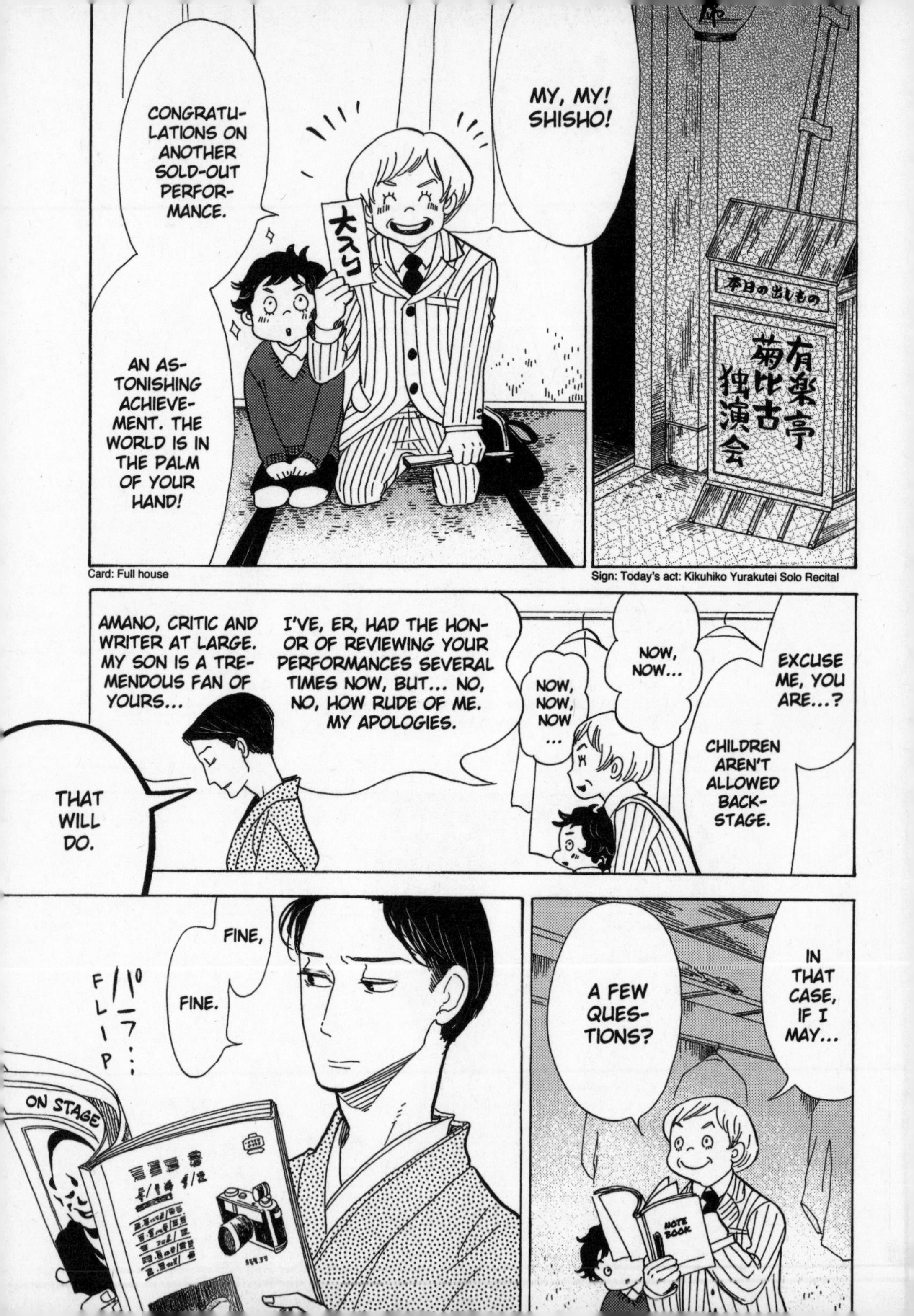

本日の出しもの
有楽亭菊比古独演会
MY, MY! SHISHO!
CONGRATULATIONS ON ANOTHER SOLD-OUT PERFORMANCE.
大入リ
AN ASTONISHING ACHIEVEMENT. THE WORLD IS IN THE PALM OF YOUR HAND!
Card: Full house
Sign: Today's act: Kikuhiko Yurakutei Solo Recital
EXCUSE ME, YOU ARE...?
CHILDREN AREN'T ALLOWED BACKSTAGE.
NOW, NOW...
NOW, NOW, NOW...
I'VE, ER, HAD THE HONOR OF REVIEWING YOUR PERFORMANCES SEVERAL TIMES NOW, BUT... NO, NO, HOW RUDE OF ME. MY APOLOGIES.
AMANO, CRITIC AND WRITER AT LARGE. MY SON IS A TREMENDOUS FAN OF YOURS...
THAT WILL DO.
IN THAT CASE, IF I MAY...
A FEW QUESTIONS?
NOTE BOOK
FINE,
FINE.
FLIP
ON STAGE

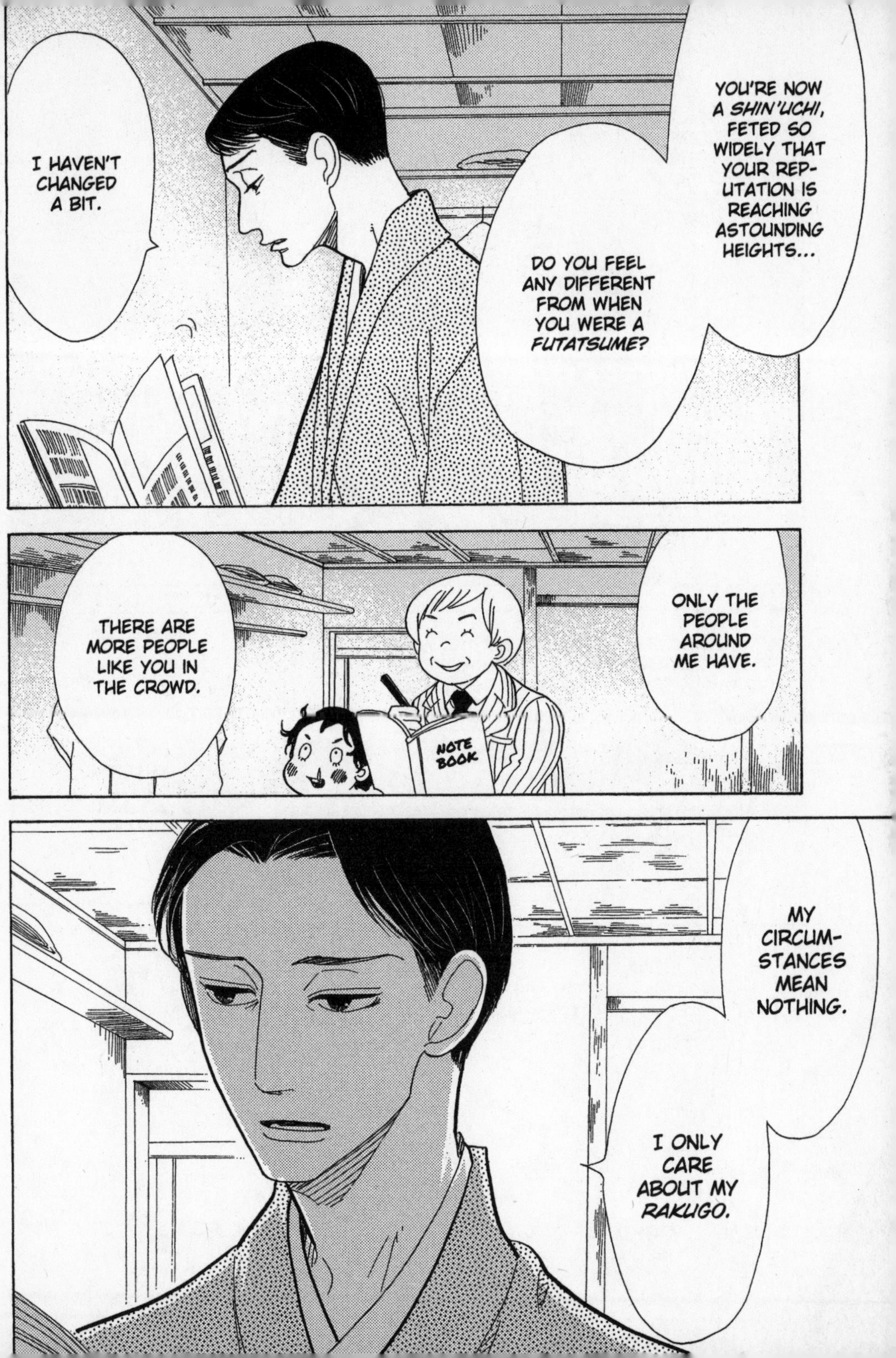
YOU'RE NOW A *SHIN'UCHI*, FETED SO WIDELY THAT YOUR REPUTATION IS REACHING ASTOUNDING HEIGHTS...
DO YOU FEEL ANY DIFFERENT FROM WHEN YOU WERE A *FUTATSUME*?
I HAVEN'T CHANGED A BIT.
ONLY THE PEOPLE AROUND ME HAVE.
THERE ARE MORE PEOPLE LIKE YOU IN THE CROWD.
NOTE BOOK
MY CIRCUMSTANCES MEAN NOTHING.
I ONLY CARE ABOUT MY *RAKUGO*.

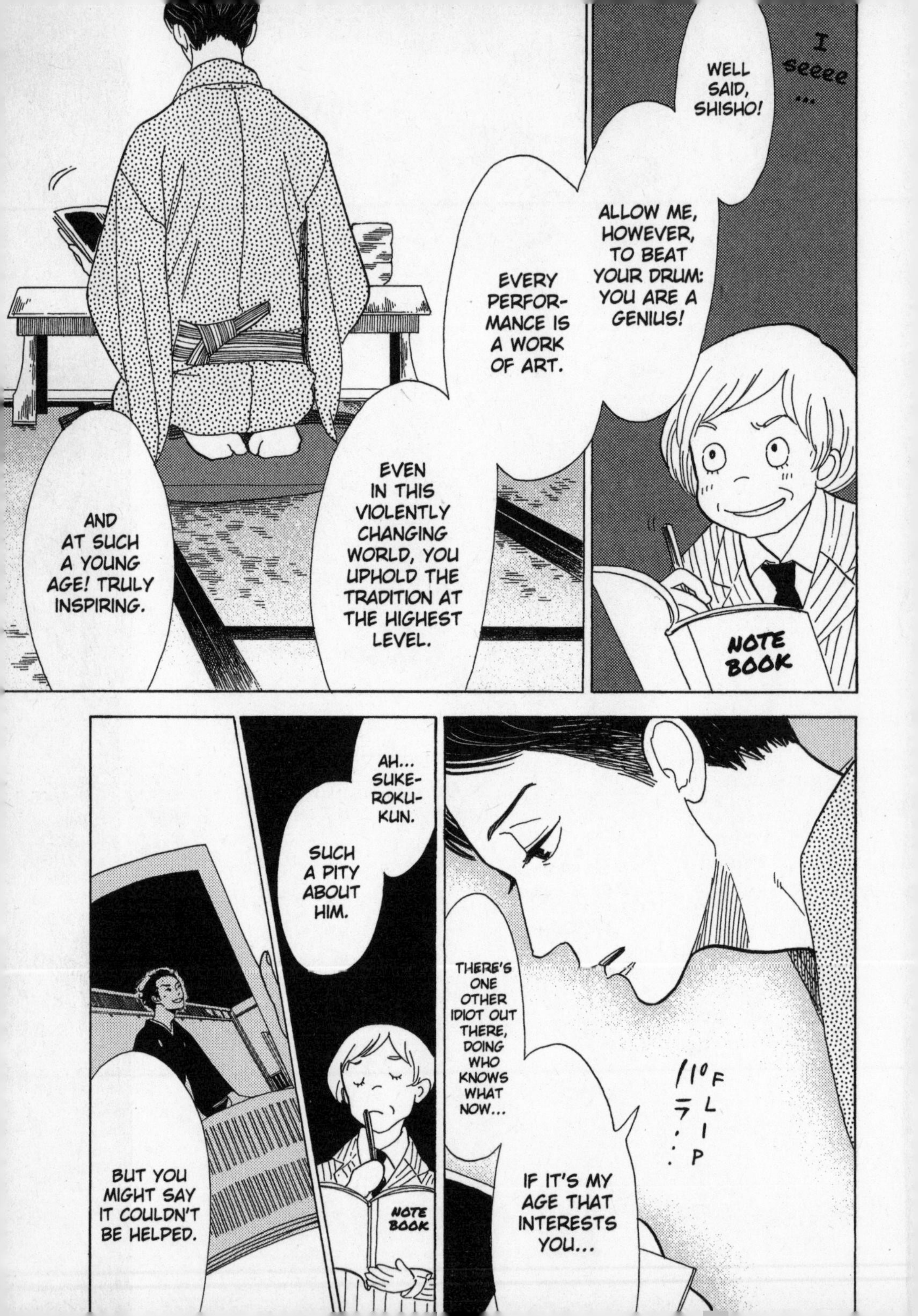
I seeee...
WELL SAID, SHISHO!
ALLOW ME, HOWEVER, TO BEAT YOUR DRUM: YOU ARE A GENIUS!
NOTE BOOK
EVERY PERFORMANCE IS A WORK OF ART.
EVEN IN THIS VIOLENTLY CHANGING WORLD, YOU UPHOLD THE TRADITION AT THE HIGHEST LEVEL.
AND AT SUCH A YOUNG AGE! TRULY INSPIRING.
THERE'S ONE OTHER IDIOT OUT THERE, DOING WHO KNOWS WHAT NOW...
FLIP
IF IT'S MY AGE THAT INTERESTS YOU...
AH... SUKE-ROKU-KUN.
SUCH A PITY ABOUT HIM.
BUT YOU MIGHT SAY IT COULDN'T BE HELPED.
NOTE BOOK

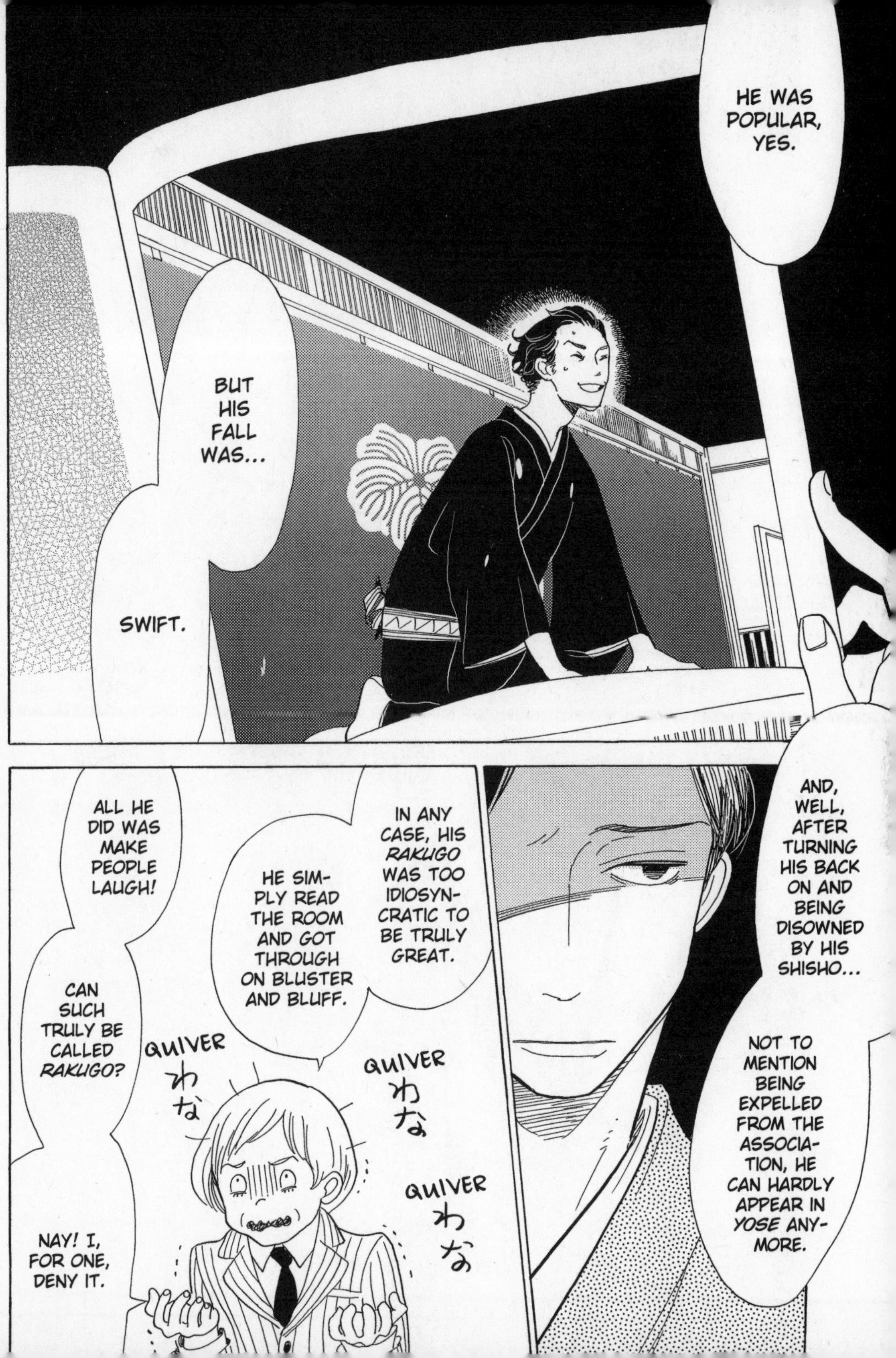
HE WAS POPULAR, YES.
BUT HIS FALL WAS...
SWIFT.
AND, WELL, AFTER TURNING HIS BACK ON AND BEING DISOWNED BY HIS SHISHO...
NOT TO MENTION BEING EXPELLED FROM THE ASSOCIATION, HE CAN HARDLY APPEAR IN *YOSE* ANYMORE.
IN ANY CASE, HIS *RAKUGO* WAS TOO IDIOSYNCRATIC TO BE TRULY GREAT.
HE SIMPLY READ THE ROOM AND GOT THROUGH ON BLUSTER AND BLUFF.
ALL HE DID WAS MAKE PEOPLE LAUGH!
CAN SUCH TRULY BE CALLED *RAKUGO*?
QUIVER わな
QUIVER わな
QUIVER わな
NAY! I, FOR ONE, DENY IT.

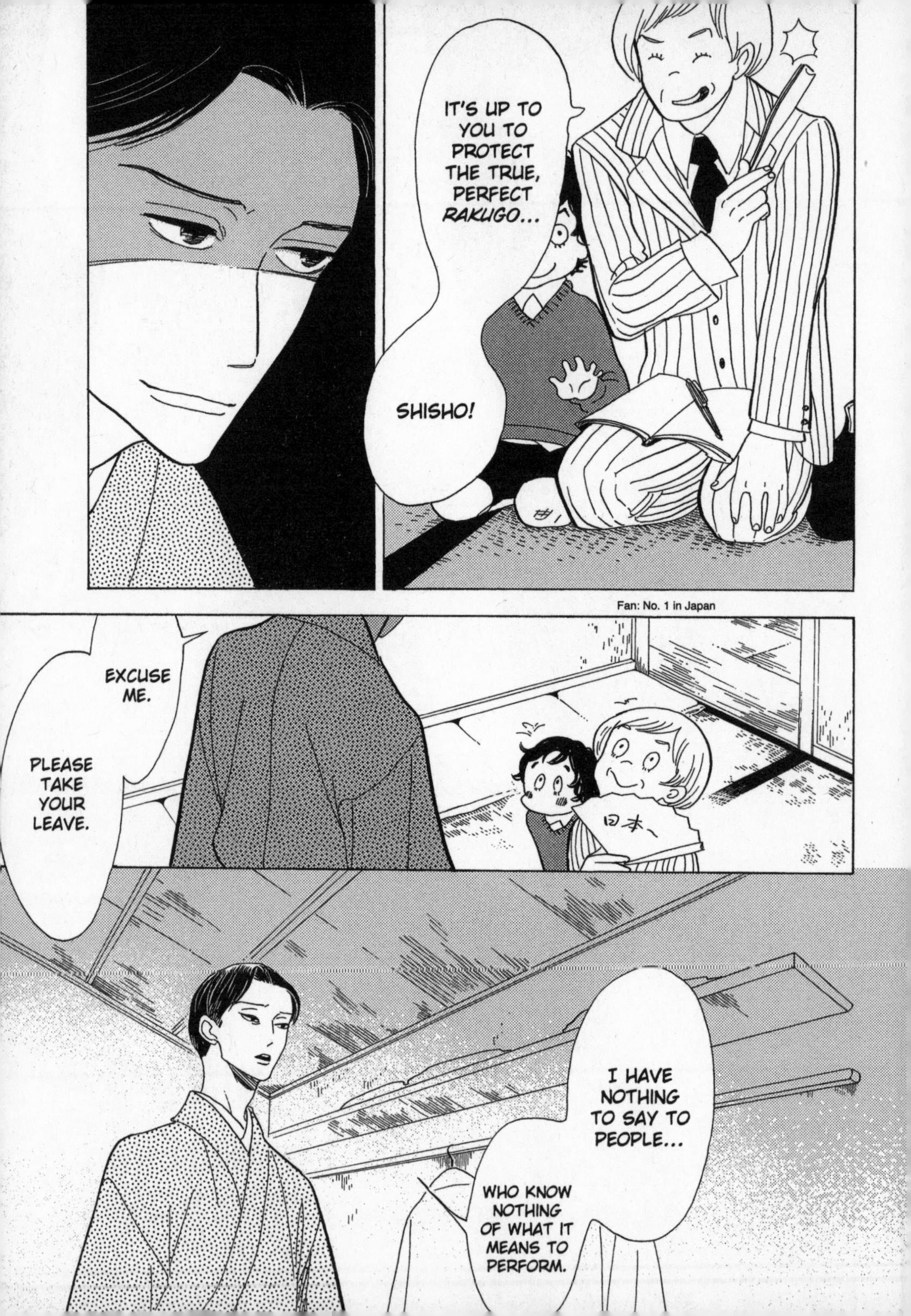
IT'S UP TO YOU TO PROTECT THE TRUE, PERFECT *RAKUGO*...
SHISHO!
Fan: No. 1 in Japan
EXCUSE ME.
PLEASE TAKE YOUR LEAVE.
I HAVE NOTHING TO SAY TO PEOPLE...
WHO KNOW NOTHING OF WHAT IT MEANS TO PERFORM.

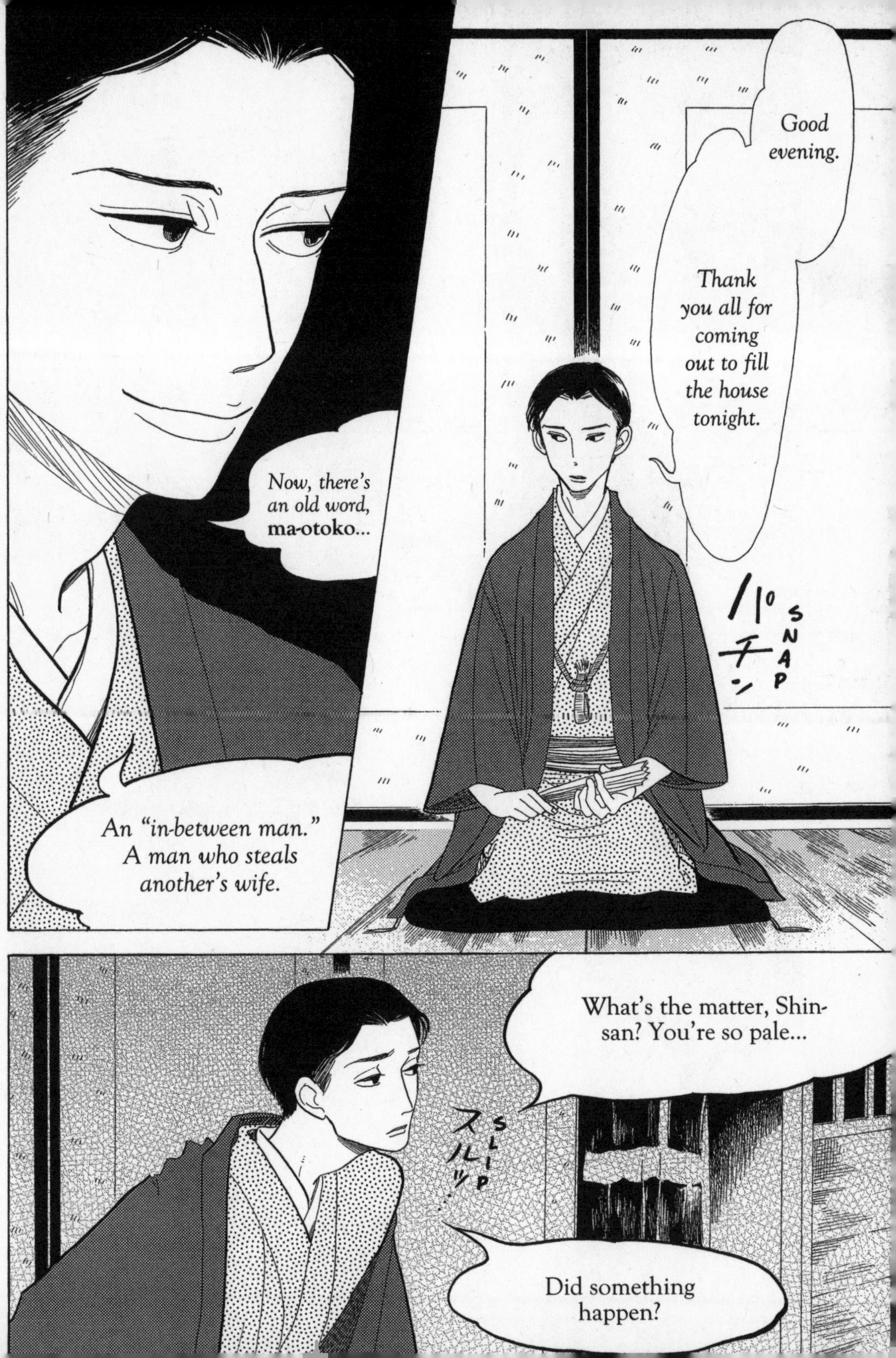
Good evening.
Thank you all for coming out to fill the house tonight.
パチン
SNAP
Now, there's an old word, **ma-otoko**...
An "in-between man." A man who steals another's wife.
What's the matter, Shin-san? You're so pale...
スルッ
SLIP
Did something happen?

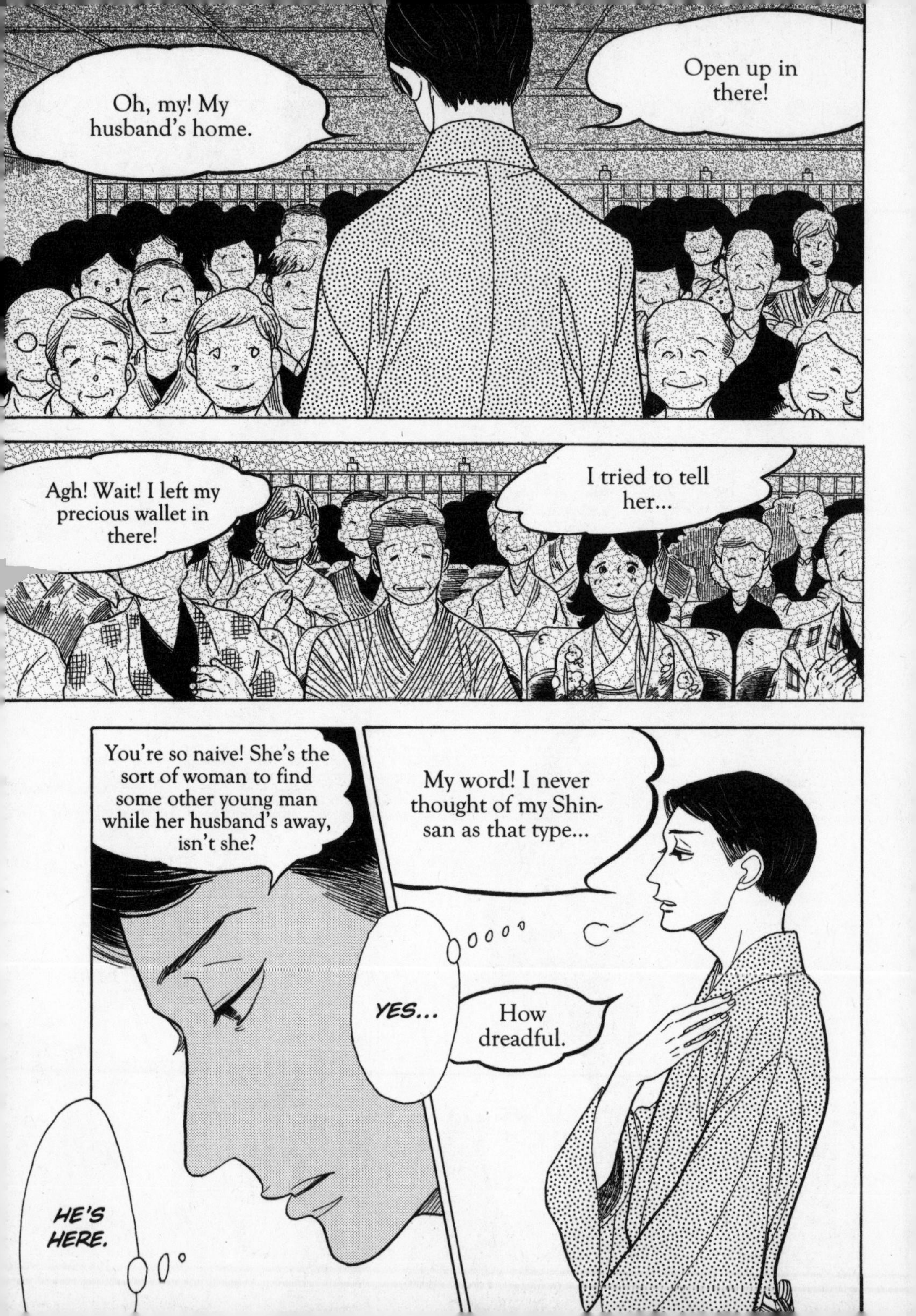
Open up in there!
Oh, my! My husband's home.
I tried to tell her...
Agh! Wait! I left my precious wallet in there!
My word! I never thought of my Shin-san as that type...
How dreadful.
You're so naive! She's the sort of woman to find some other young man while her husband's away, isn't she?
YES...
HE'S HERE.

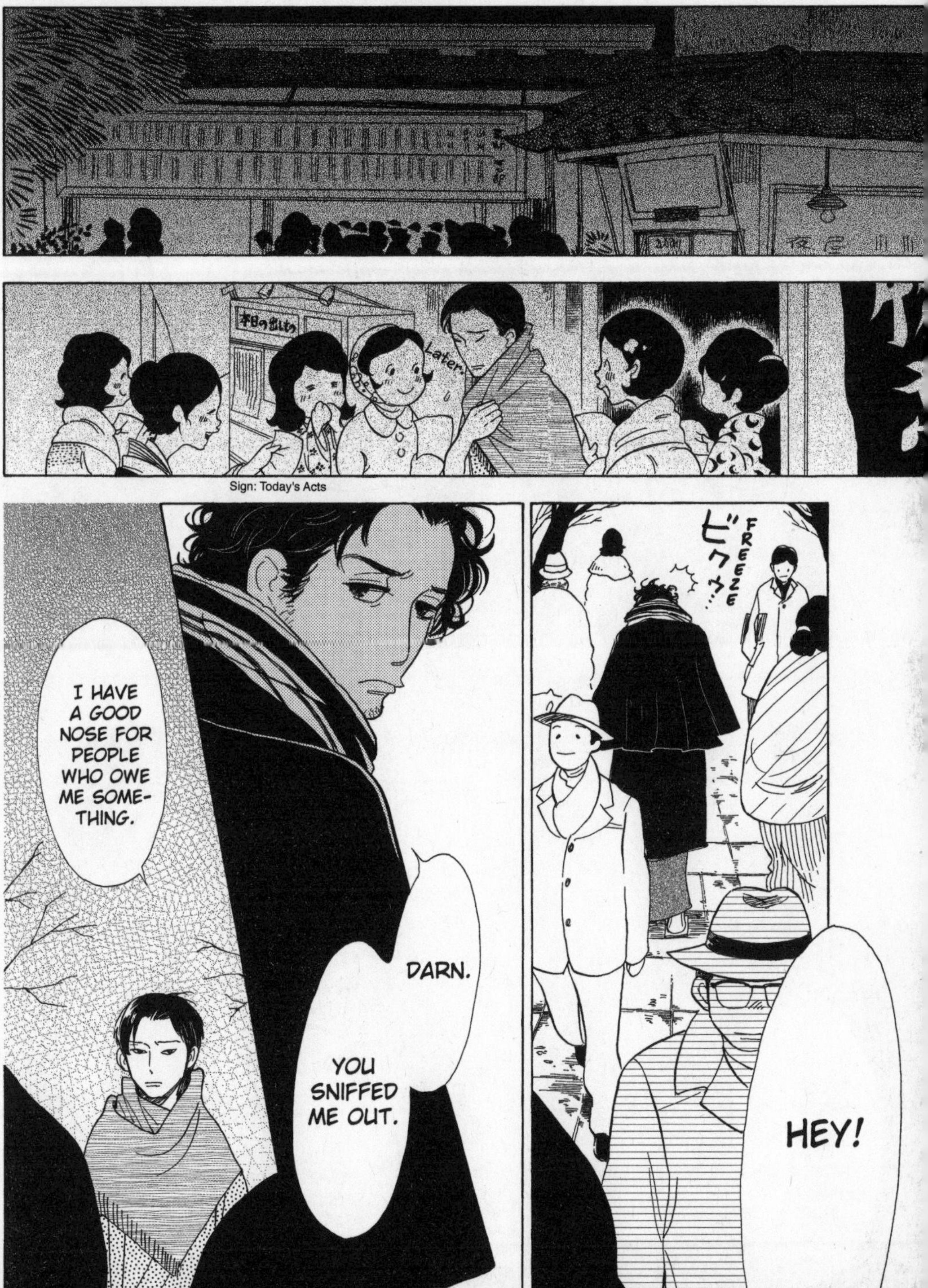
Later.
Sign: Today's Acts
FREEZE
HEY!
DARN.
YOU SNIFFED ME OUT.
I HAVE A GOOD NOSE FOR PEOPLE WHO OWE ME SOME-THING.

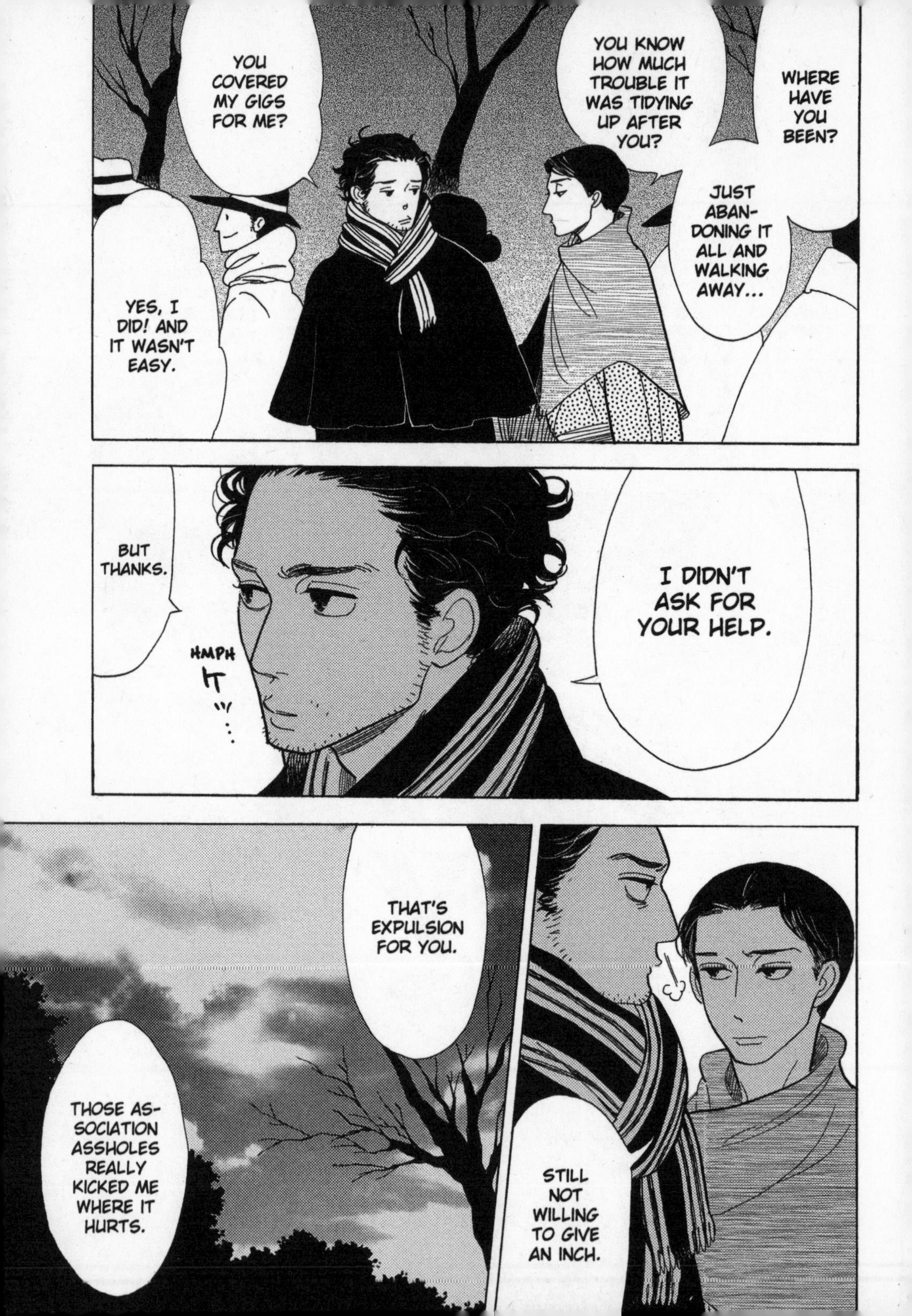
WHERE HAVE YOU BEEN?
JUST ABAN-DONING IT ALL AND WALKING AWAY...
YOU KNOW HOW MUCH TROUBLE IT WAS TIDYING UP AFTER YOU?
YOU COVERED MY GIGS FOR ME?
YES, I DID! AND IT WASN'T EASY.
I DIDN'T ASK FOR YOUR HELP.
HMPH
BUT THANKS.
STILL NOT WILLING TO GIVE AN INCH.
THAT'S EXPULSION FOR YOU.
THOSE AS-SOCIATION ASSHOLES REALLY KICKED ME WHERE IT HURTS.

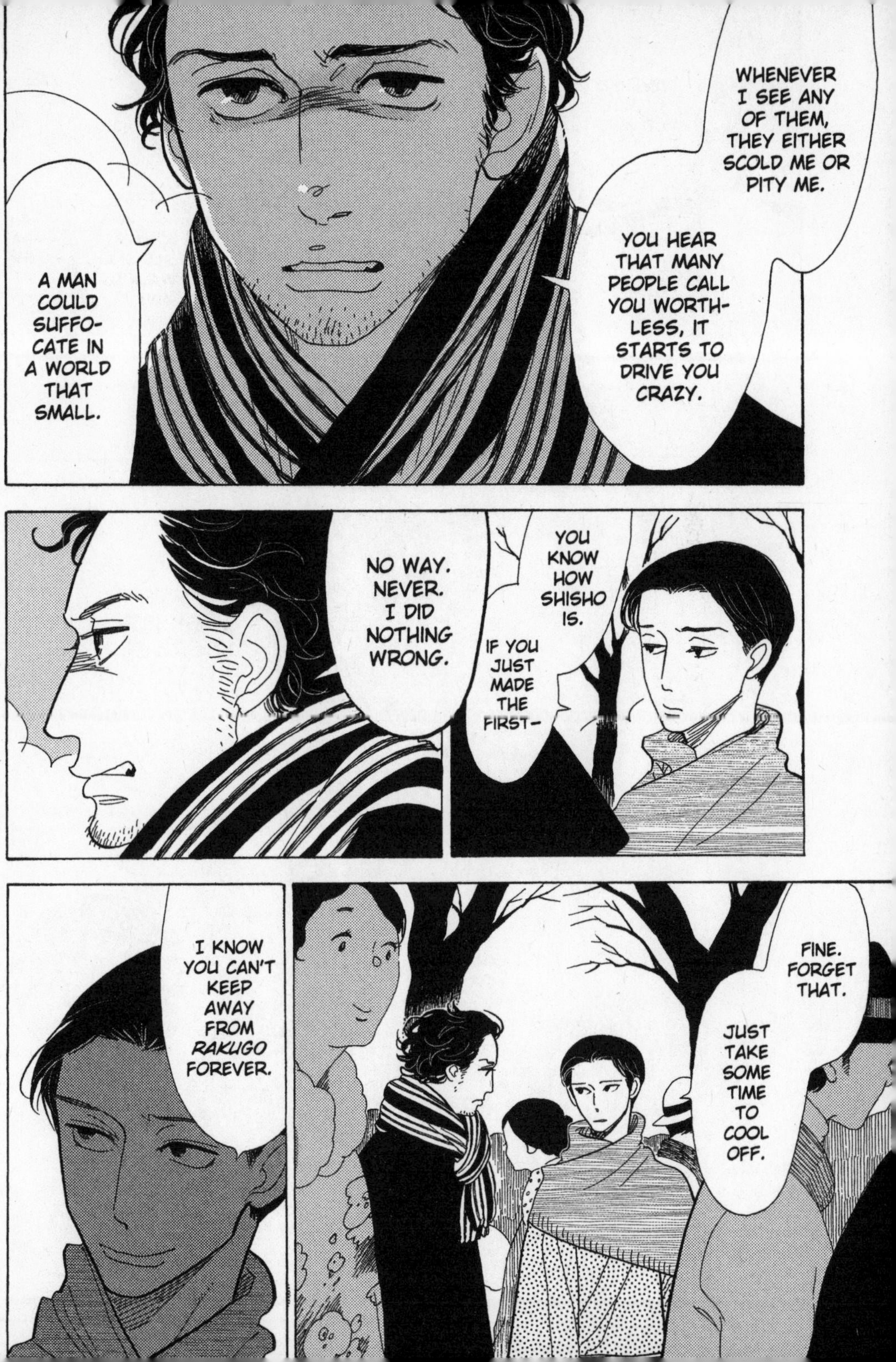
WHENEVER I SEE ANY OF THEM, THEY EITHER SCOLD ME OR PITY ME.
YOU HEAR THAT MANY PEOPLE CALL YOU WORTHLESS, IT STARTS TO DRIVE YOU CRAZY.
A MAN COULD SUFFOCATE IN A WORLD THAT SMALL.
YOU KNOW HOW SHISHO IS.
IF YOU JUST MADE THE FIRST-
NO WAY. NEVER. I DID NOTHING WRONG.
FINE. FORGET THAT.
JUST TAKE SOME TIME TO COOL OFF.
I KNOW YOU CAN'T KEEP AWAY FROM *RAKUGO* FOREVER.

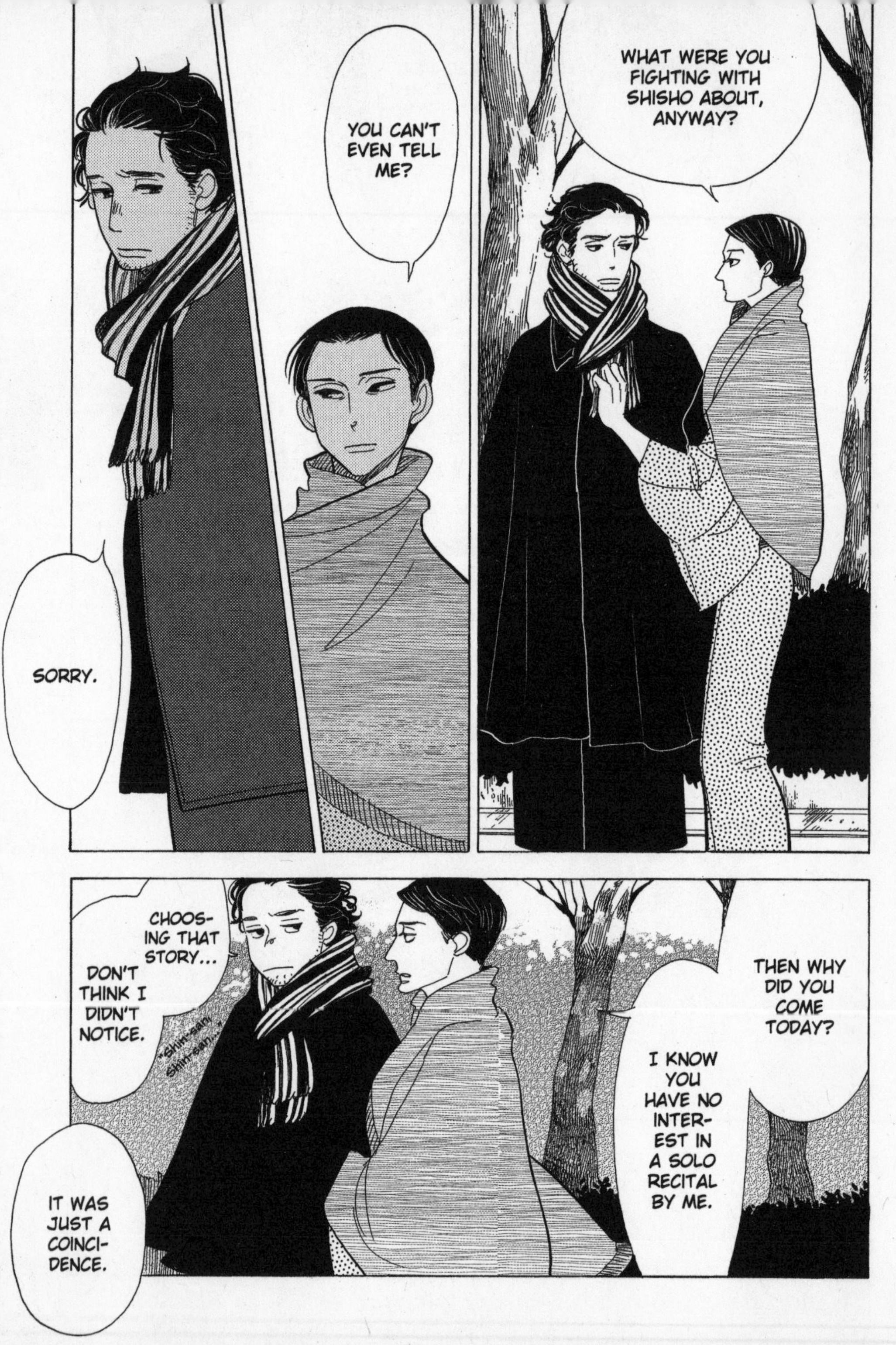
WHAT WERE YOU FIGHTING WITH SHISHO ABOUT, ANYWAY?
YOU CAN'T EVEN TELL ME?
SORRY.
THEN WHY DID YOU COME TODAY?
I KNOW YOU HAVE NO INTER-EST IN A SOLO RECITAL BY ME.
CHOOS-ING THAT STORY... DON'T THINK I DIDN'T NOTICE.
"Shin-san, Shin-san..."
IT WAS JUST A COINCI-DENCE.

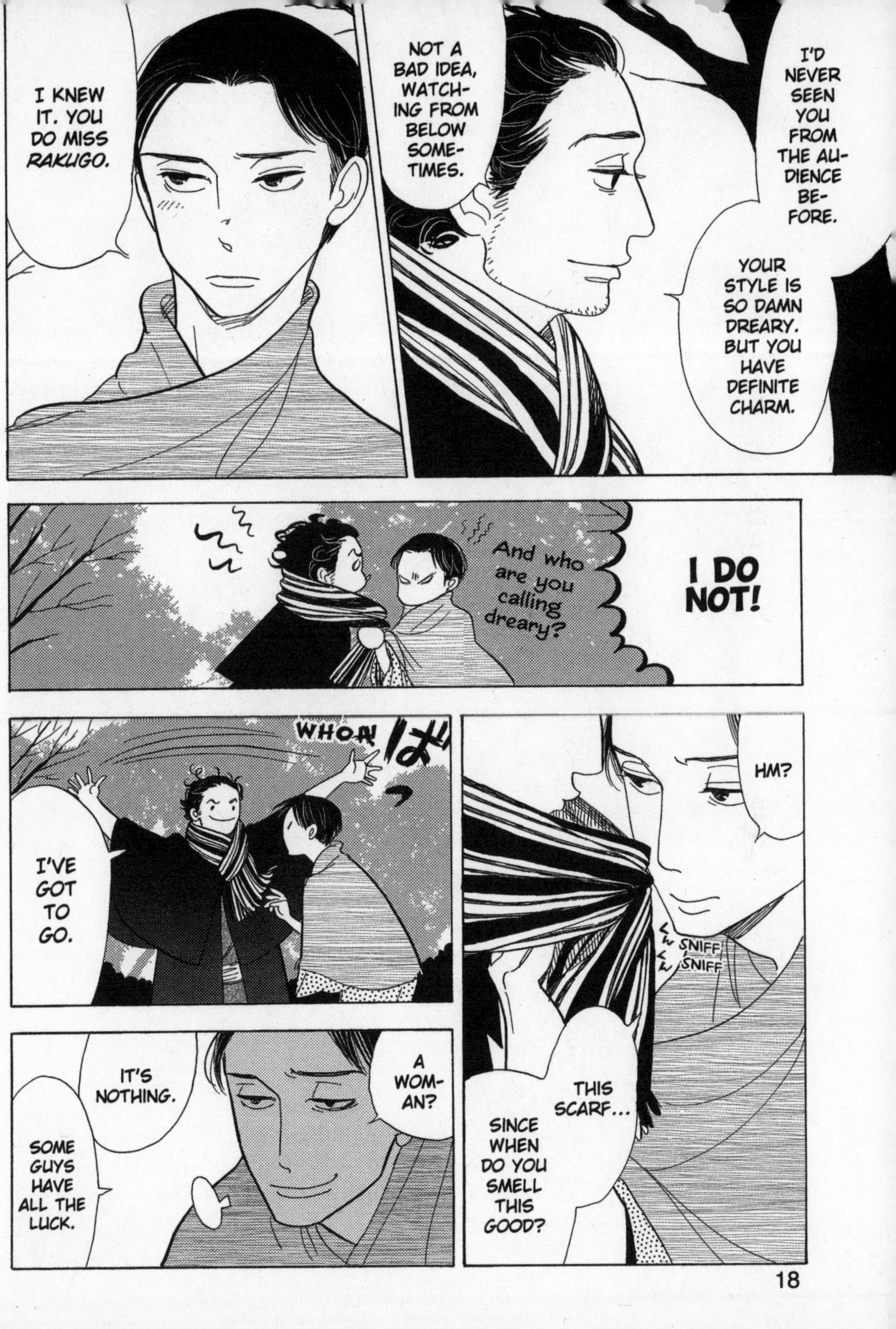
I'D NEVER SEEN YOU FROM THE AUDIENCE BEFORE.
YOUR STYLE IS SO DAMN DREARY. BUT YOU HAVE DEFINITE CHARM.
NOT A BAD IDEA, WATCHING FROM BELOW SOMETIMES.
I KNEW IT. YOU DO MISS RAKUGO.
I DO NOT!
And who are you calling dreary?
HM?
SNIFF SNIFF
THIS SCARF...
SINCE WHEN DO YOU SMELL THIS GOOD?
WHOA
I'VE GOT TO GO.
A WOMAN?
IT'S NOTHING.
SOME GUYS HAVE ALL THE LUCK.

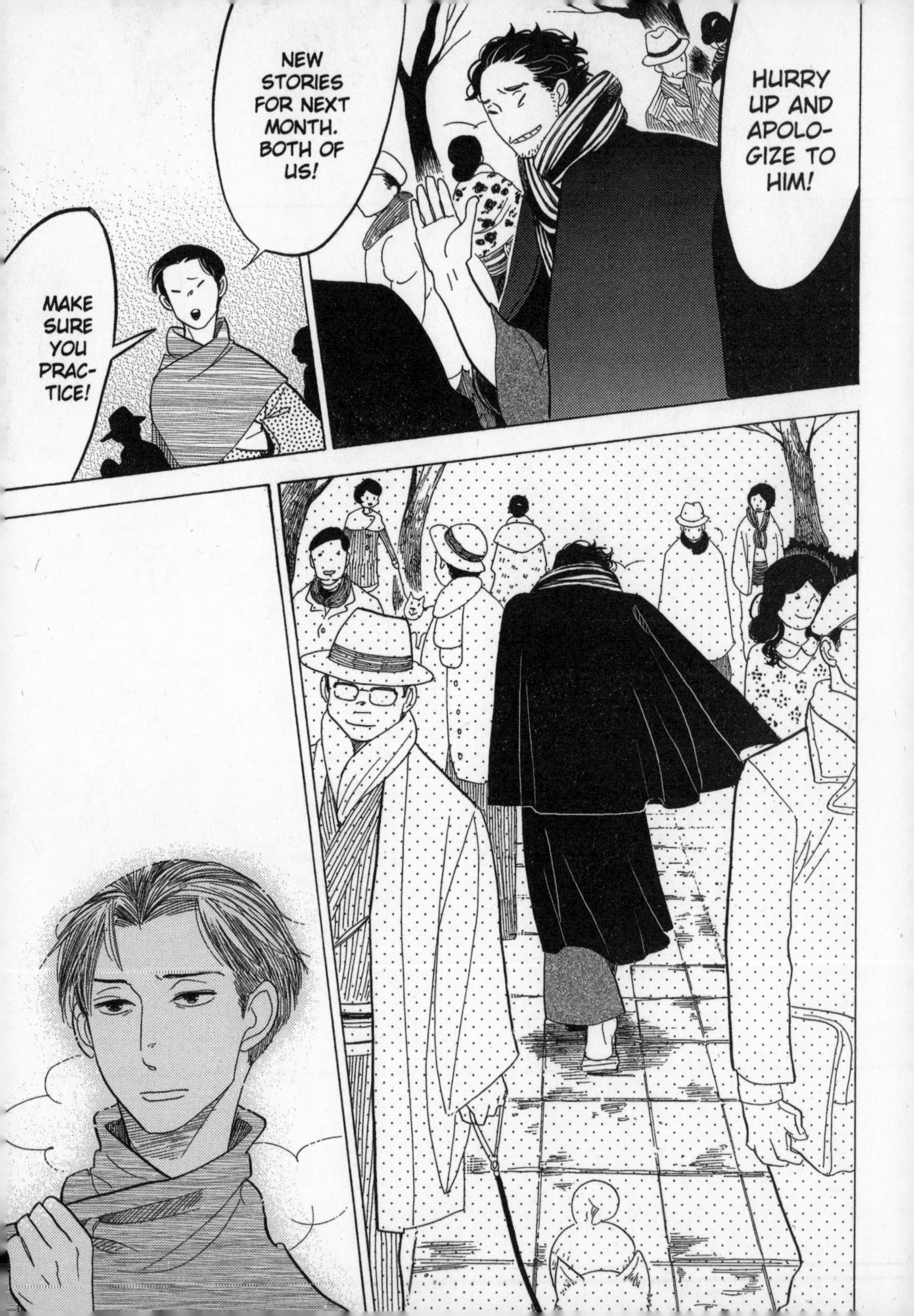
HURRY UP AND APOLOGIZE TO HIM!
NEW STORIES FOR NEXT MONTH. BOTH OF US!
MAKE SURE YOU PRACTICE!

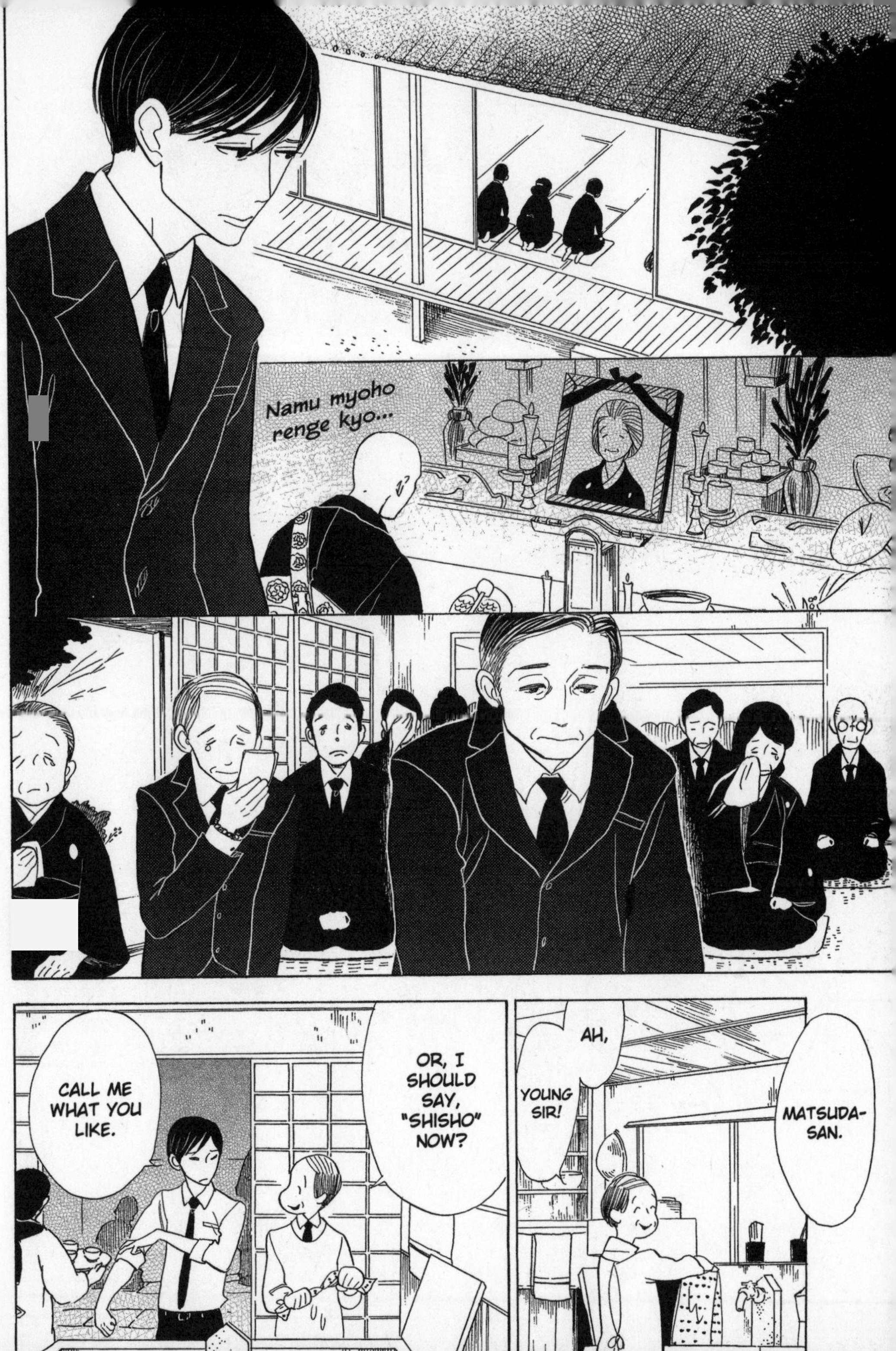
Namu myoho renge kyo...
MATSUDA-SAN.
AH,
YOUNG SIR!
OR, I SHOULD SAY, "SHISHO" NOW?
CALL ME WHAT YOU LIKE.

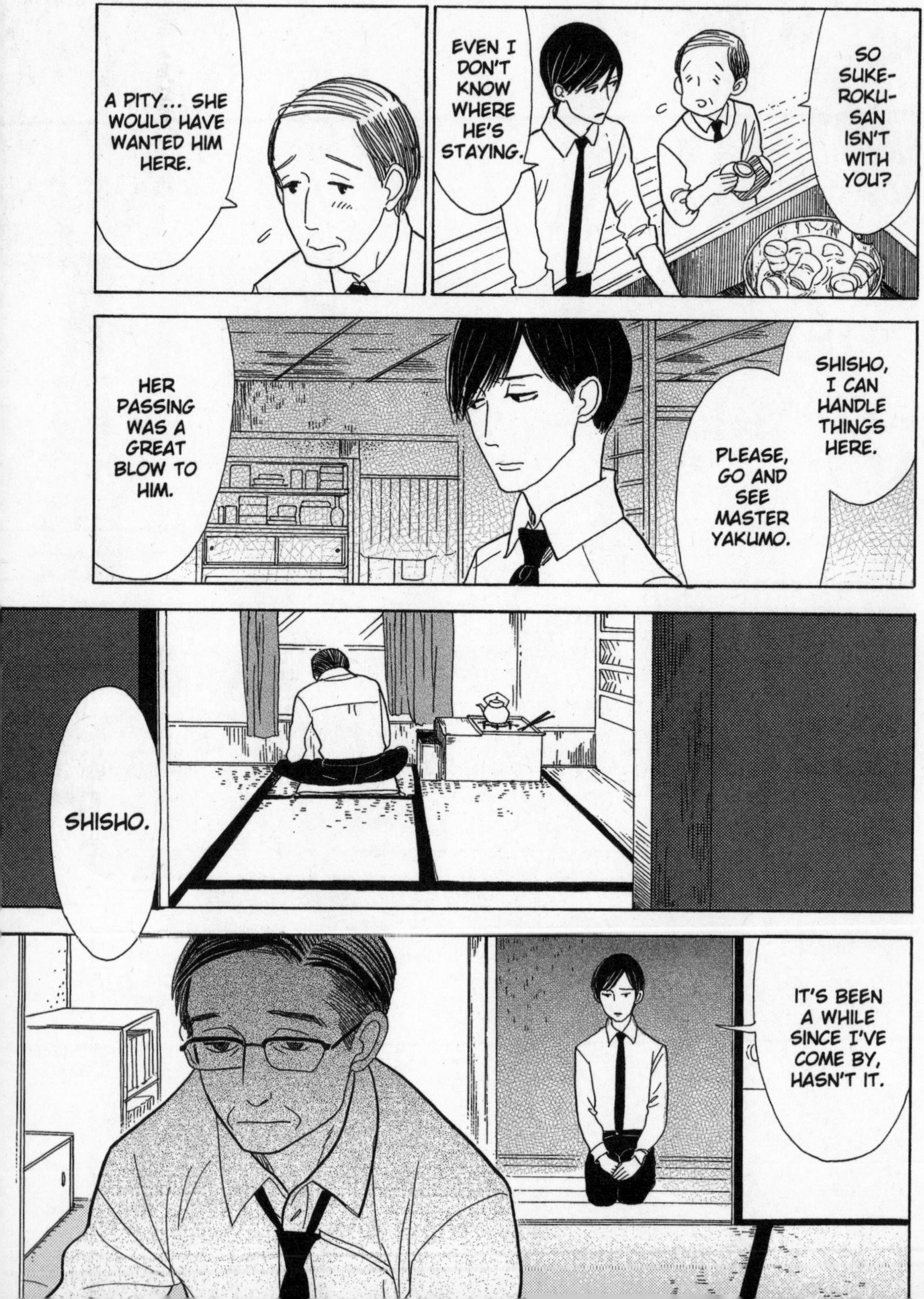
SO SUKE-ROKU-SAN ISN'T WITH YOU?
EVEN I DON'T KNOW WHERE HE'S STAYING.
A PITY... SHE WOULD HAVE WANTED HIM HERE.
SHISHO, I CAN HANDLE THINGS HERE.
PLEASE, GO AND SEE MASTER YAKUMO.
HER PASSING WAS A GREAT BLOW TO HIM.
SHISHO.
IT'S BEEN A WHILE SINCE I'VE COME BY, HASN'T IT.

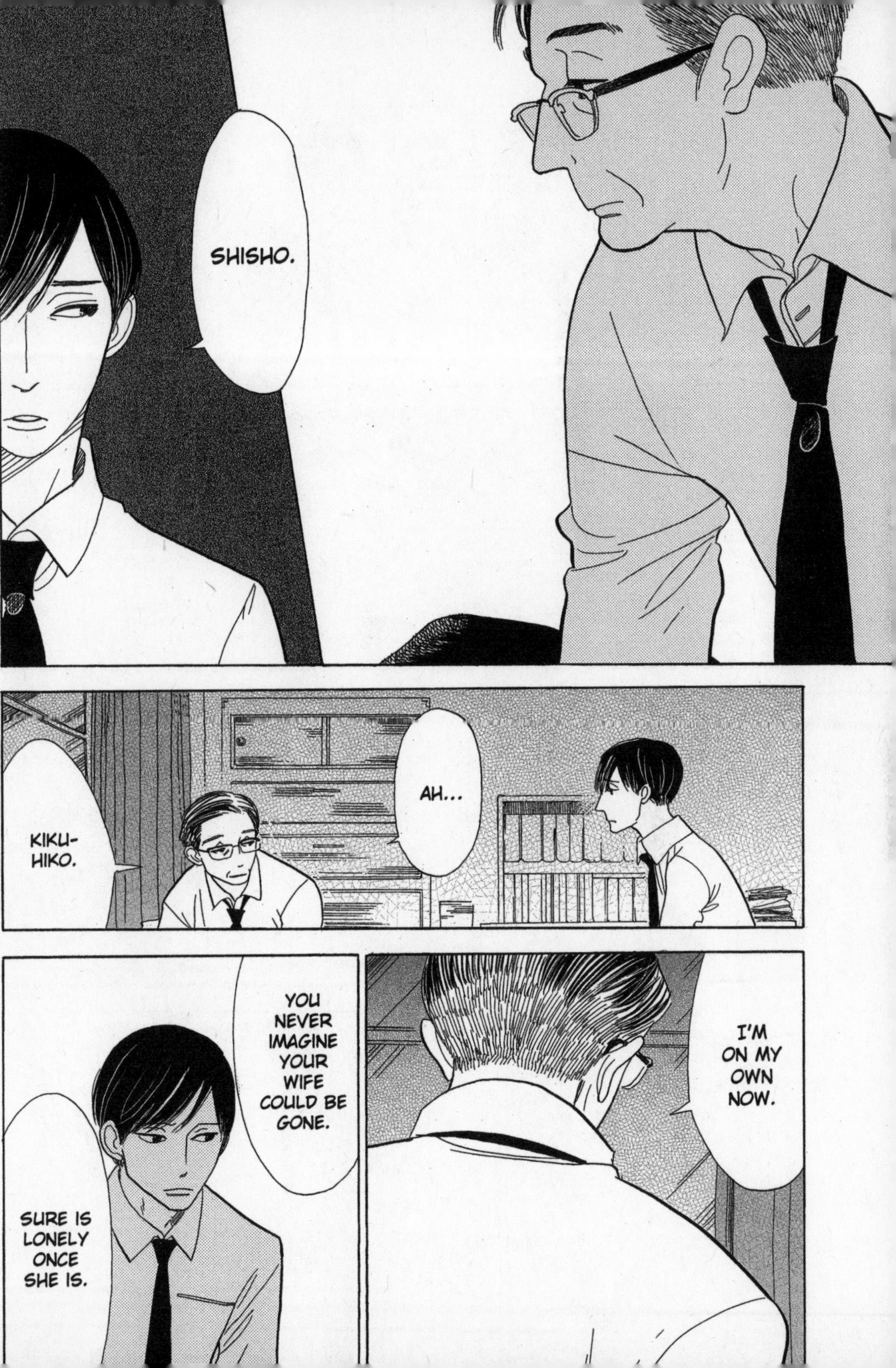
SHISHO.
AH...
KIKU-HIKO.
I'M ON MY OWN NOW.
YOU NEVER IMAGINE YOUR WIFE COULD BE GONE.
SURE IS LONELY ONCE SHE IS.

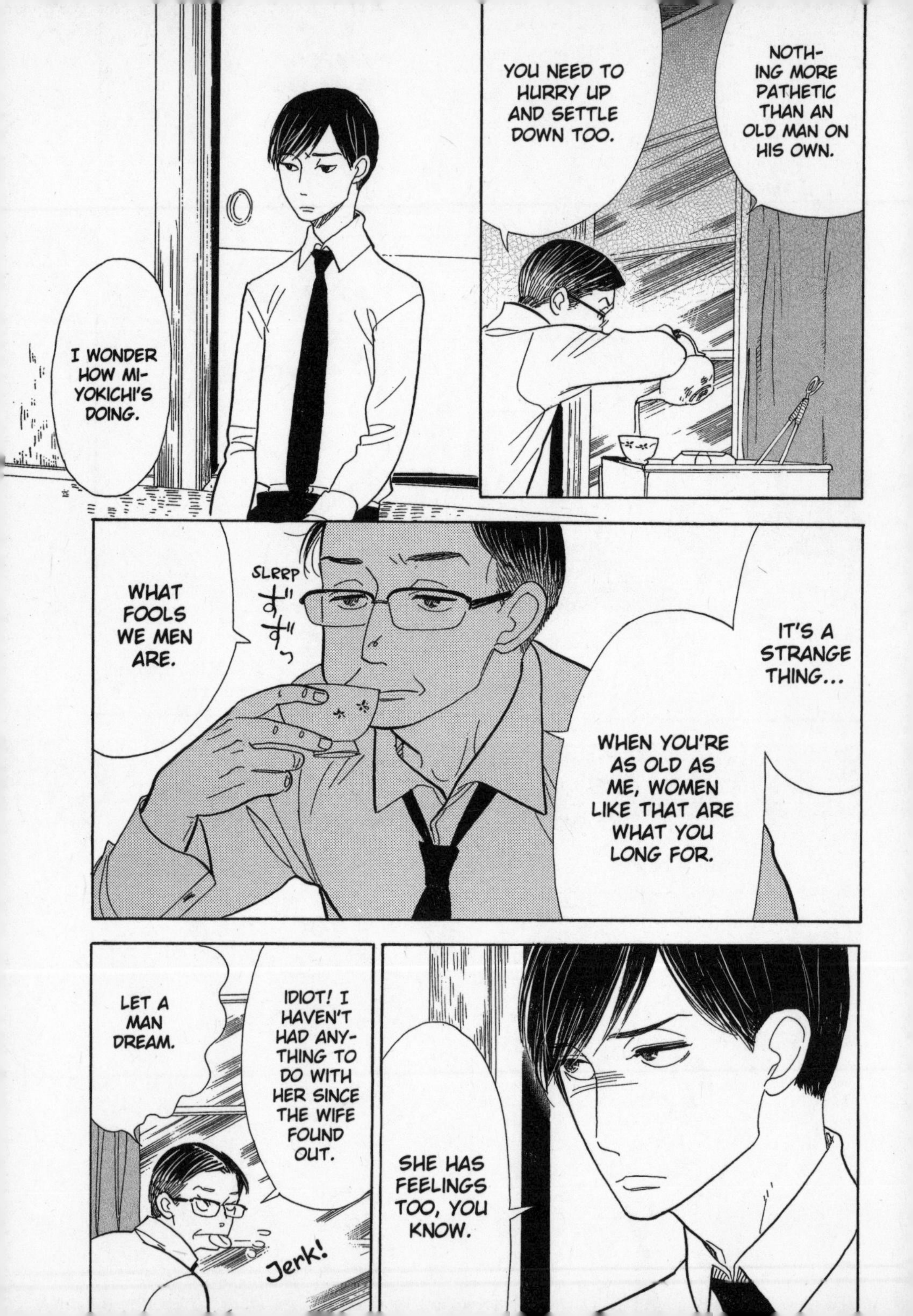
NOTHING MORE PATHETIC THAN AN OLD MAN ON HIS OWN.
YOU NEED TO HURRY UP AND SETTLE DOWN TOO.
I WONDER HOW MIYOKICHI'S DOING.
IT'S A STRANGE THING...
WHEN YOU'RE AS OLD AS ME, WOMEN LIKE THAT ARE WHAT YOU LONG FOR.
SLRRP
ずず
WHAT FOOLS WE MEN ARE.
SHE HAS FEELINGS TOO, YOU KNOW.
IDIOT! I HAVEN'T HAD ANYTHING TO DO WITH HER SINCE THE WIFE FOUND OUT.
LET A MAN DREAM.
Jerk!

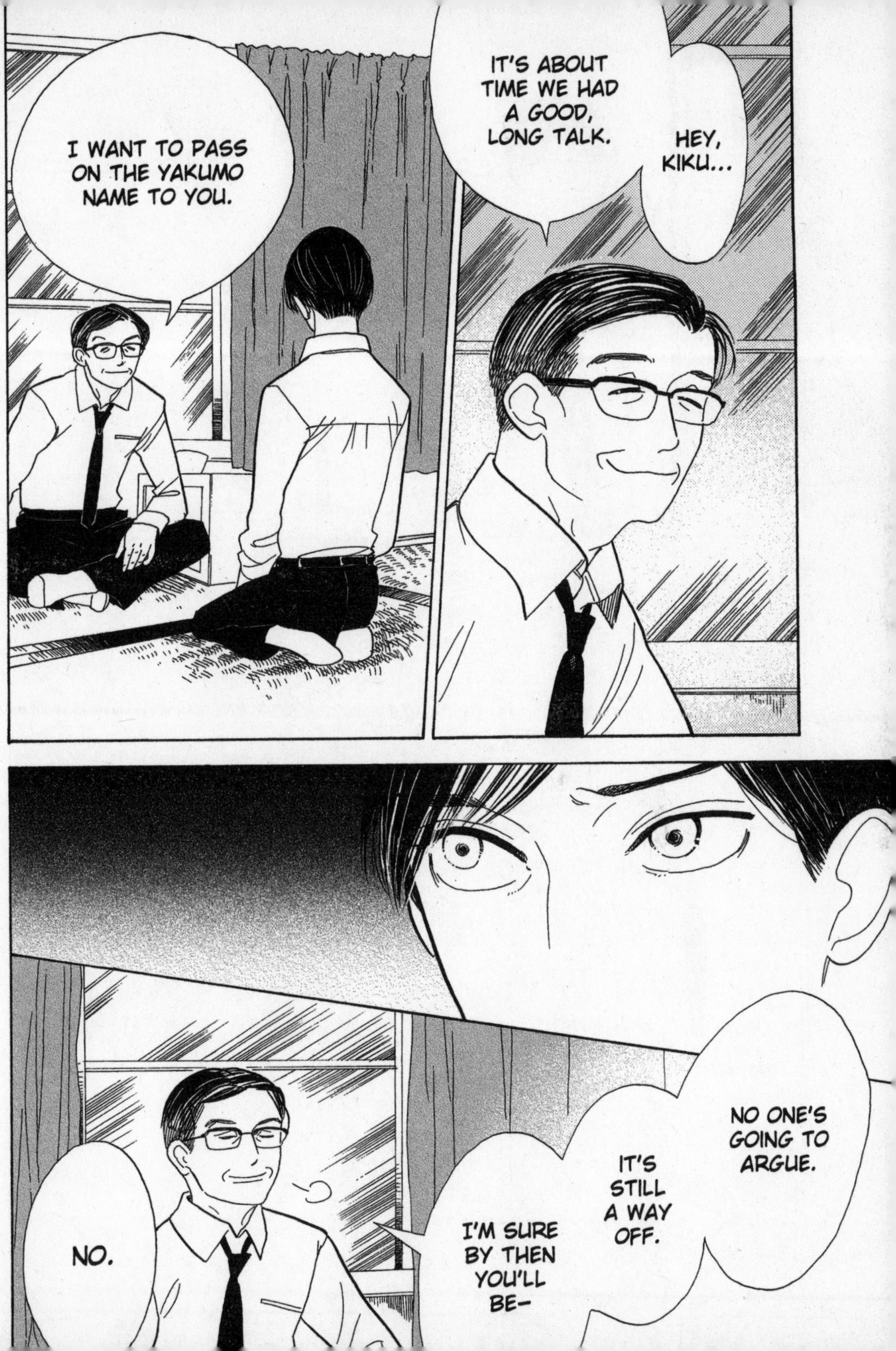
HEY, KIKU...
IT'S ABOUT TIME WE HAD A GOOD, LONG TALK.
I WANT TO PASS ON THE YAKUMO NAME TO YOU.
NO ONE'S GOING TO ARGUE.
IT'S STILL A WAY OFF.
I'M SURE BY THEN YOU'LL BE-
NO.

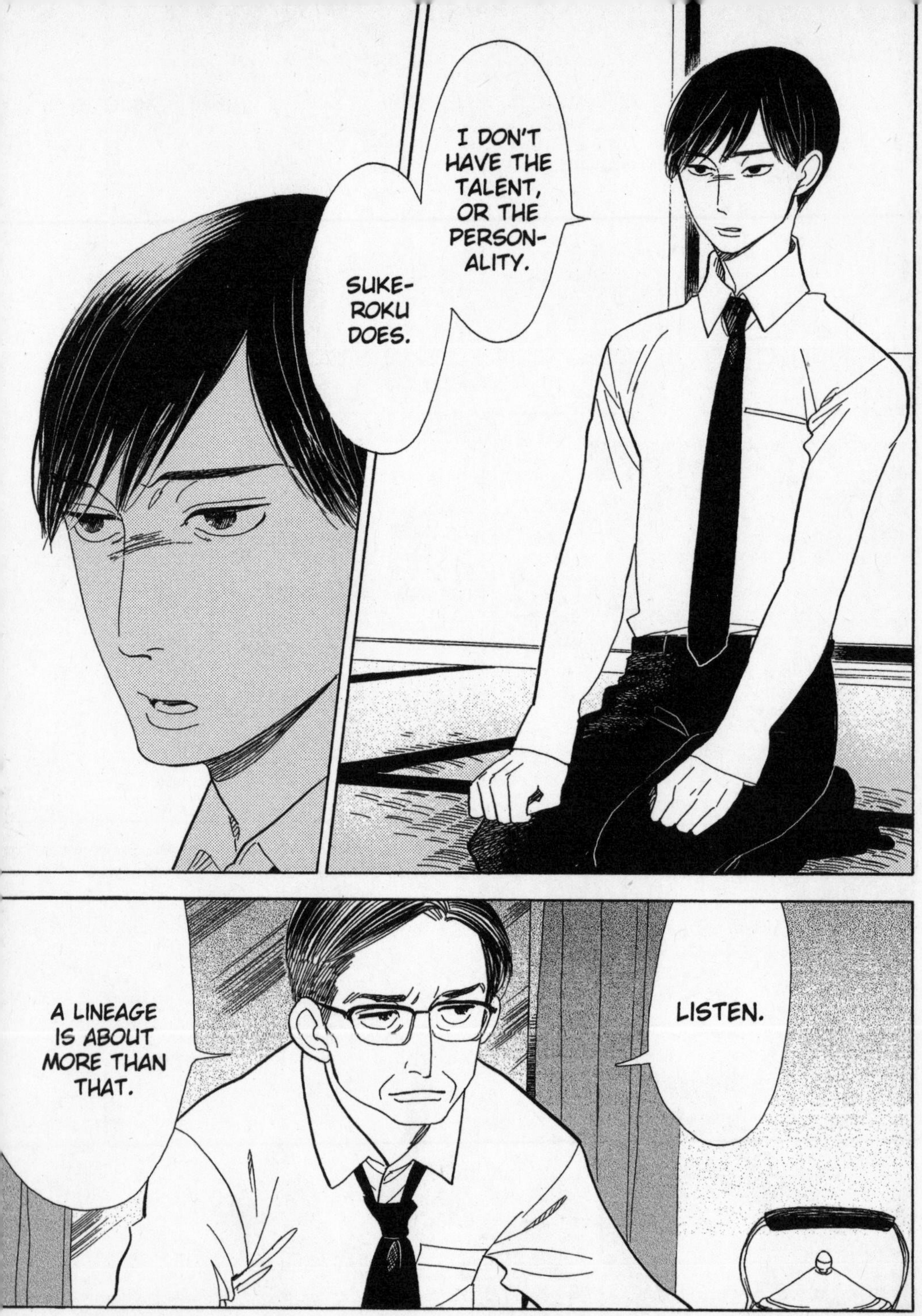
I DON'T HAVE THE TALENT, OR THE PERSONALITY.
SUKE-ROKU DOES.
LISTEN.
A LINEAGE IS ABOUT MORE THAN THAT.

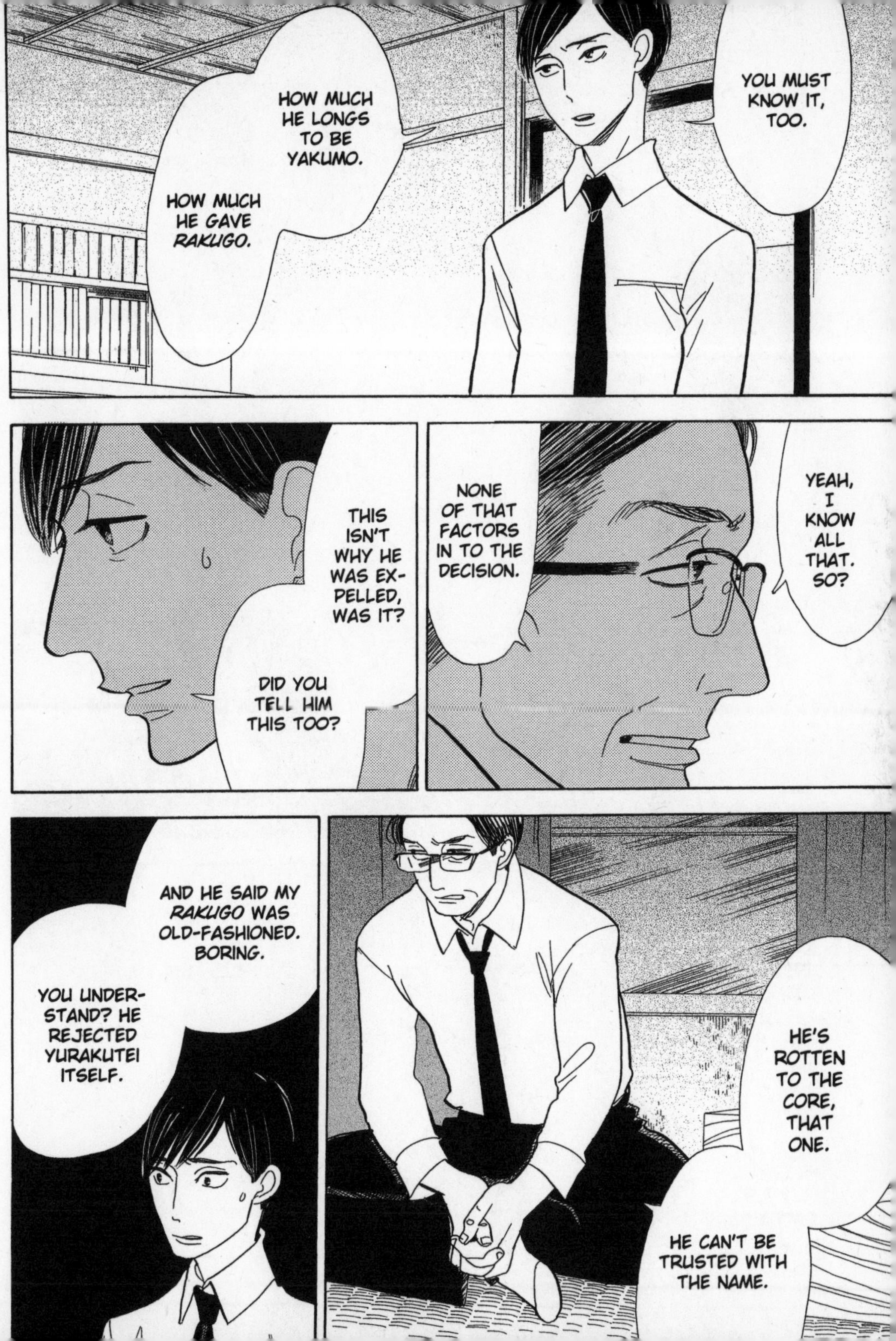
YOU MUST KNOW IT, TOO.
HOW MUCH HE LONGS TO BE YAKUMO.
HOW MUCH HE GAVE *RAKUGO*.
YEAH, I KNOW ALL THAT. SO?
NONE OF THAT FACTORS IN TO THE DECISION.
THIS ISN'T WHY HE WAS EX-PELLED, WAS IT?
DID YOU TELL HIM THIS TOO?
HE'S ROTTEN TO THE CORE, THAT ONE.
HE CAN'T BE TRUSTED WITH THE NAME.
AND HE SAID MY *RAKUGO* WAS OLD-FASHIONED. BORING.
YOU UNDER-STAND? HE REJECTED YURAKUTEI ITSELF.

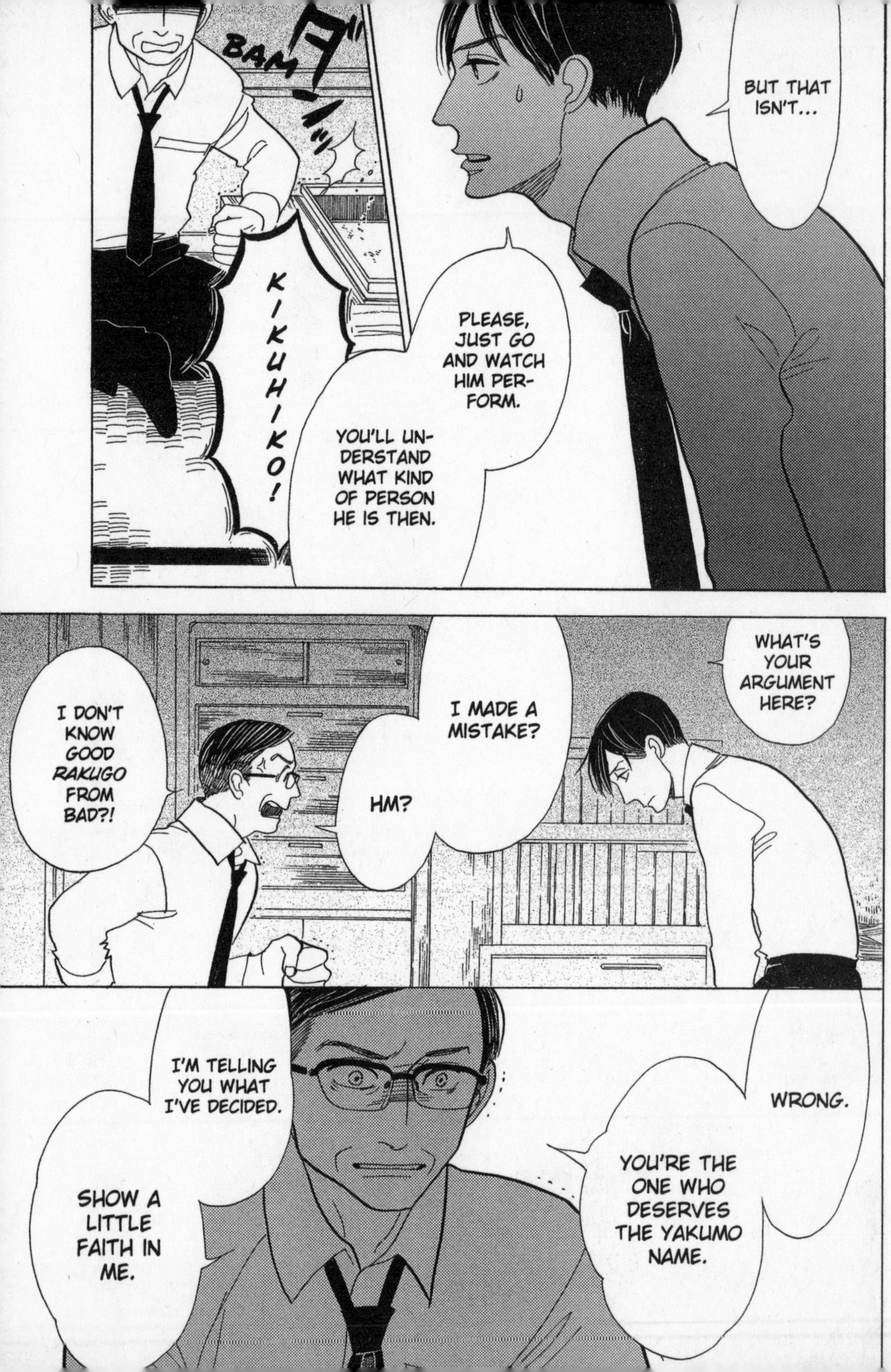
BUT THAT ISN'T...
PLEASE, JUST GO AND WATCH HIM PER-FORM.
YOU'LL UN-DERSTAND WHAT KIND OF PERSON HE IS THEN.
BAM
KIKUHIKO!
WHAT'S YOUR ARGUMENT HERE?
I MADE A MISTAKE?
HM?
I DON'T KNOW GOOD RAKUGO FROM BAD?!
WRONG.
YOU'RE THE ONE WHO DESERVES THE YAKUMO NAME.
I'M TELLING YOU WHAT I'VE DECIDED.
SHOW A LITTLE FAITH IN ME.

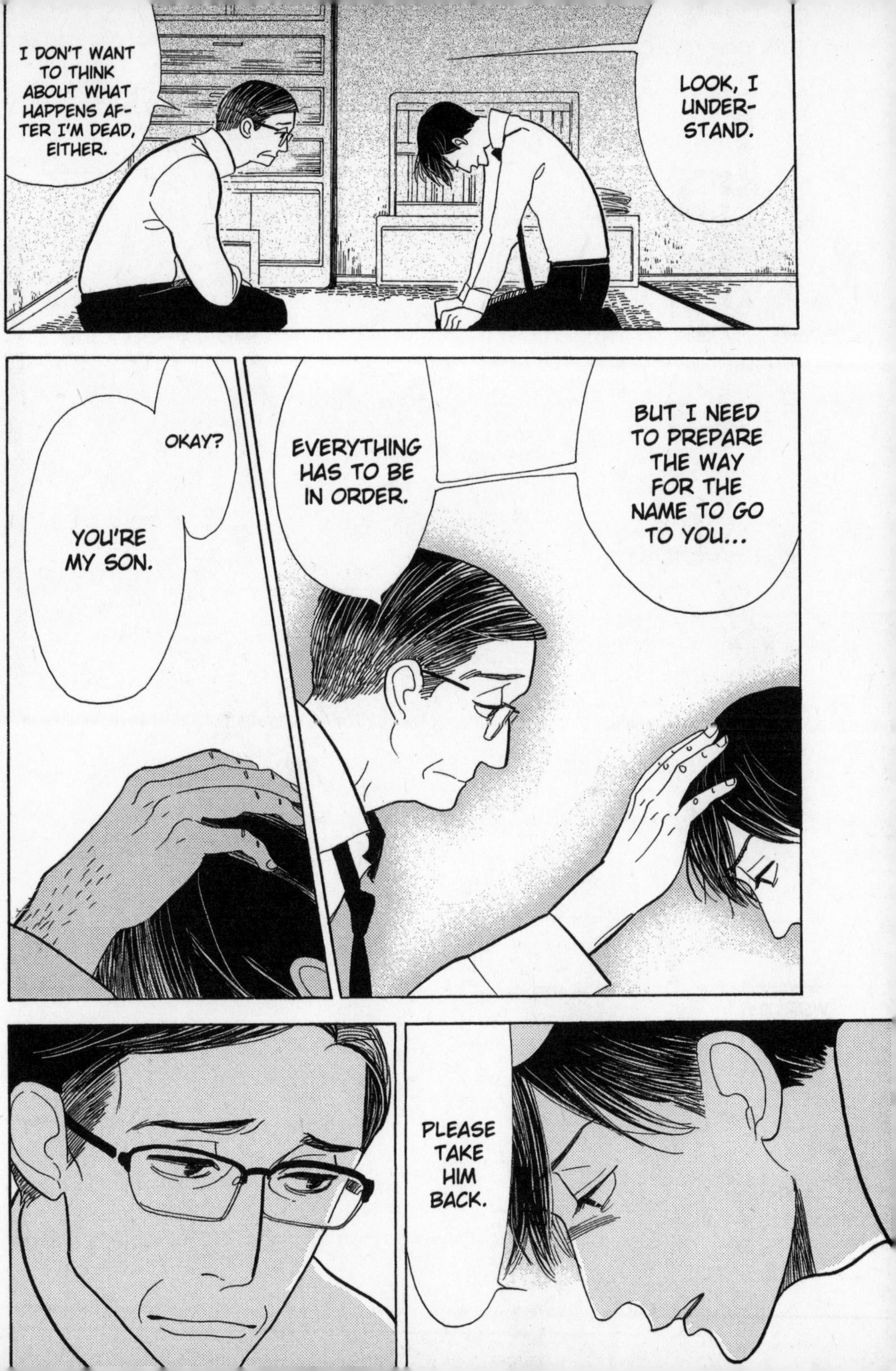
LOOK, I UNDERSTAND.
I DON'T WANT TO THINK ABOUT WHAT HAPPENS AFTER I'M DEAD, EITHER.
BUT I NEED TO PREPARE THE WAY FOR THE NAME TO GO TO YOU...
EVERYTHING HAS TO BE IN ORDER.
OKAY?
YOU'RE MY SON.
PLEASE TAKE HIM BACK.

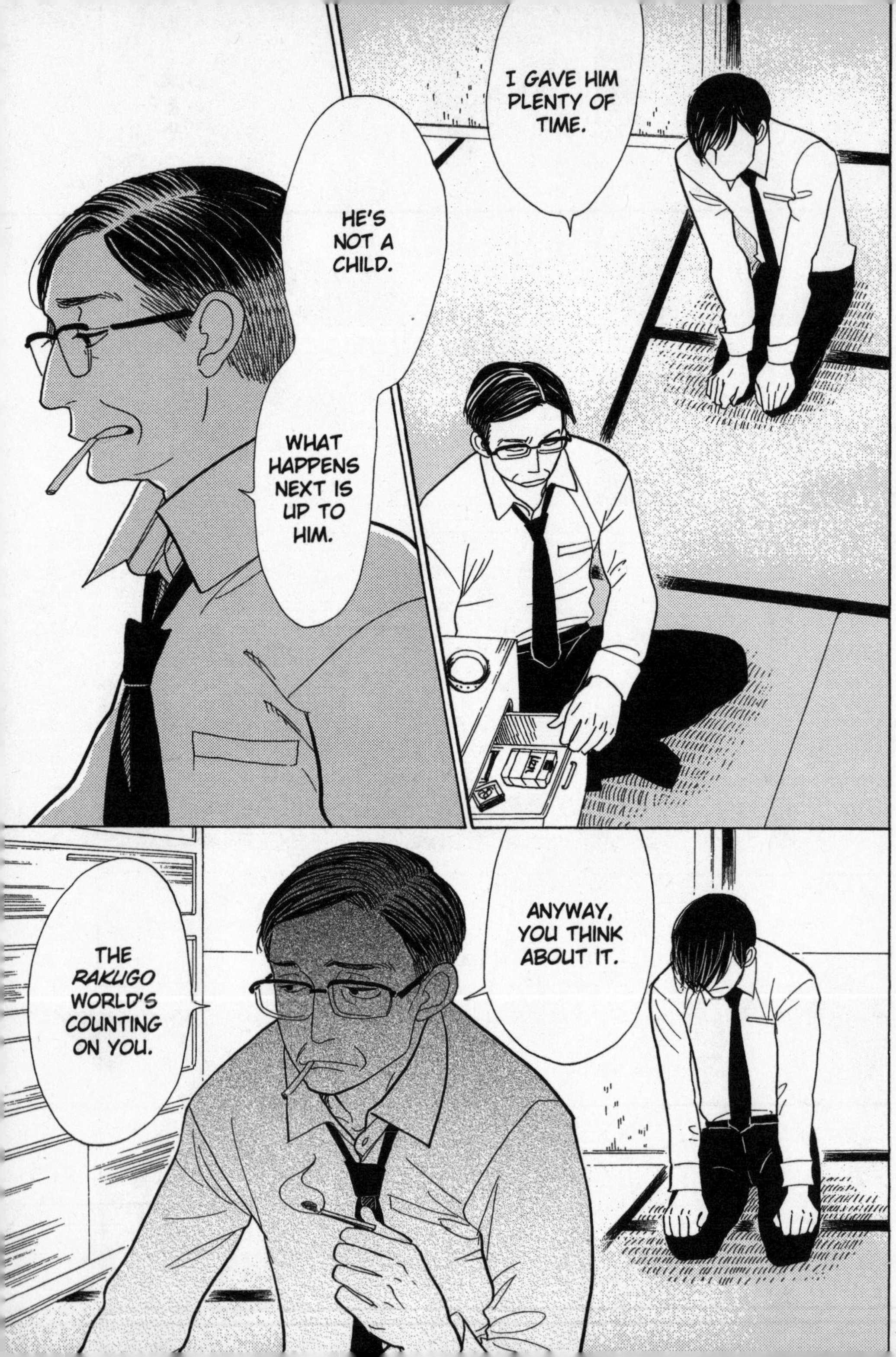
I GAVE HIM PLENTY OF TIME.
HE'S NOT A CHILD.
WHAT HAPPENS NEXT IS UP TO HIM.
ANYWAY, YOU THINK ABOUT IT.
THE *RAKUGO* WORLD'S COUNTING ON YOU.

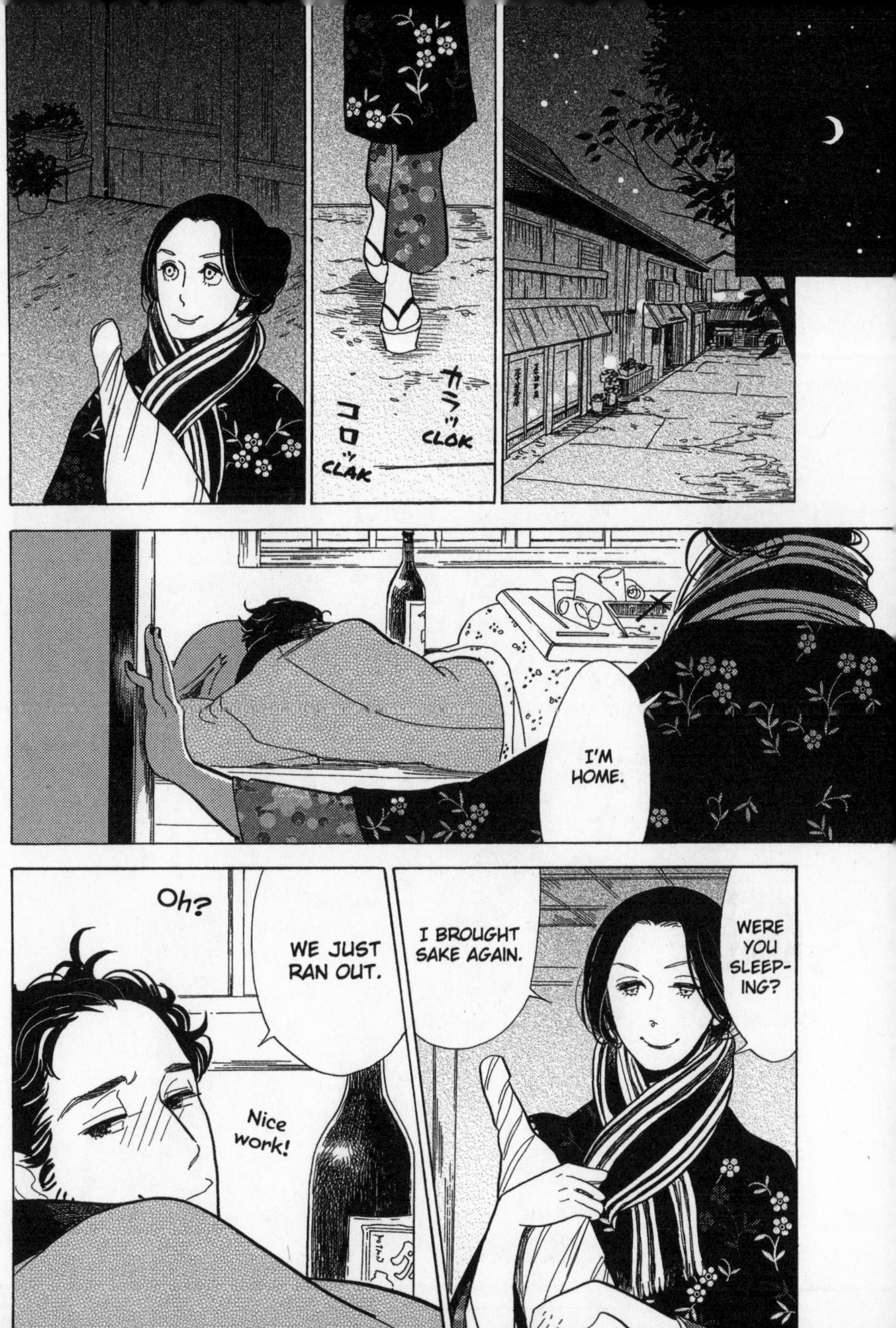
カラッ
CLOK
コロッ
CLAK
I'M HOME.
WERE YOU SLEEP-ING?
I BROUGHT SAKE AGAIN.
Oh?
WE JUST RAN OUT.
Nice work!

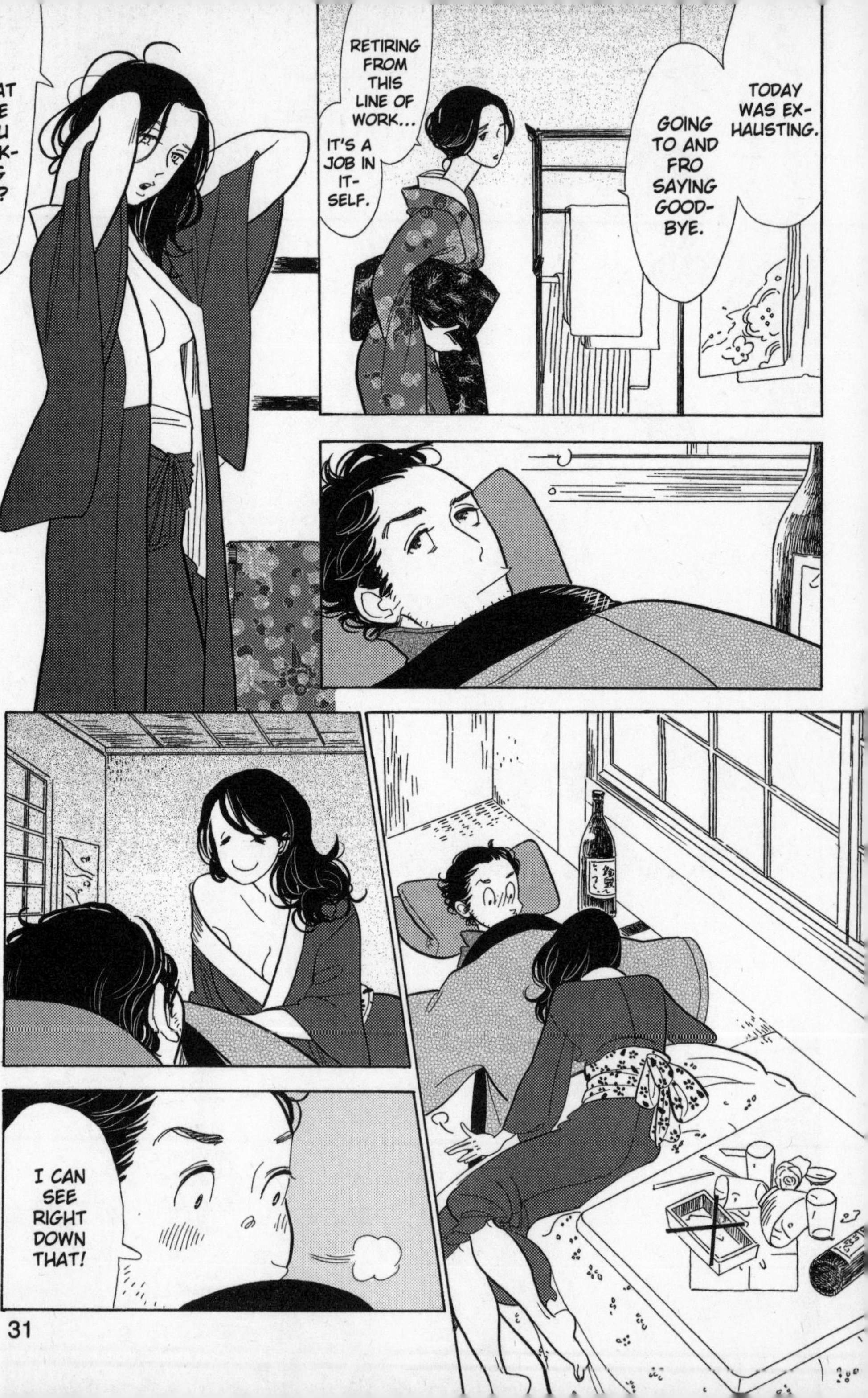
TODAY WAS EX-HAUSTING.
GOING TO AND FRO SAYING GOOD-BYE.
RETIRING FROM THIS LINE OF WORK...
IT'S A JOB IN IT-SELF.
WHAT ARE YOU LOOK-ING AT?
I CAN SEE RIGHT DOWN THAT!

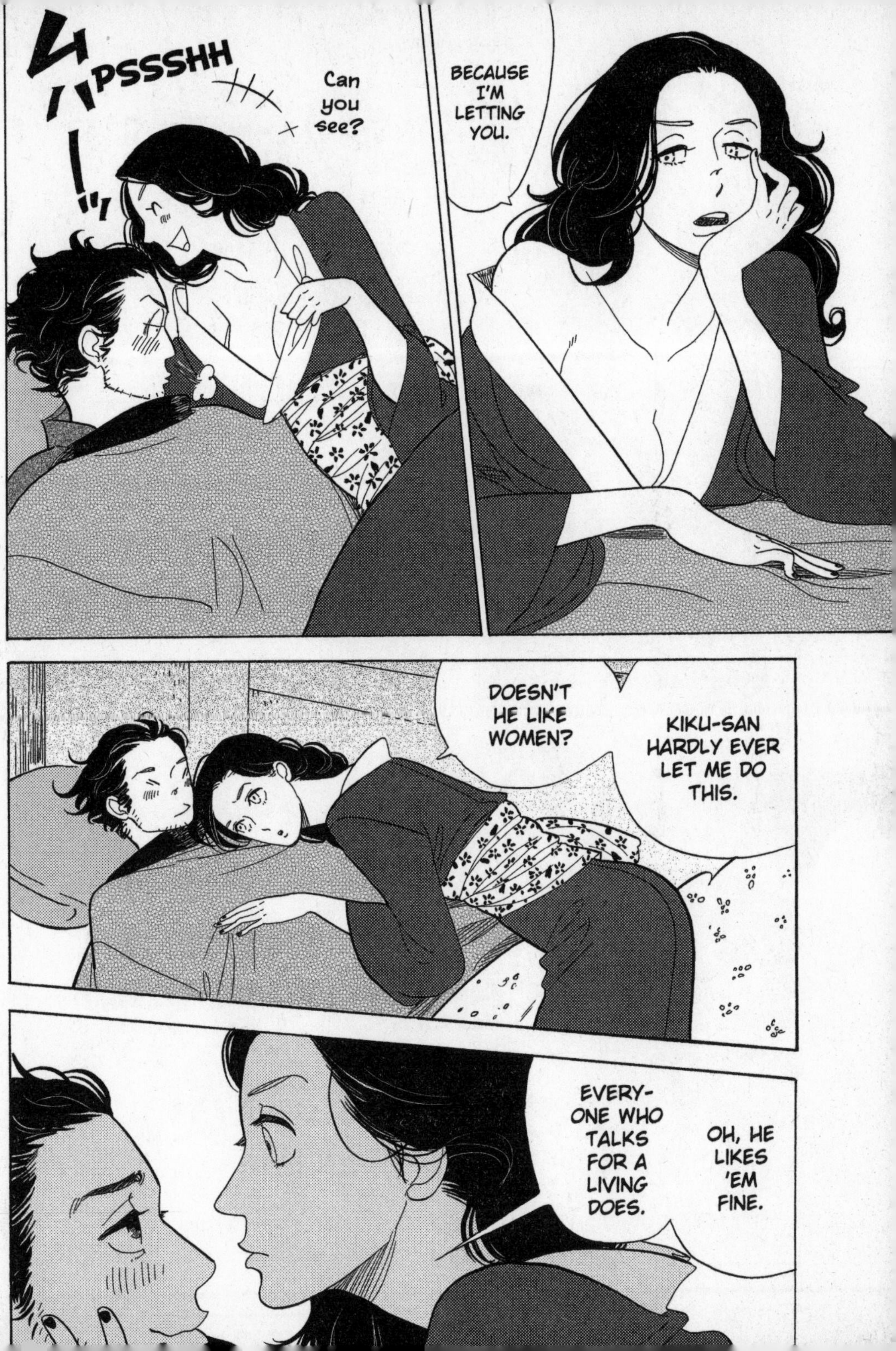
BECAUSE I'M LETTING YOU.
Can you see?
PSSSHH
KIKU-SAN HARDLY EVER LET ME DO THIS.
DOESN'T HE LIKE WOMEN?
OH, HE LIKES 'EM FINE.
EVERY-ONE WHO TALKS FOR A LIVING DOES.

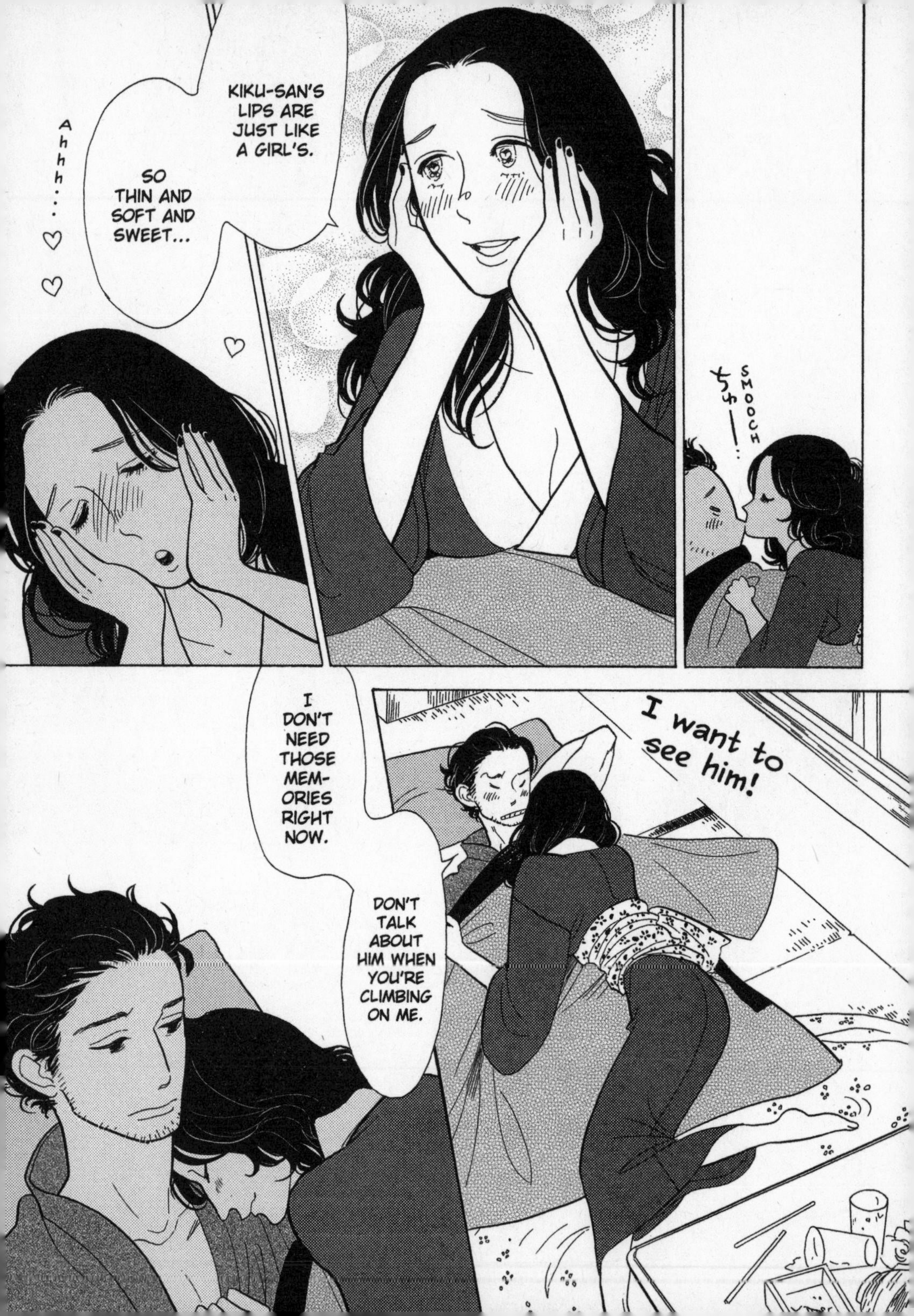
SMOOCH
ちゅー
KIKU-SAN'S LIPS ARE JUST LIKE A GIRL'S.
SO THIN AND SOFT AND SWEET...
Ahhh...
I want to see him!
I DON'T NEED THOSE MEMORIES RIGHT NOW.
DON'T TALK ABOUT HIM WHEN YOU'RE CLIMBING ON ME.

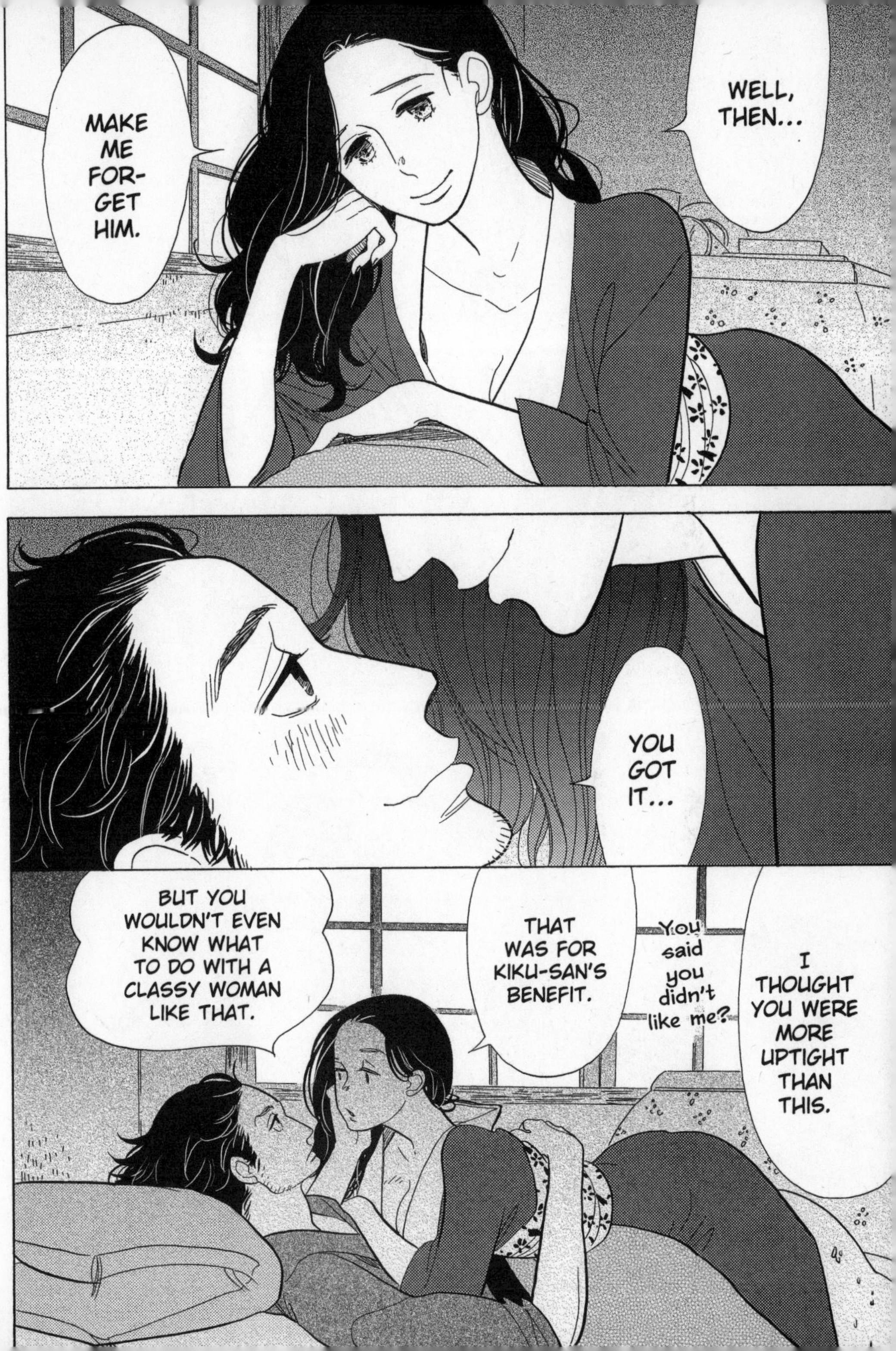
WELL, THEN...
MAKE ME FOR-GET HIM.
YOU GOT IT...
I THOUGHT YOU WERE MORE UPTIGHT THAN THIS.
You said you didn't like me?
THAT WAS FOR KIKU-SAN'S BENEFIT.
BUT YOU WOULDN'T EVEN KNOW WHAT TO DO WITH A CLASSY WOMAN LIKE THAT.

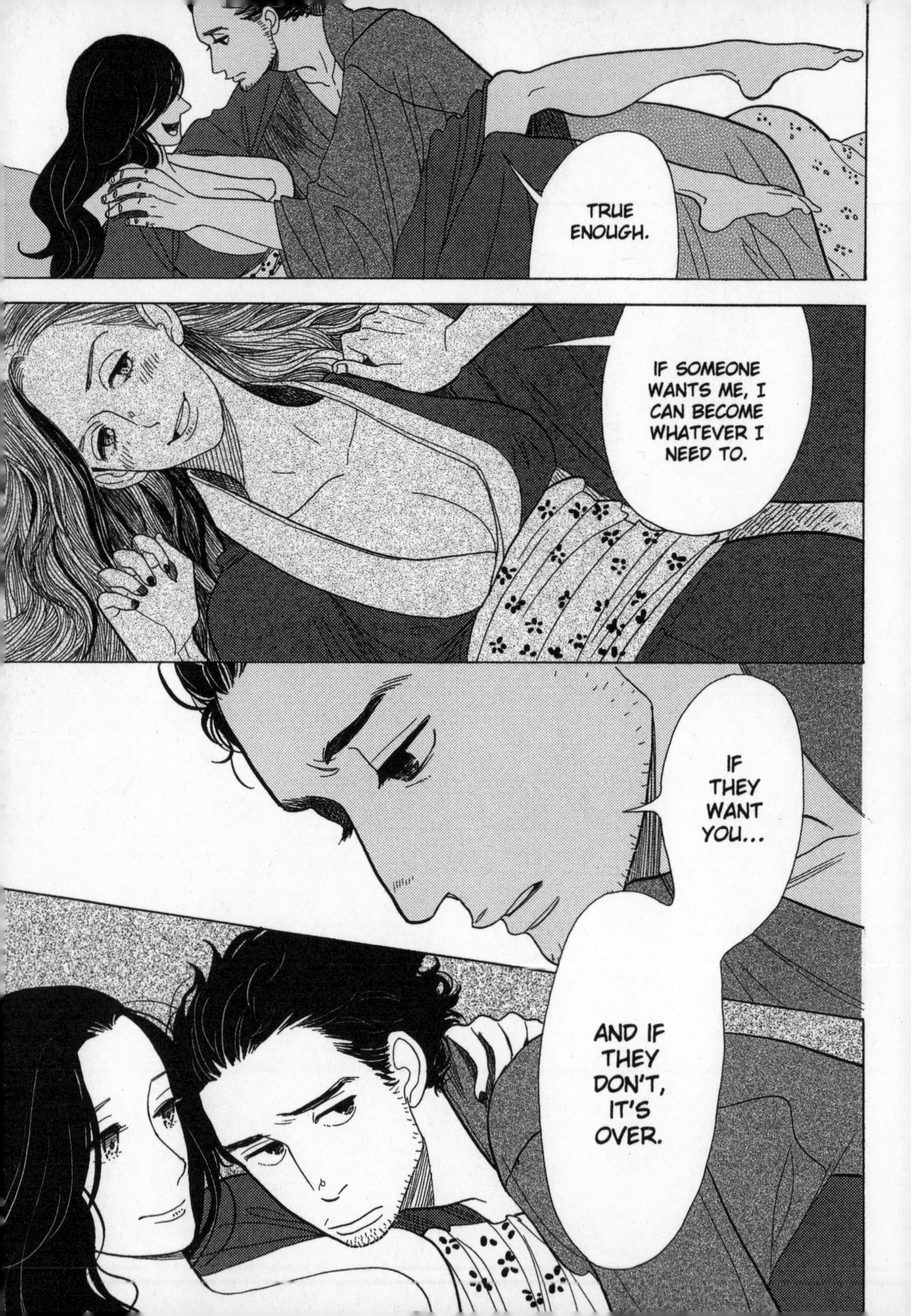
TRUE ENOUGH.
IF SOMEONE WANTS ME, I CAN BECOME WHATEVER I NEED TO.
IF THEY WANT YOU...
AND IF THEY DON'T, IT'S OVER.

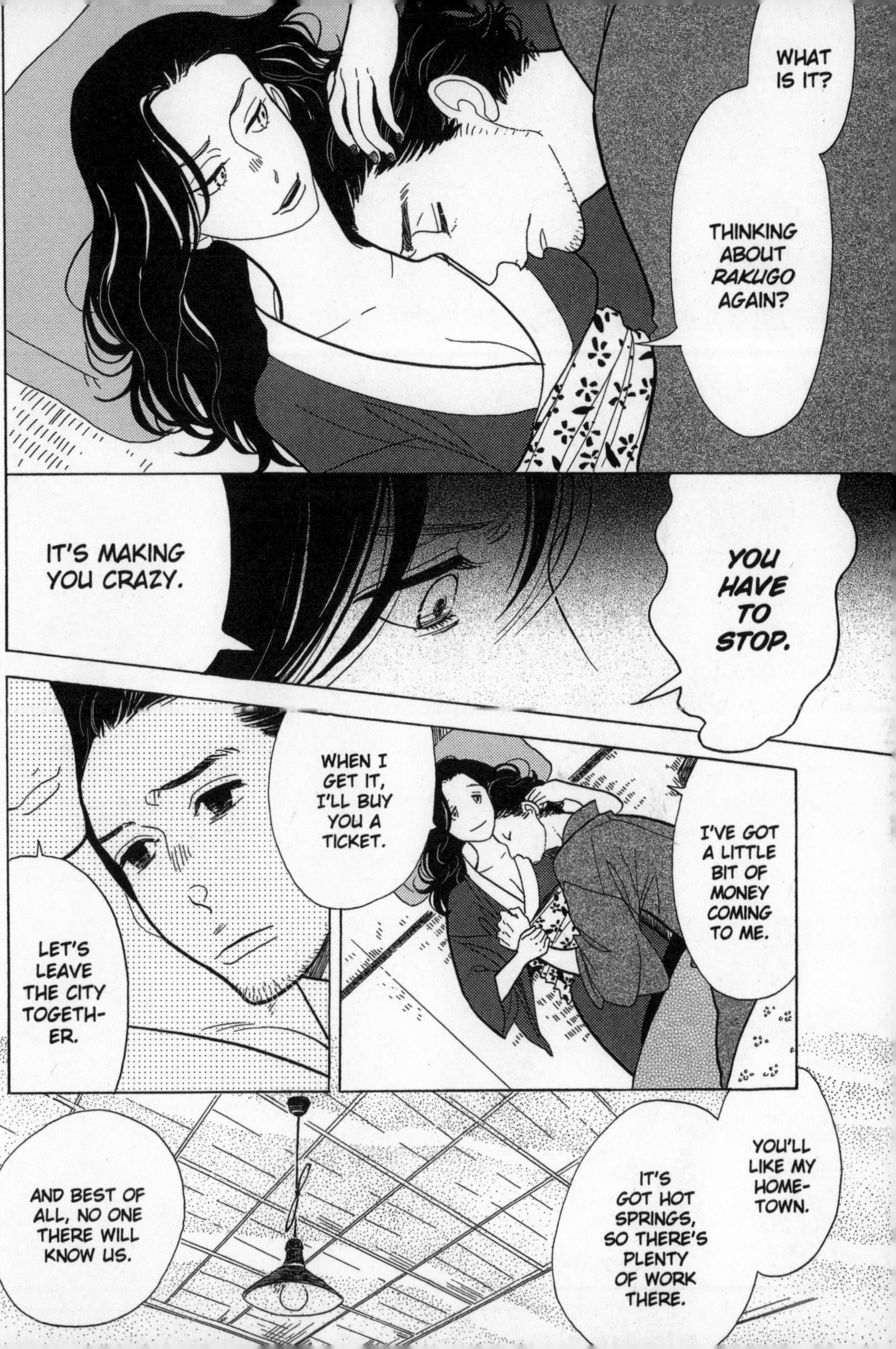
WHAT IS IT?
THINKING ABOUT RAKUGO AGAIN?
YOU HAVE TO STOP.
IT'S MAKING YOU CRAZY.
I'VE GOT A LITTLE BIT OF MONEY COMING TO ME.
WHEN I GET IT, I'LL BUY YOU A TICKET.
LET'S LEAVE THE CITY TOGETH-ER.
YOU'LL LIKE MY HOME-TOWN.
IT'S GOT HOT SPRINGS, SO THERE'S PLENTY OF WORK THERE.
AND BEST OF ALL, NO ONE THERE WILL KNOW US.

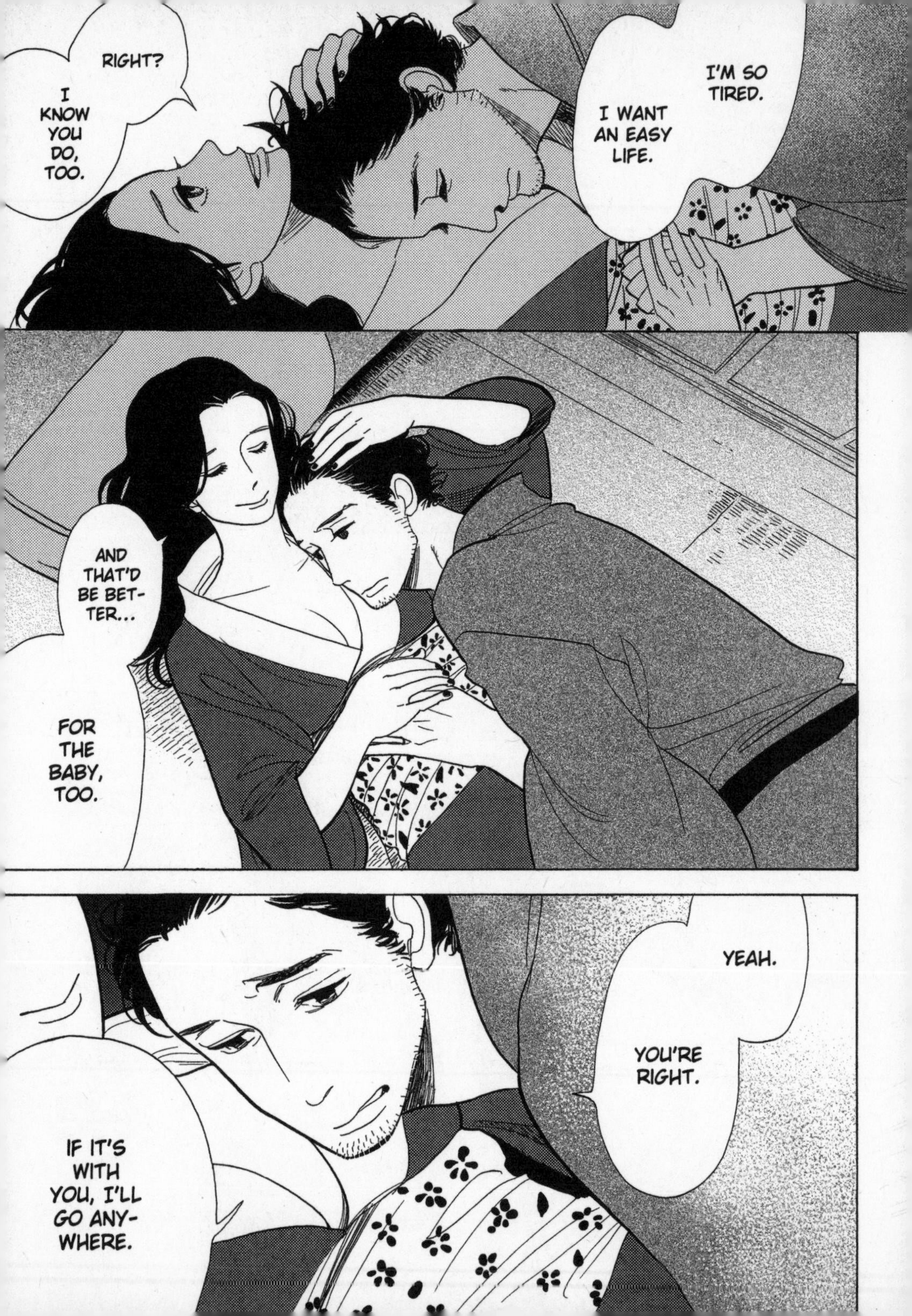
I'M SO TIRED. I WANT AN EASY LIFE.
RIGHT? I KNOW YOU DO, TOO.
AND THAT'D BE BET-TER...
FOR THE BABY, TOO.
YEAH. YOU'RE RIGHT.
IF IT'S WITH YOU, I'LL GO ANY-WHERE.

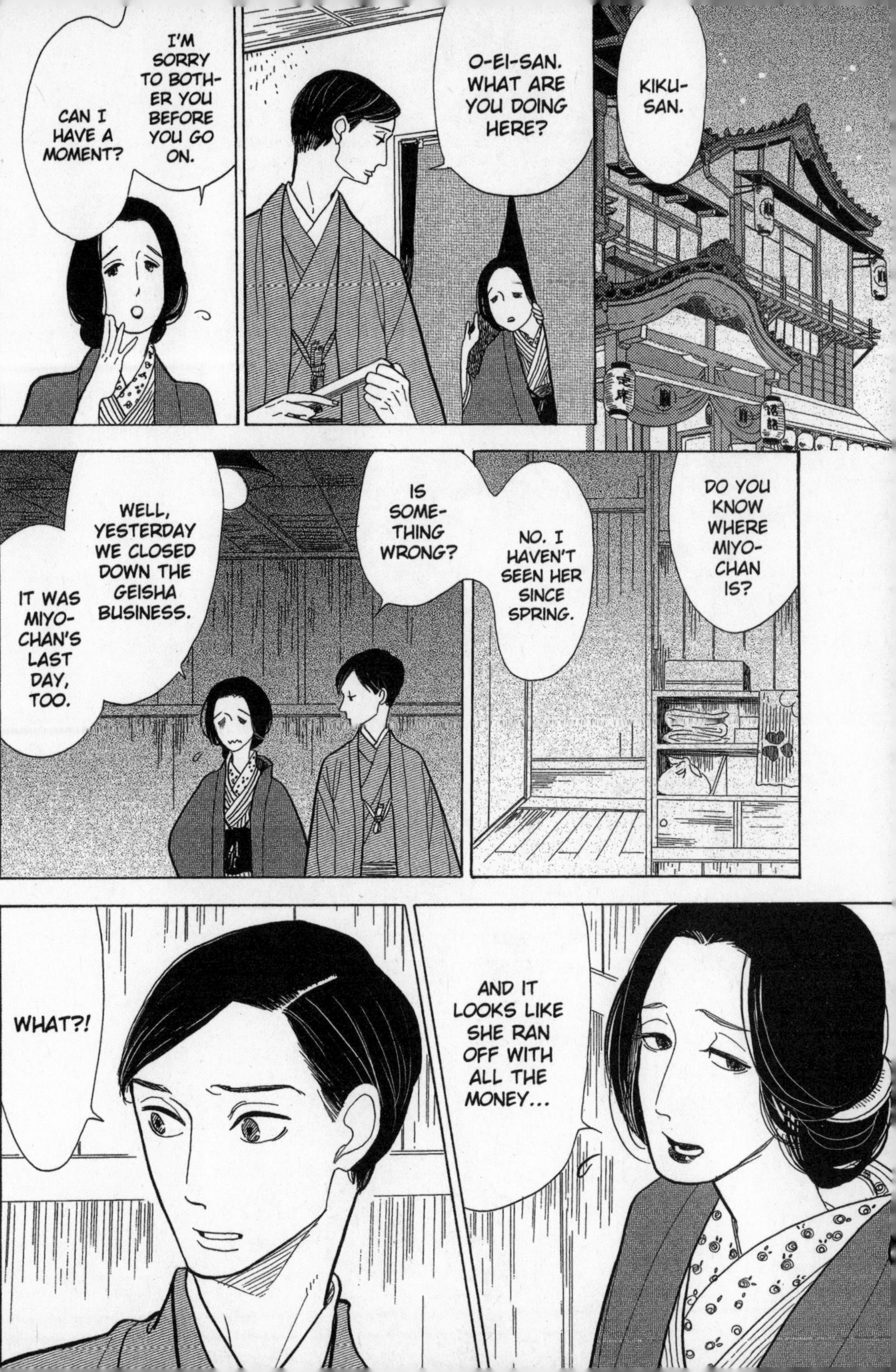
KIKU-SAN.
O-EI-SAN. WHAT ARE YOU DOING HERE?
I'M SORRY TO BOTHER YOU BEFORE YOU GO ON.
CAN I HAVE A MOMENT?
DO YOU KNOW WHERE MIYO-CHAN IS?
NO. I HAVEN'T SEEN HER SINCE SPRING.
IS SOMETHING WRONG?
WELL, YESTERDAY WE CLOSED DOWN THE GEISHA BUSINESS.
IT WAS MIYO-CHAN'S LAST DAY, TOO.
AND IT LOOKS LIKE SHE RAN OFF WITH ALL THE MONEY...
WHAT?!

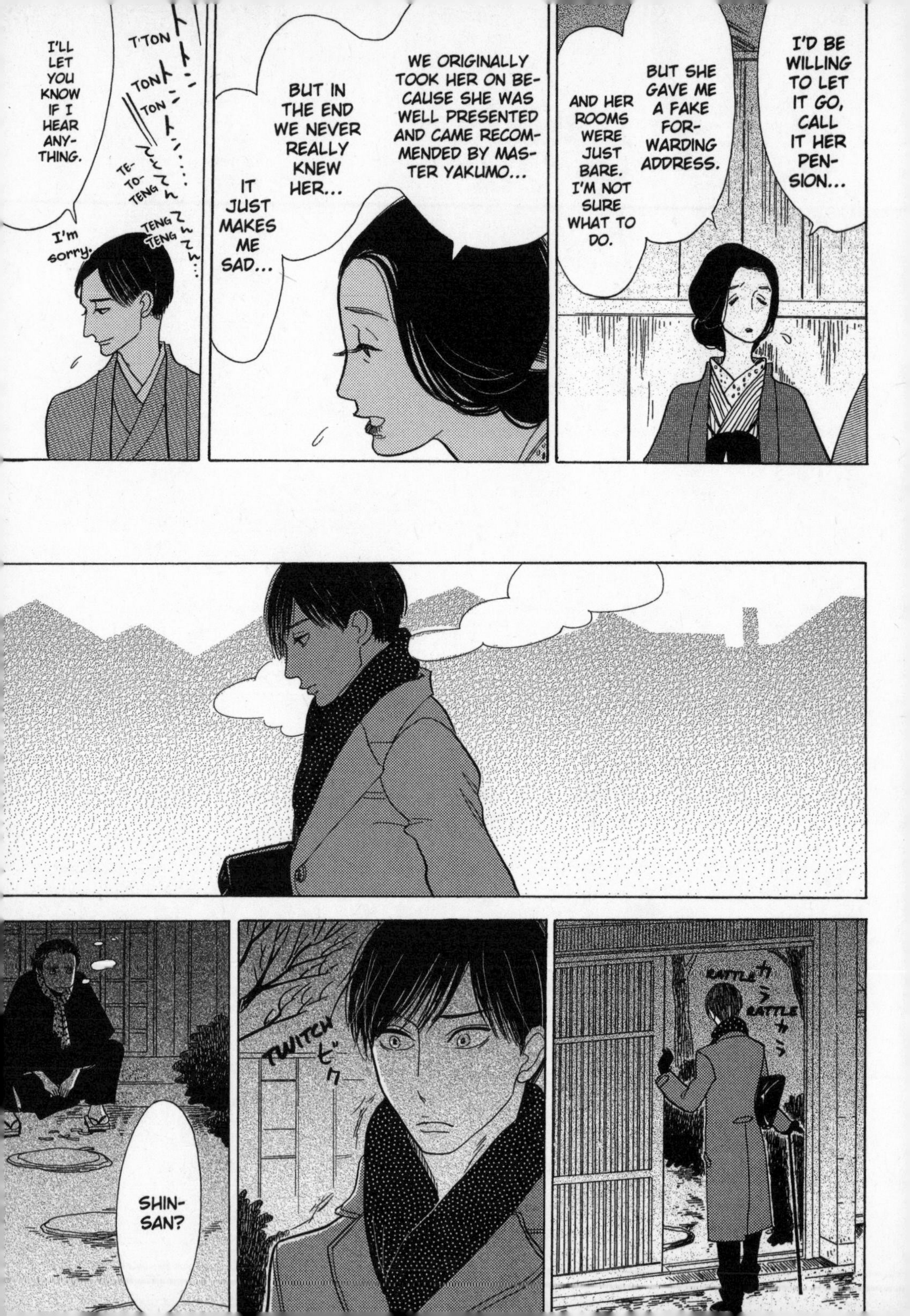
I'D BE WILLING TO LET IT GO, CALL IT HER PENSION...
BUT SHE GAVE ME A FAKE FORWARDING ADDRESS.
AND HER ROOMS WERE JUST BARE. I'M NOT SURE WHAT TO DO.
WE ORIGINALLY TOOK HER ON BECAUSE SHE WAS WELL PRESENTED AND CAME RECOMMENDED BY MASTER YAKUMO...
BUT IN THE END WE NEVER REALLY KNEW HER...
IT JUST MAKES ME SAD...
T'TON
TON
TON
TE-TO-TENG
TENG TENG
I'LL LET YOU KNOW IF I HEAR ANYTHING.
I'm sorry.
RATTLE
RATTLE
TWITCH
SHIN-SAN?

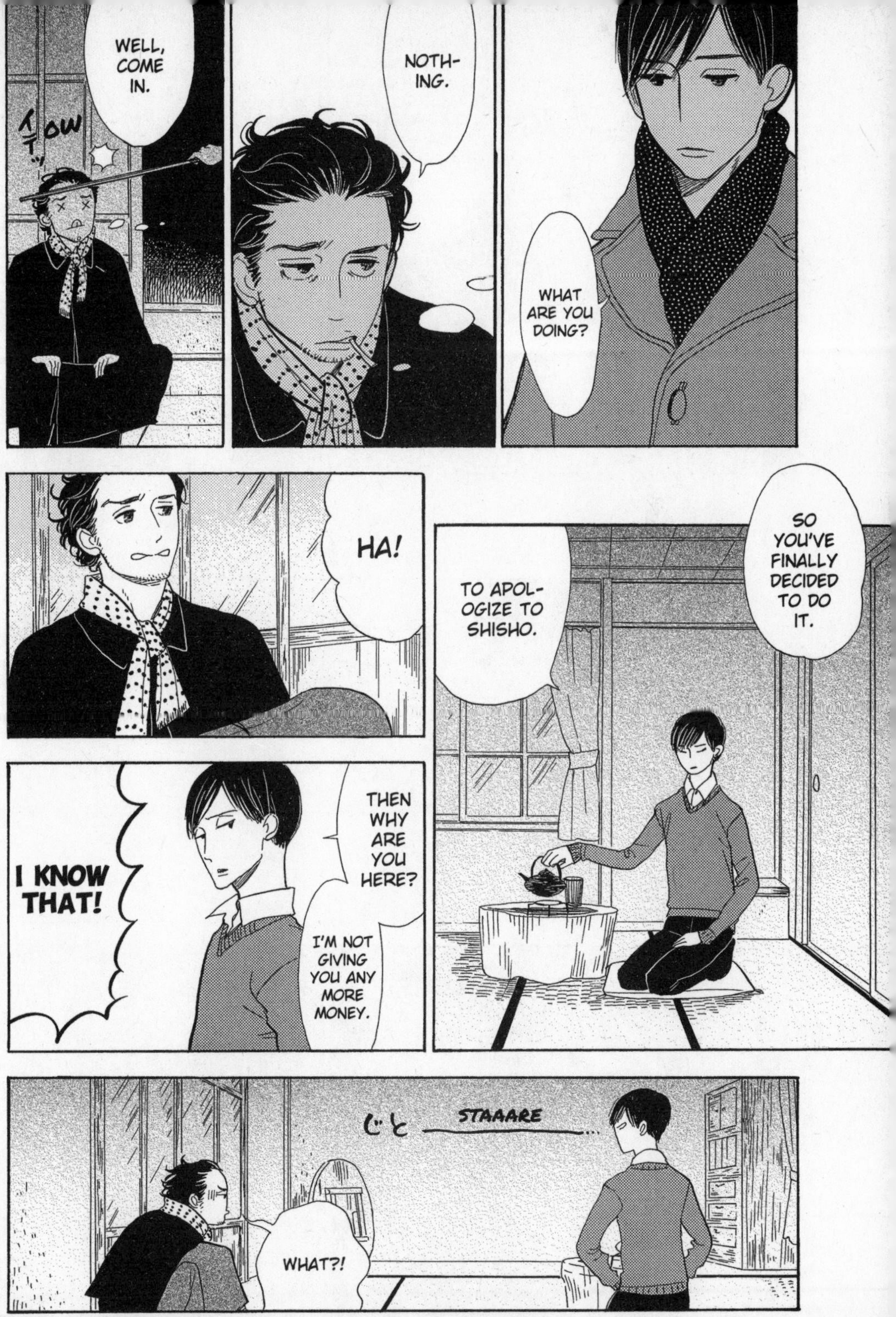
WHAT ARE YOU DOING?
NOTH-ING.
WELL, COME IN.
イテッ
OW
SO YOU'VE FINALLY DECIDED TO DO IT.
TO APOL-OGIZE TO SHISHO.
HA!
THEN WHY ARE YOU HERE?
I'M NOT GIVING YOU ANY MORE MONEY.
I KNOW THAT!
じと
STAAARE
WHAT?!

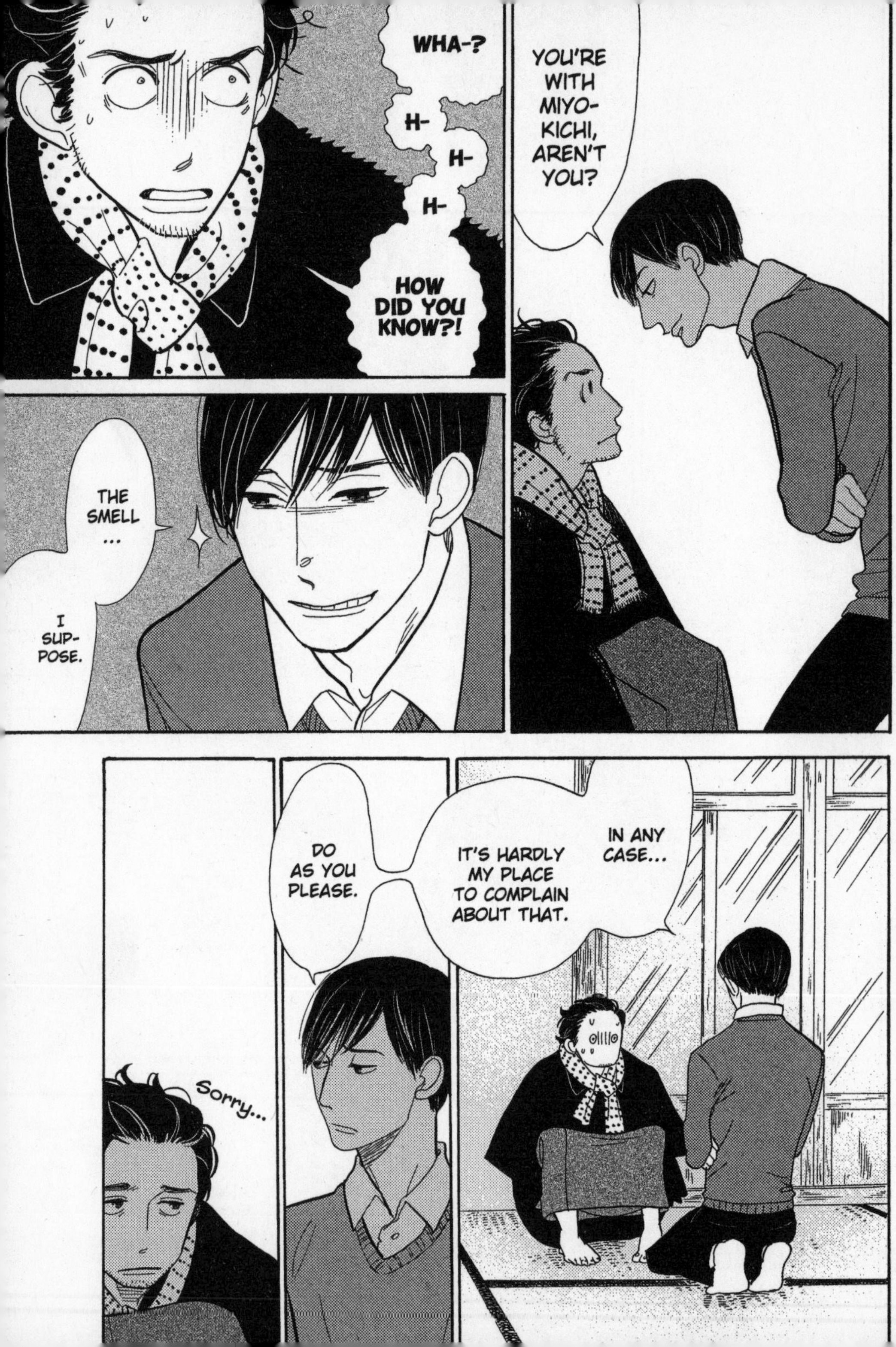
YOU'RE WITH MIYO-KICHI, AREN'T YOU?
WHA-?
H-
H-
H-
HOW DID YOU KNOW?!
THE SMELL...
I SUPPOSE.
IN ANY CASE...
IT'S HARDLY MY PLACE TO COMPLAIN ABOUT THAT.
DO AS YOU PLEASE.
Sorry...

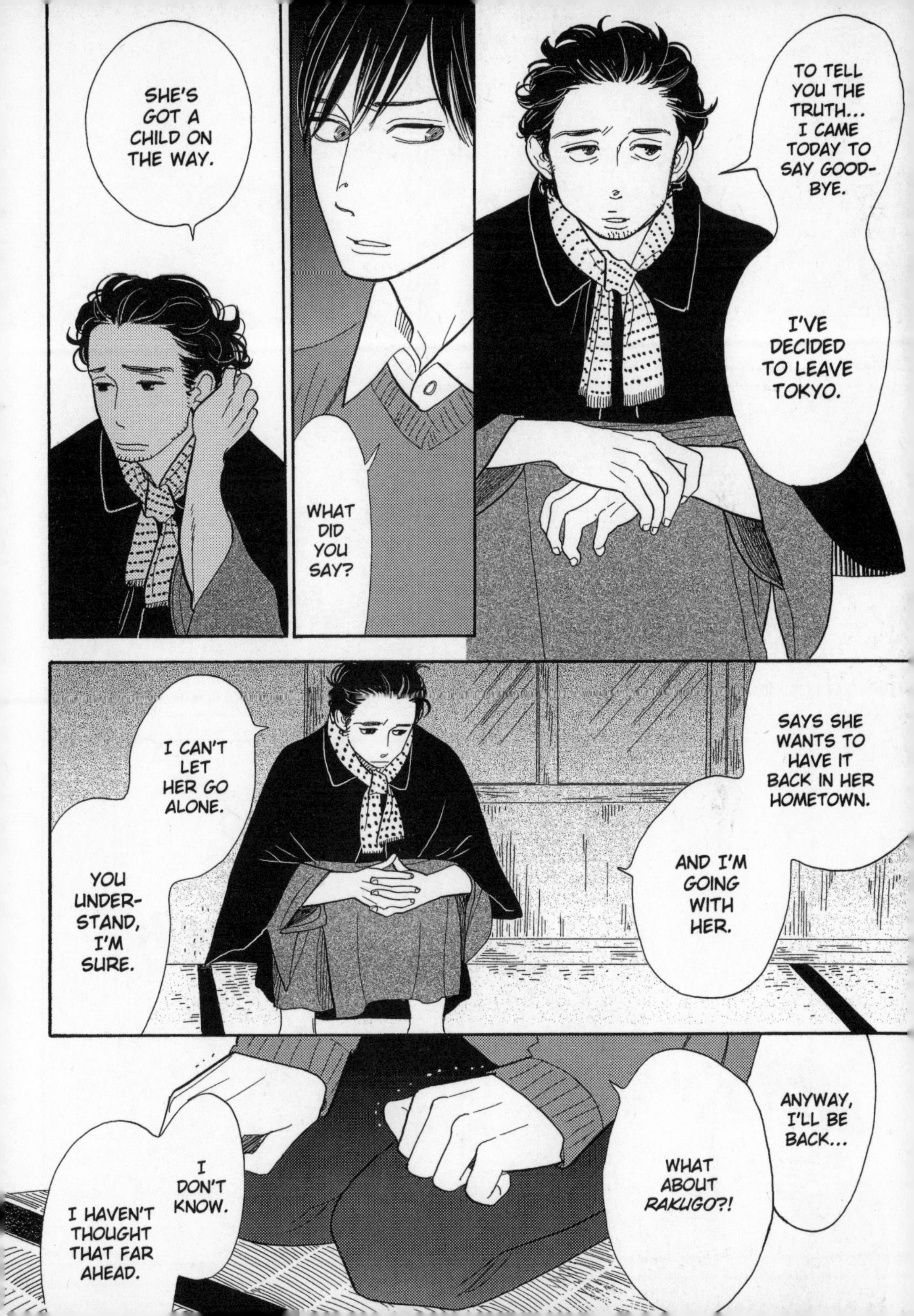
TO TELL YOU THE TRUTH... I CAME TODAY TO SAY GOOD-BYE.
I'VE DECIDED TO LEAVE TOKYO.
WHAT DID YOU SAY?
SHE'S GOT A CHILD ON THE WAY.
SAYS SHE WANTS TO HAVE IT BACK IN HER HOMETOWN.
AND I'M GOING WITH HER.
I CAN'T LET HER GO ALONE.
YOU UNDER-STAND, I'M SURE.
ANYWAY, I'LL BE BACK...
WHAT ABOUT *RAKUGO*?!
I DON'T KNOW.
I HAVEN'T THOUGHT THAT FAR AHEAD.

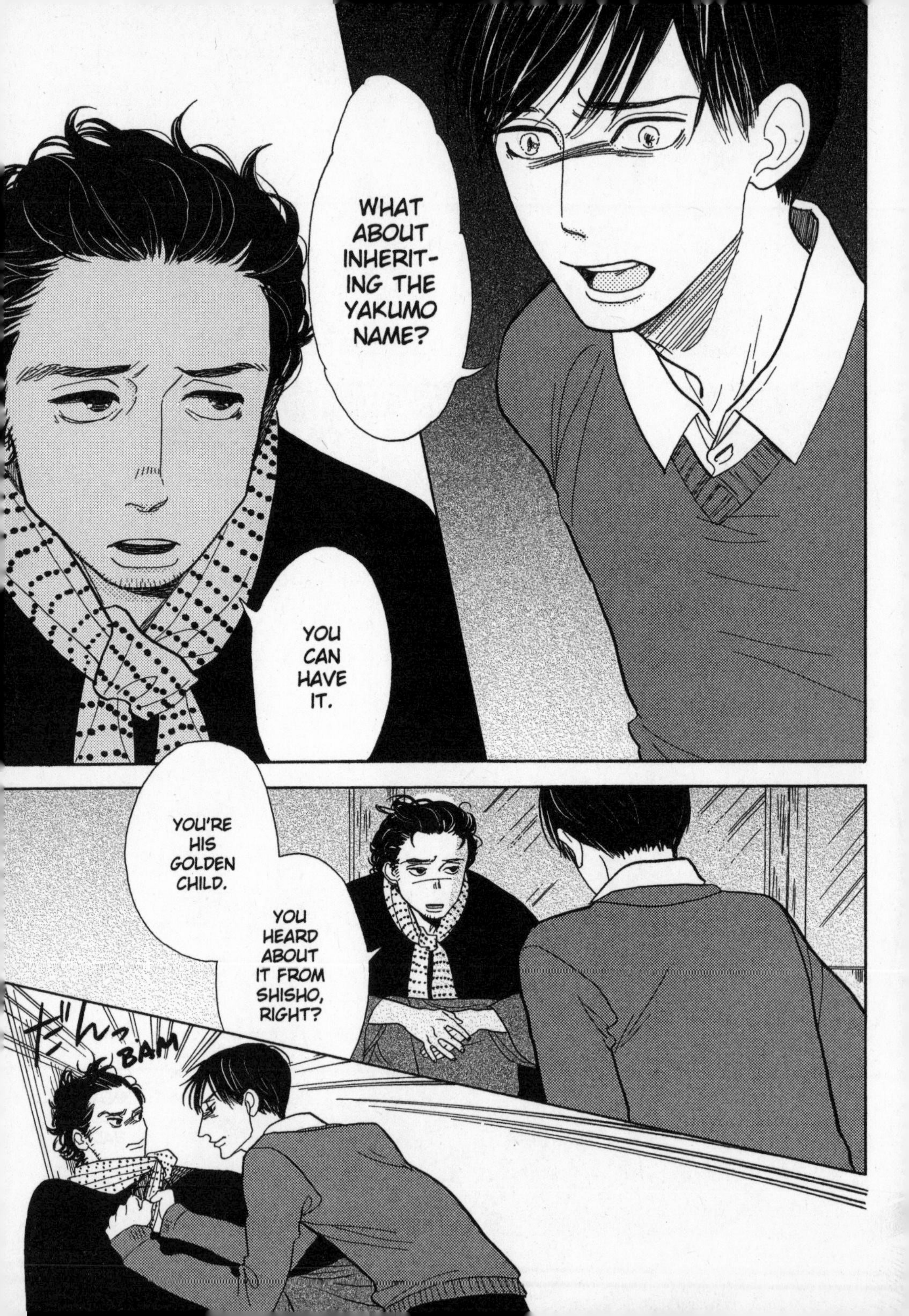
WHAT ABOUT INHERIT-ING THE YAKUMO NAME?
YOU CAN HAVE IT.
YOU'RE HIS GOLDEN CHILD.
YOU HEARD ABOUT IT FROM SHISHO, RIGHT?
だんっ
BAM

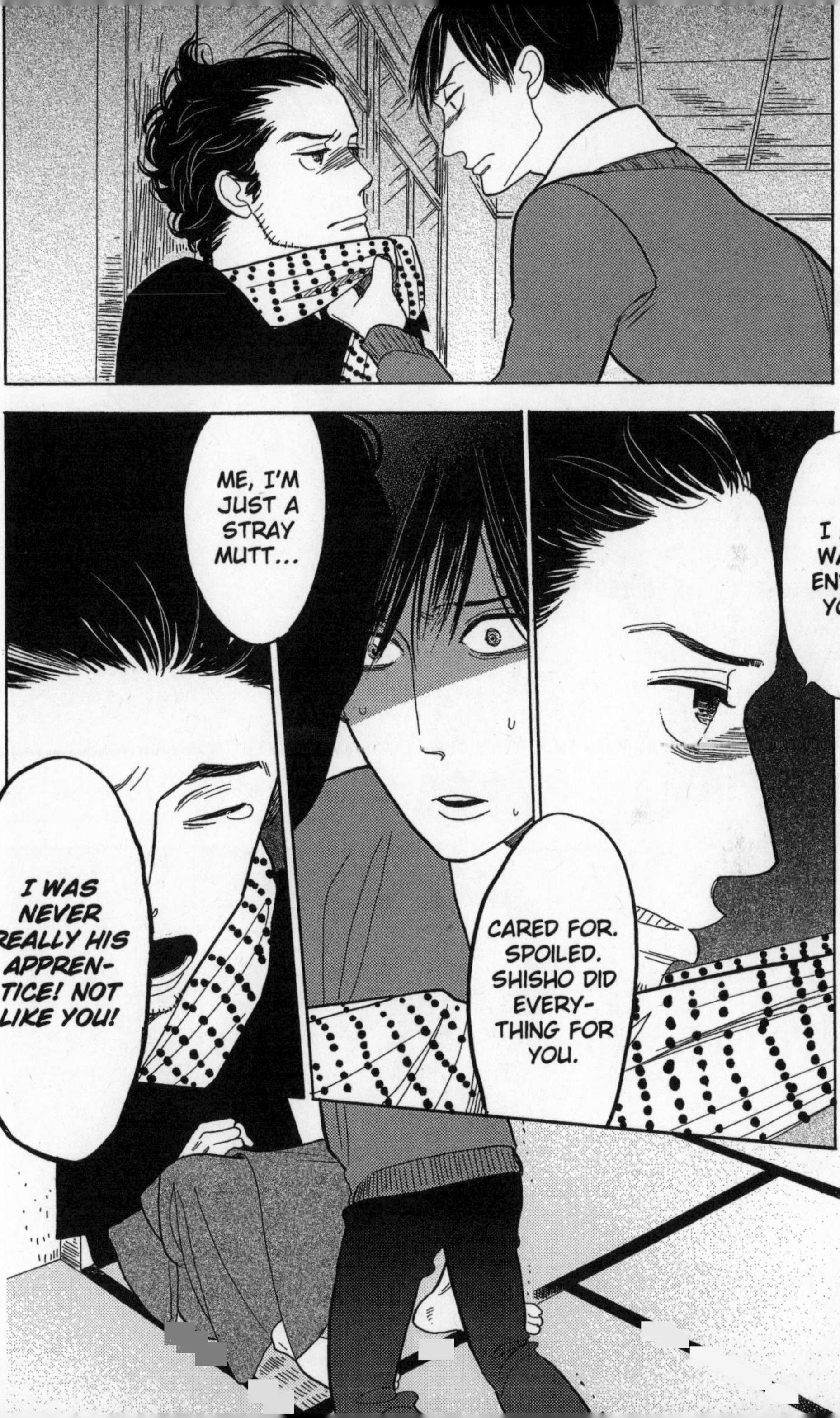
I AL-WAYS ENVIED YOU.
CARED FOR. SPOILED. SHISHO DID EVERY-THING FOR YOU.
ME, I'M JUST A STRAY MUTT...
I WAS NEVER REALLY HIS APPREN-TICE! NOT LIKE YOU!

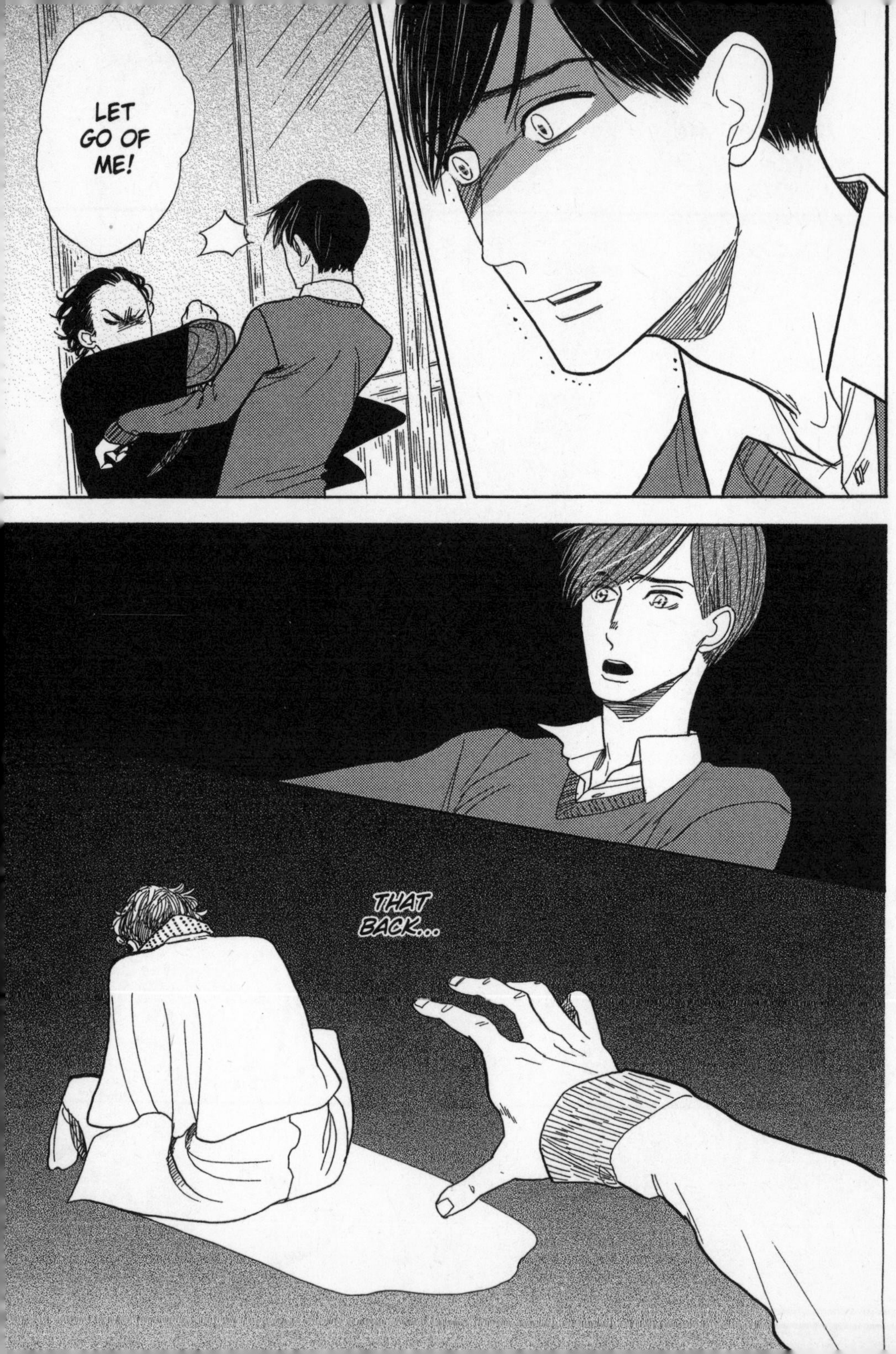
LET GO OF ME!
THAT BACK...

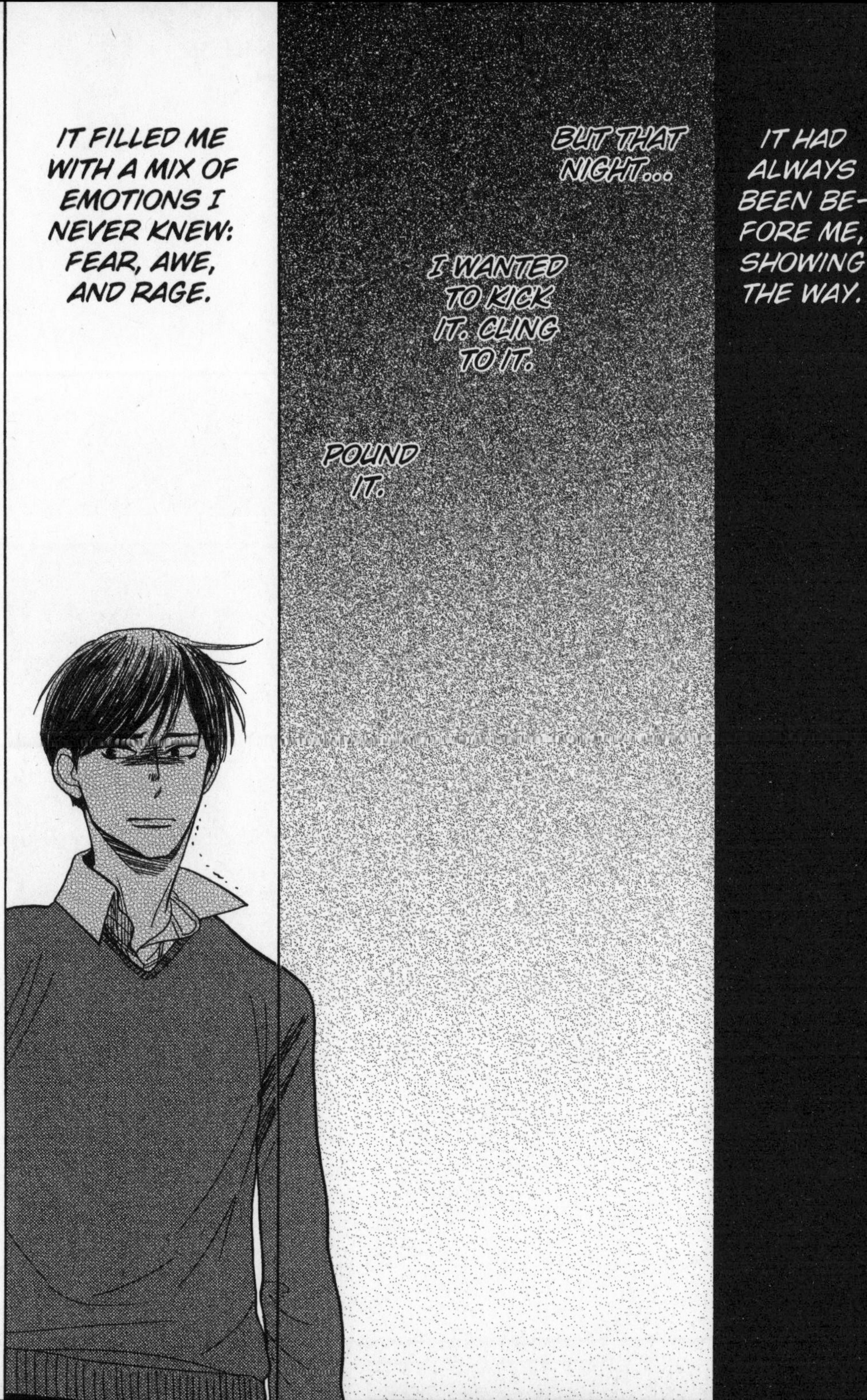
IT HAD ALWAYS BEEN BE-FORE ME, SHOWING THE WAY.
BUT THAT NIGHT...
I WANTED TO KICK IT. CLING TO IT.
POUND IT.
IT FILLED ME WITH A MIX OF EMOTIONS I NEVER KNEW: FEAR, AWE, AND RAGE.

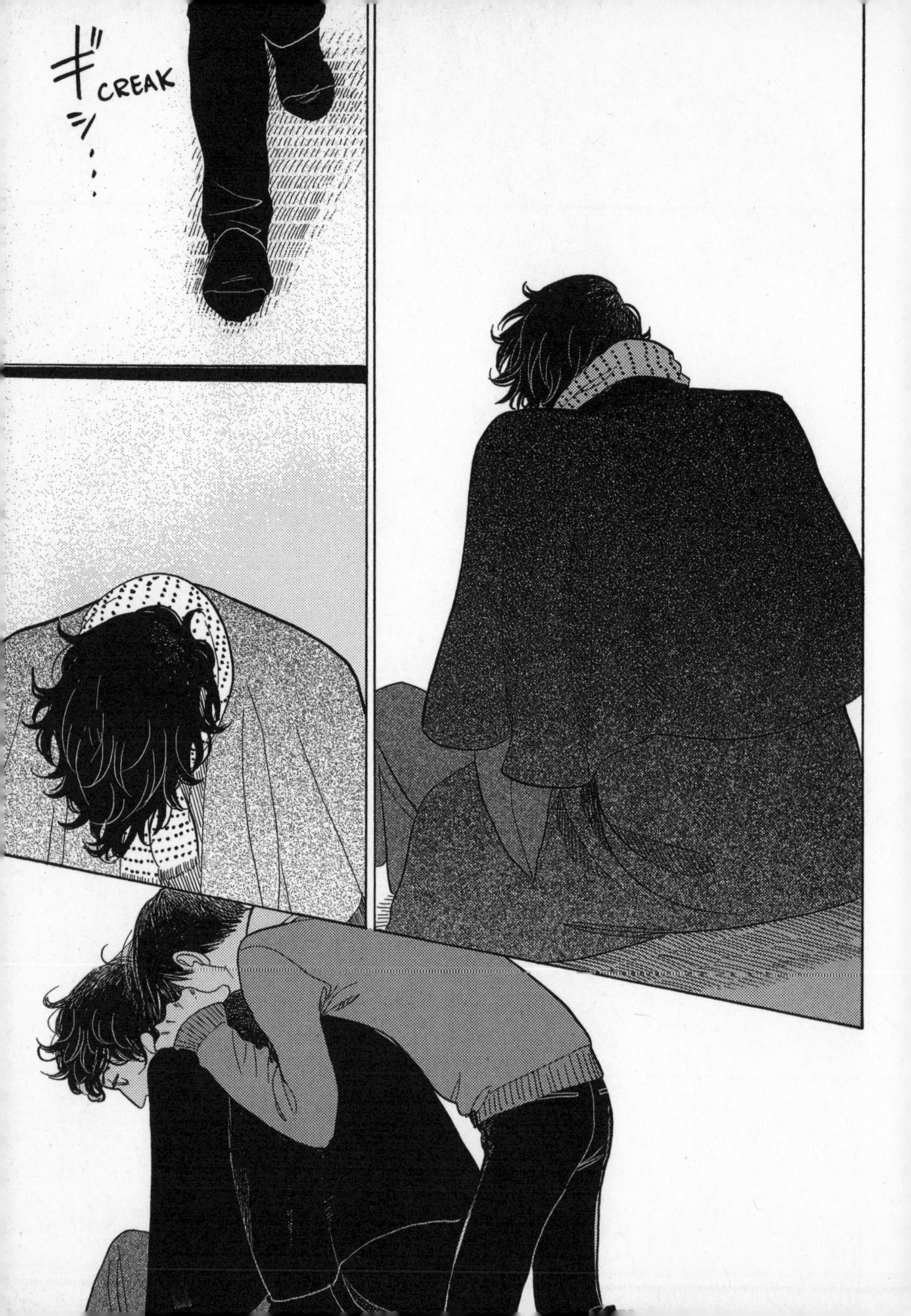
ギシ…
CREAK

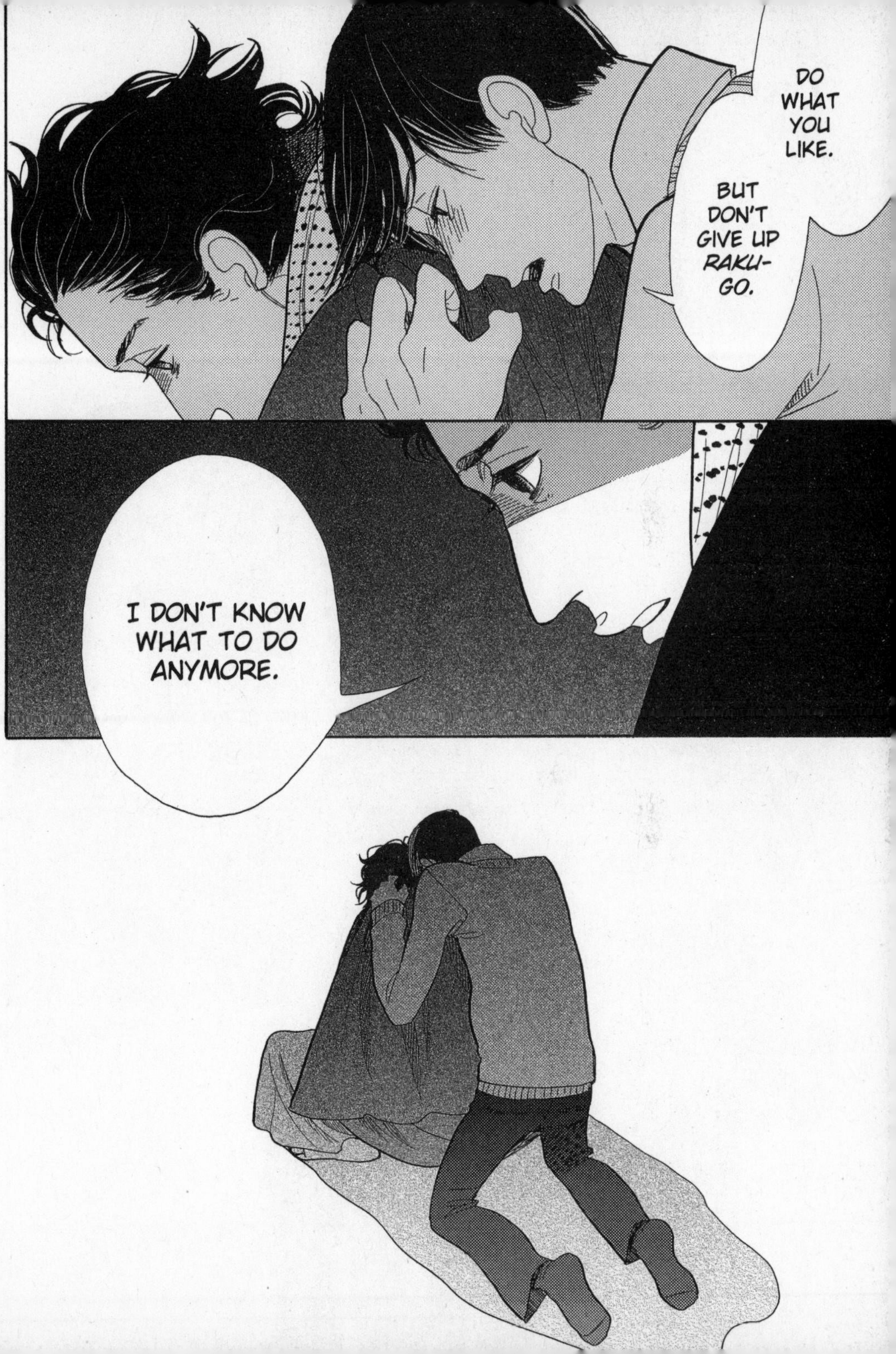
DO WHAT YOU LIKE.
BUT DON'T GIVE UP RAKU-GO.
I DON'T KNOW WHAT TO DO ANYMORE.

DESCENDING
STORIES

SHOWA
GENROKU
RAKUGO
SHINJU

HARUKO KUMOTA

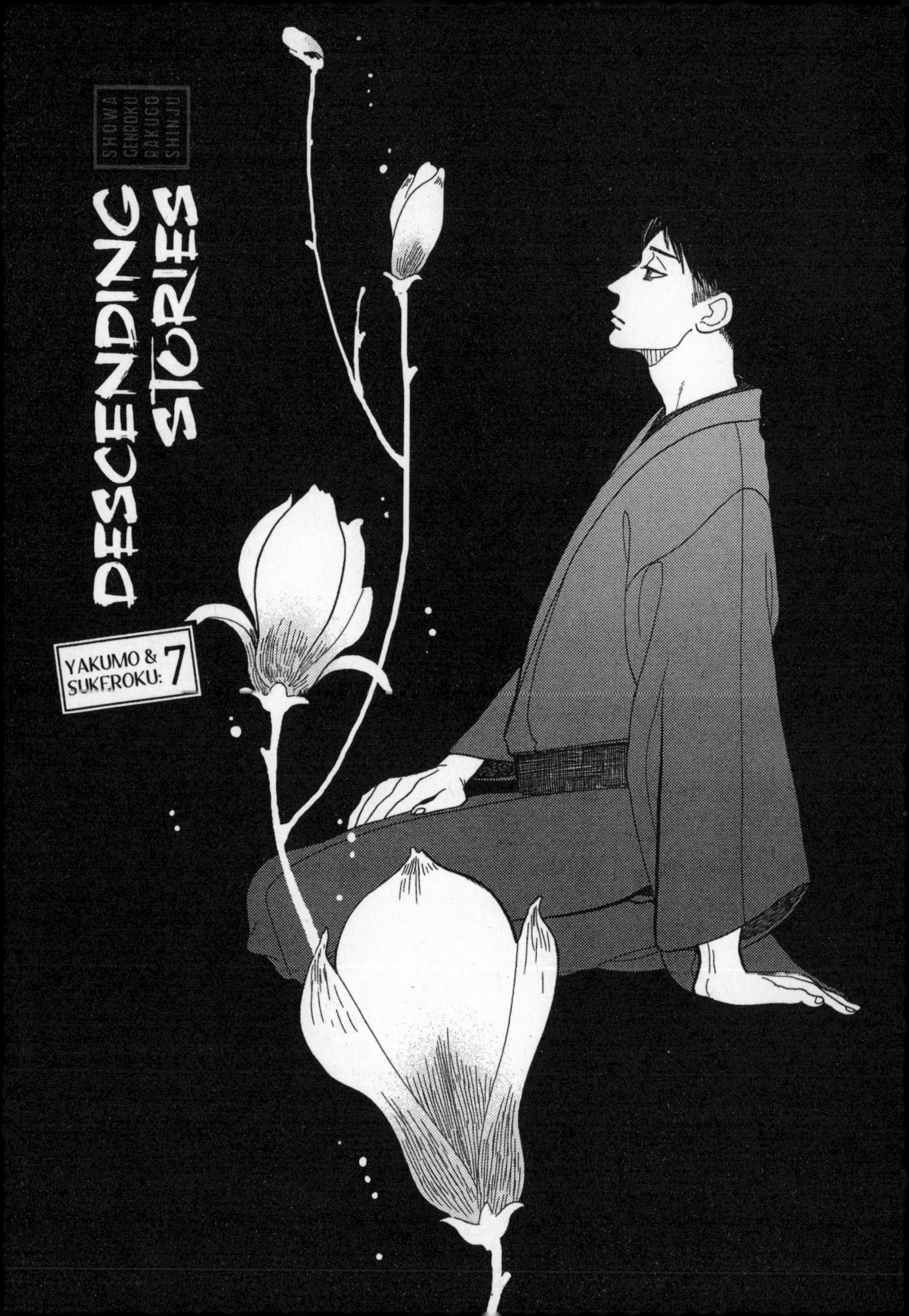
SHOWA GENROKU RAKUGO SHINJU
DESCENDING STORIES
YAKUMO & SUKEROKU: 7

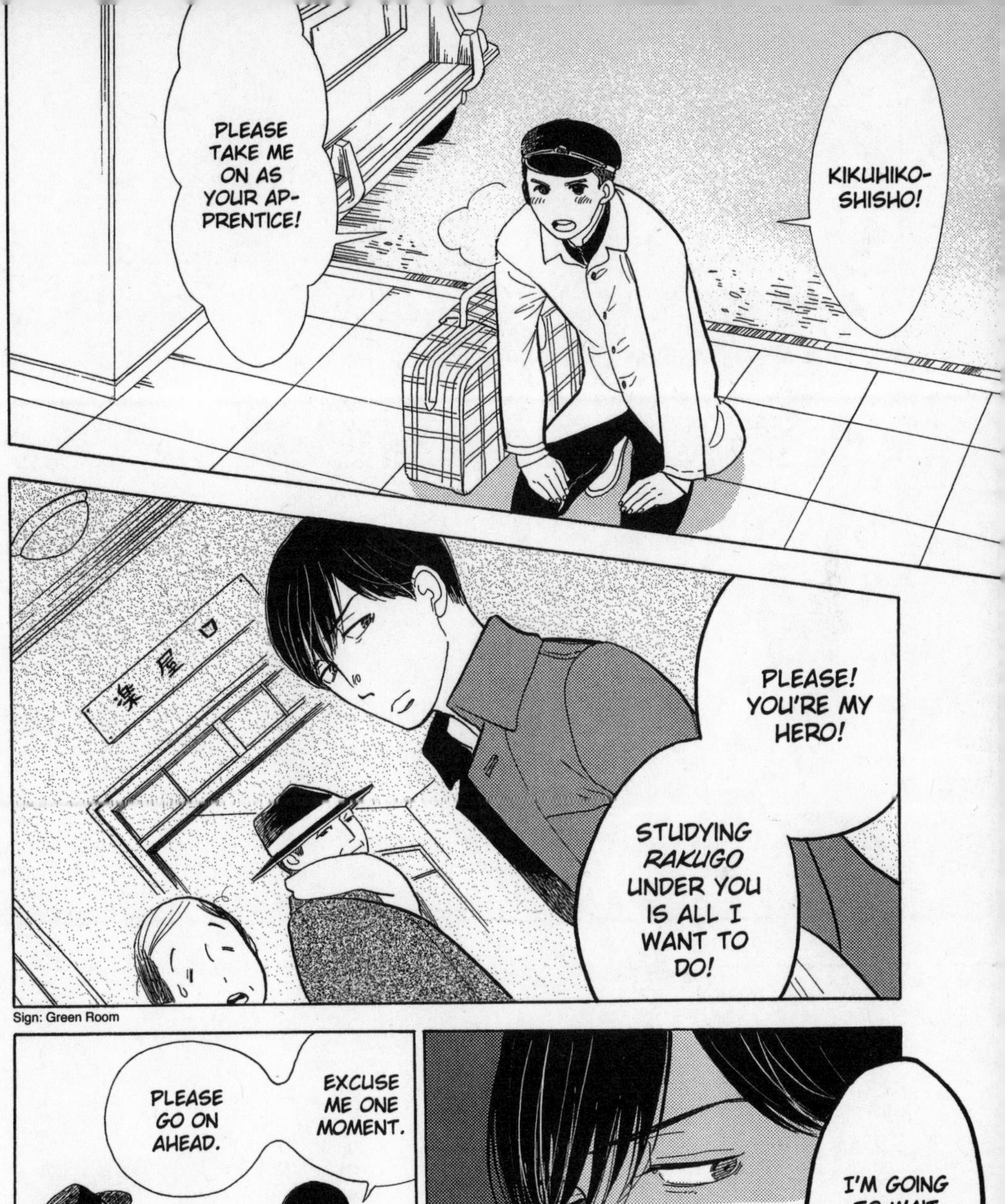
KIKUHIKO-SHISHO!
PLEASE TAKE ME ON AS YOUR AP-PRENTICE!
楽屋口
PLEASE! YOU'RE MY HERO!
STUDYING *RAKUGO* UNDER YOU IS ALL I WANT TO DO!
Sign: Green Room

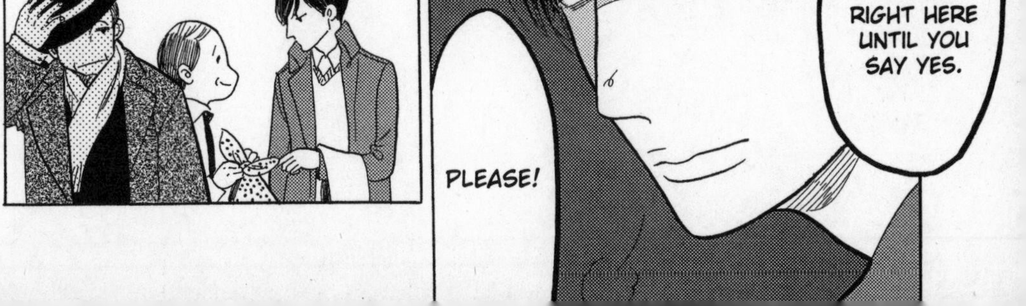
I'M GOING TO WAIT RIGHT HERE UNTIL YOU SAY YES.
PLEASE!
EXCUSE ME ONE MOMENT.
PLEASE GO ON AHEAD.

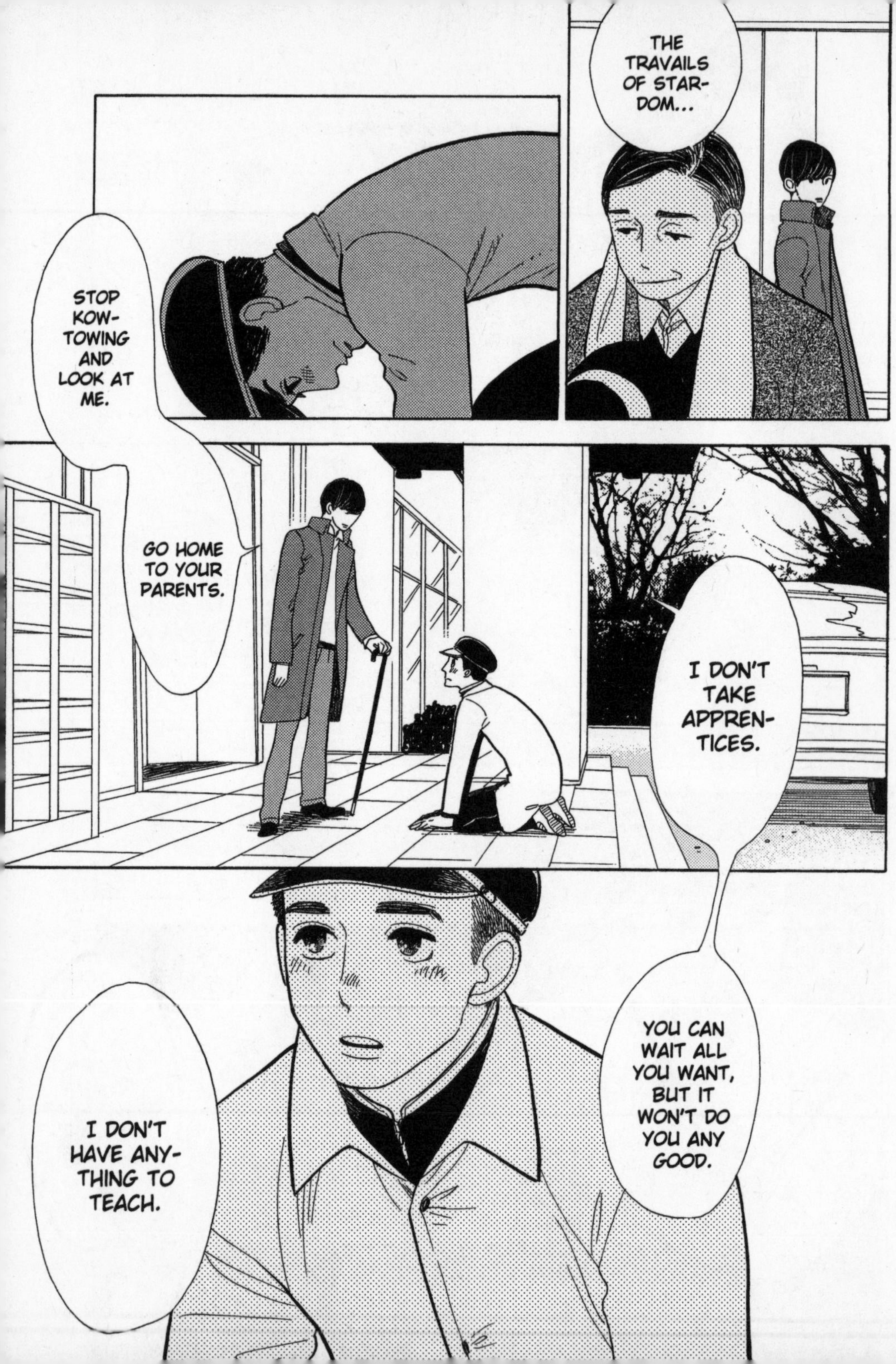
THE TRAVAILS OF STAR-DOM...
STOP KOW-TOWING AND LOOK AT ME.
GO HOME TO YOUR PARENTS.
I DON'T TAKE APPREN-TICES.
YOU CAN WAIT ALL YOU WANT, BUT IT WON'T DO YOU ANY GOOD.
I DON'T HAVE ANY-THING TO TEACH.

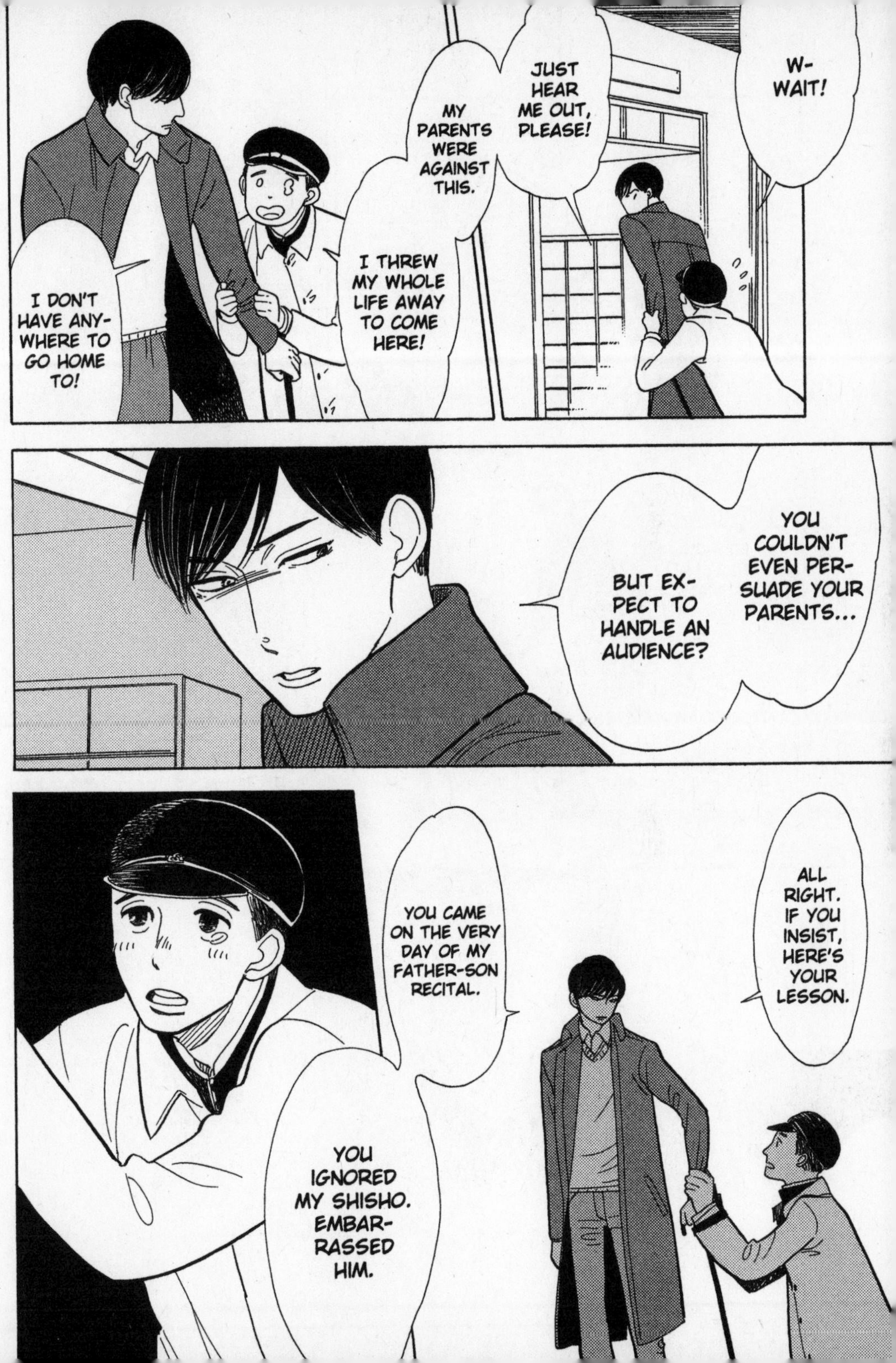
W- WAIT!
JUST HEAR ME OUT, PLEASE!
MY PARENTS WERE AGAINST THIS.
I THREW MY WHOLE LIFE AWAY TO COME HERE!
I DON'T HAVE ANYWHERE TO GO HOME TO!
YOU COULDN'T EVEN PERSUADE YOUR PARENTS...
BUT EXPECT TO HANDLE AN AUDIENCE?
ALL RIGHT. IF YOU INSIST, HERE'S YOUR LESSON.
YOU CAME ON THE VERY DAY OF MY FATHER-SON RECITAL.
YOU IGNORED MY SHISHO. EMBARRASSED HIM.

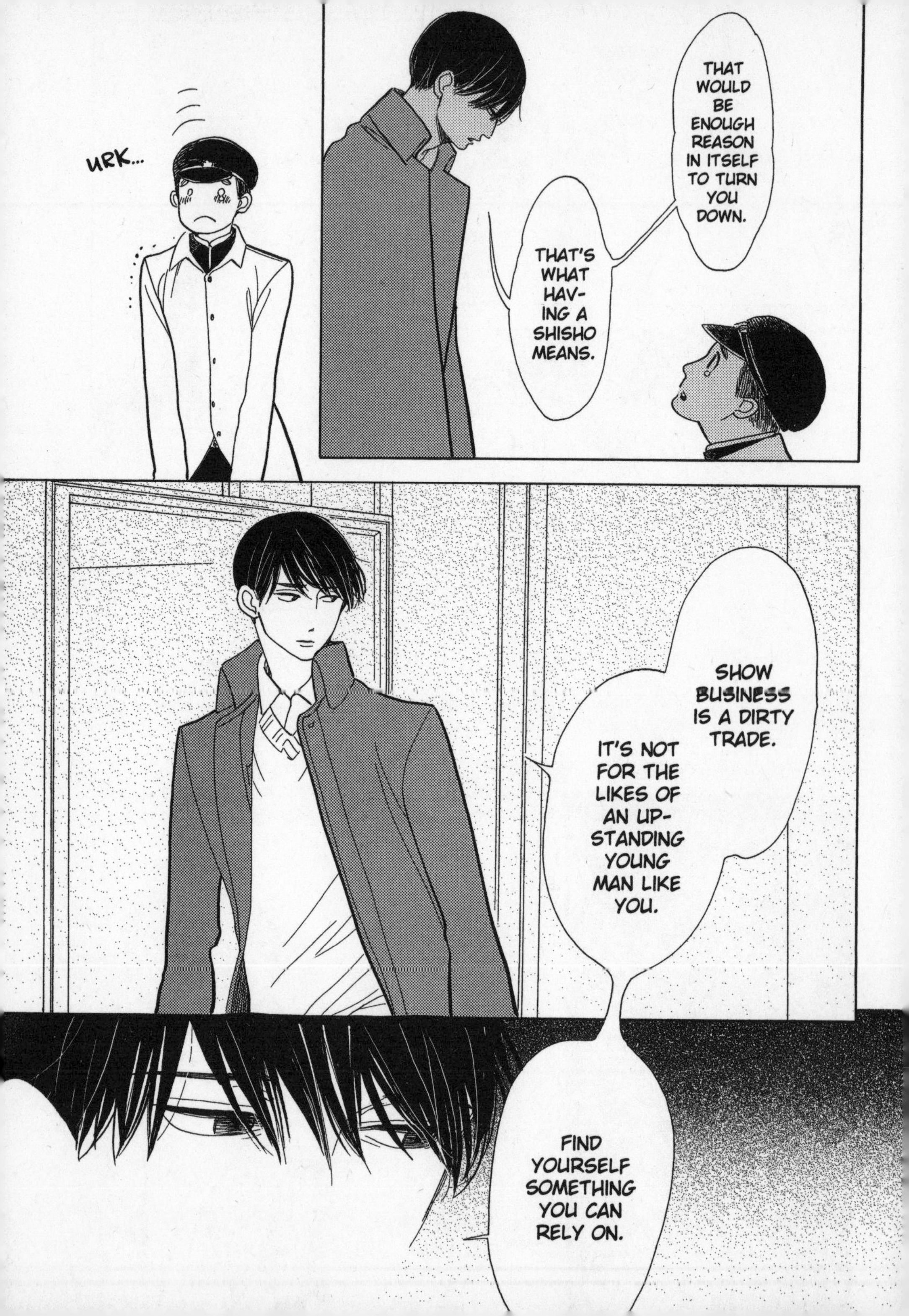
THAT WOULD BE ENOUGH REASON IN ITSELF TO TURN YOU DOWN.
THAT'S WHAT HAV-ING A SHISHO MEANS.
URK...
SHOW BUSINESS IS A DIRTY TRADE.
IT'S NOT FOR THE LIKES OF AN UP-STANDING YOUNG MAN LIKE YOU.
FIND YOURSELF SOMETHING YOU CAN RELY ON.

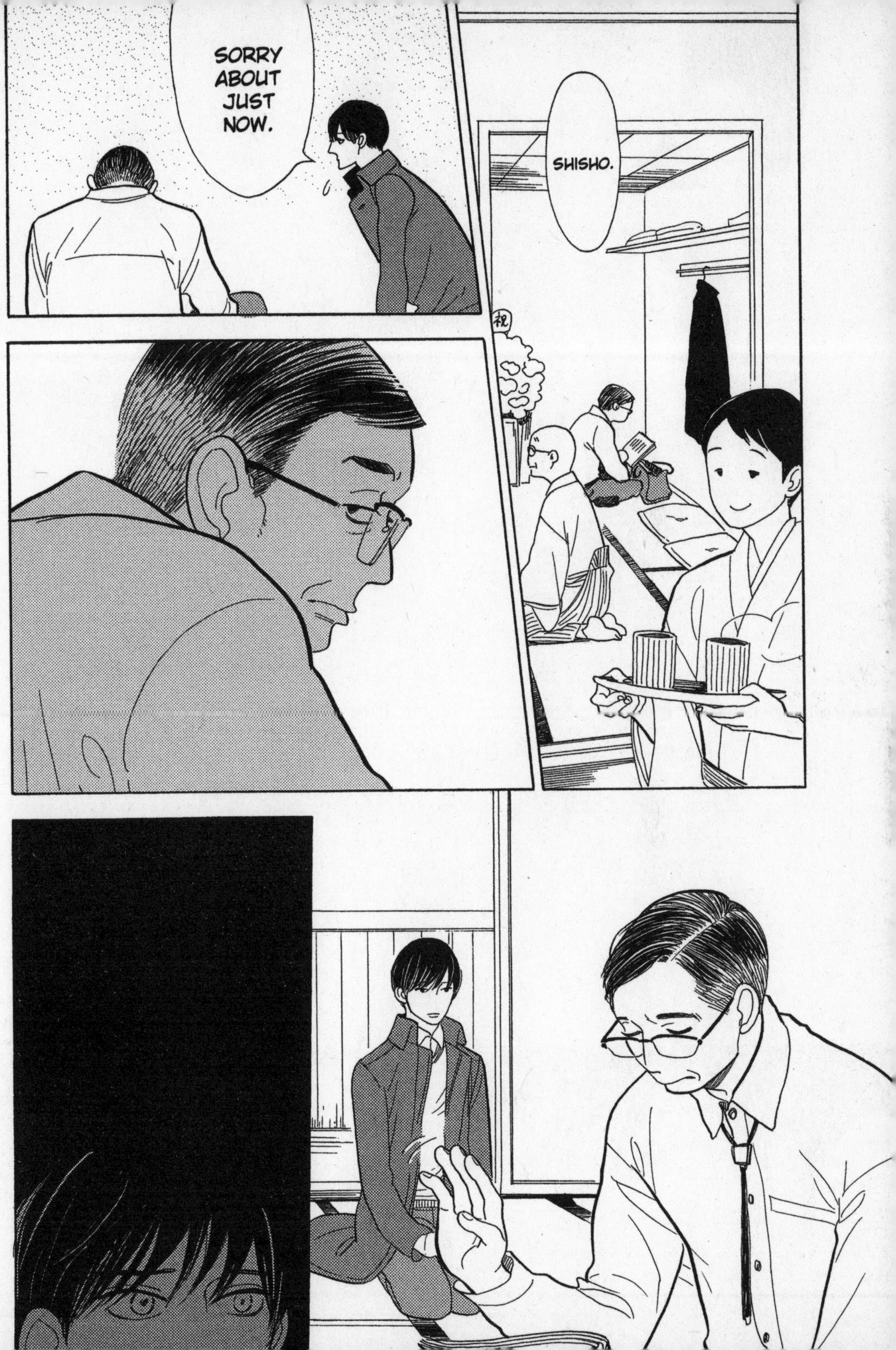
SHISHO.
SORRY ABOUT JUST NOW.

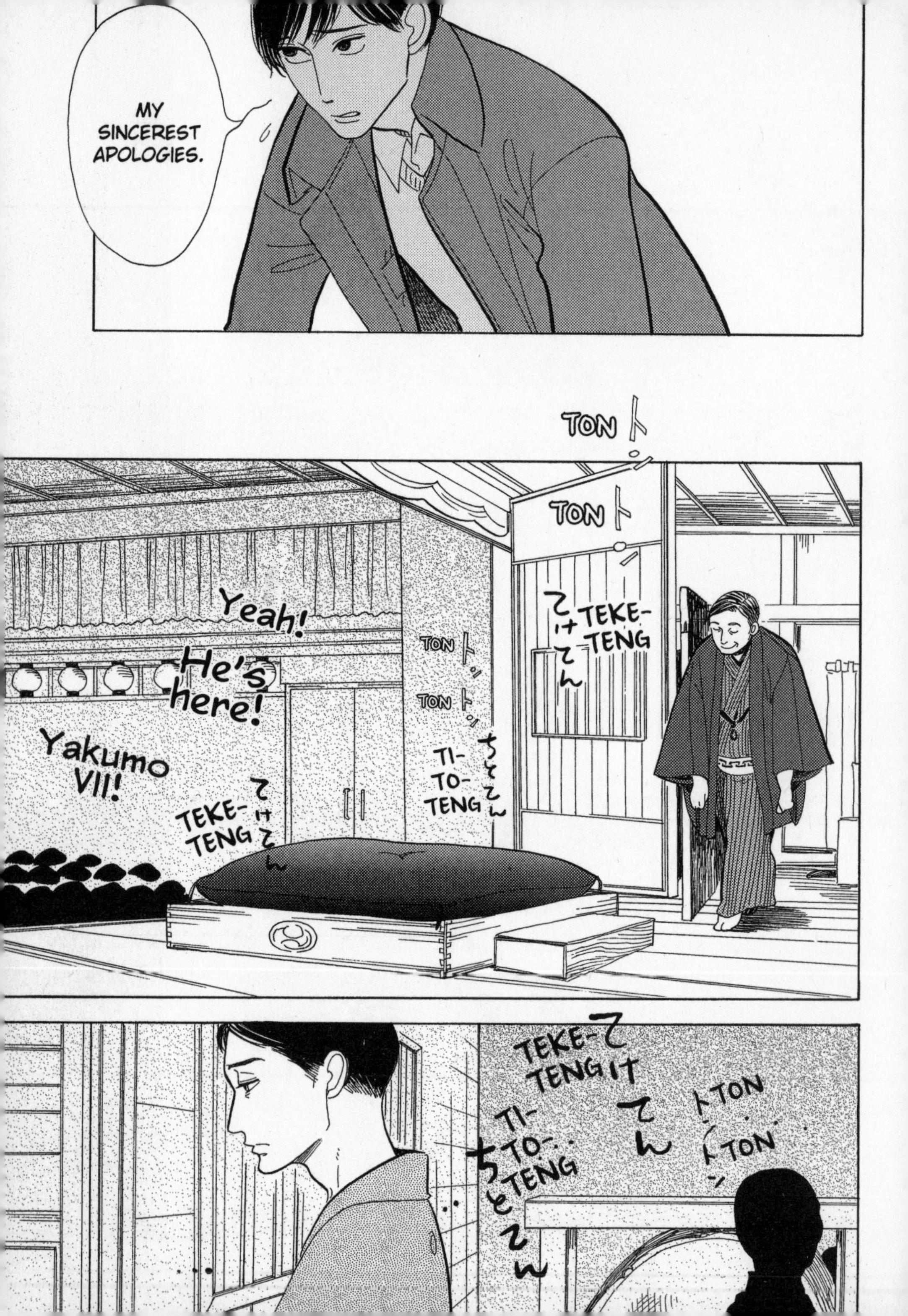
MY SINCEREST APOLOGIES.
TON
TON
TEKE-TENG
TON
TON
TI-TO-TENG
TEKE-TENG
Yeah!
He's here!
Yakumo VII!
TEKE-TENG
TI-TO-TENG
TON
TON
...

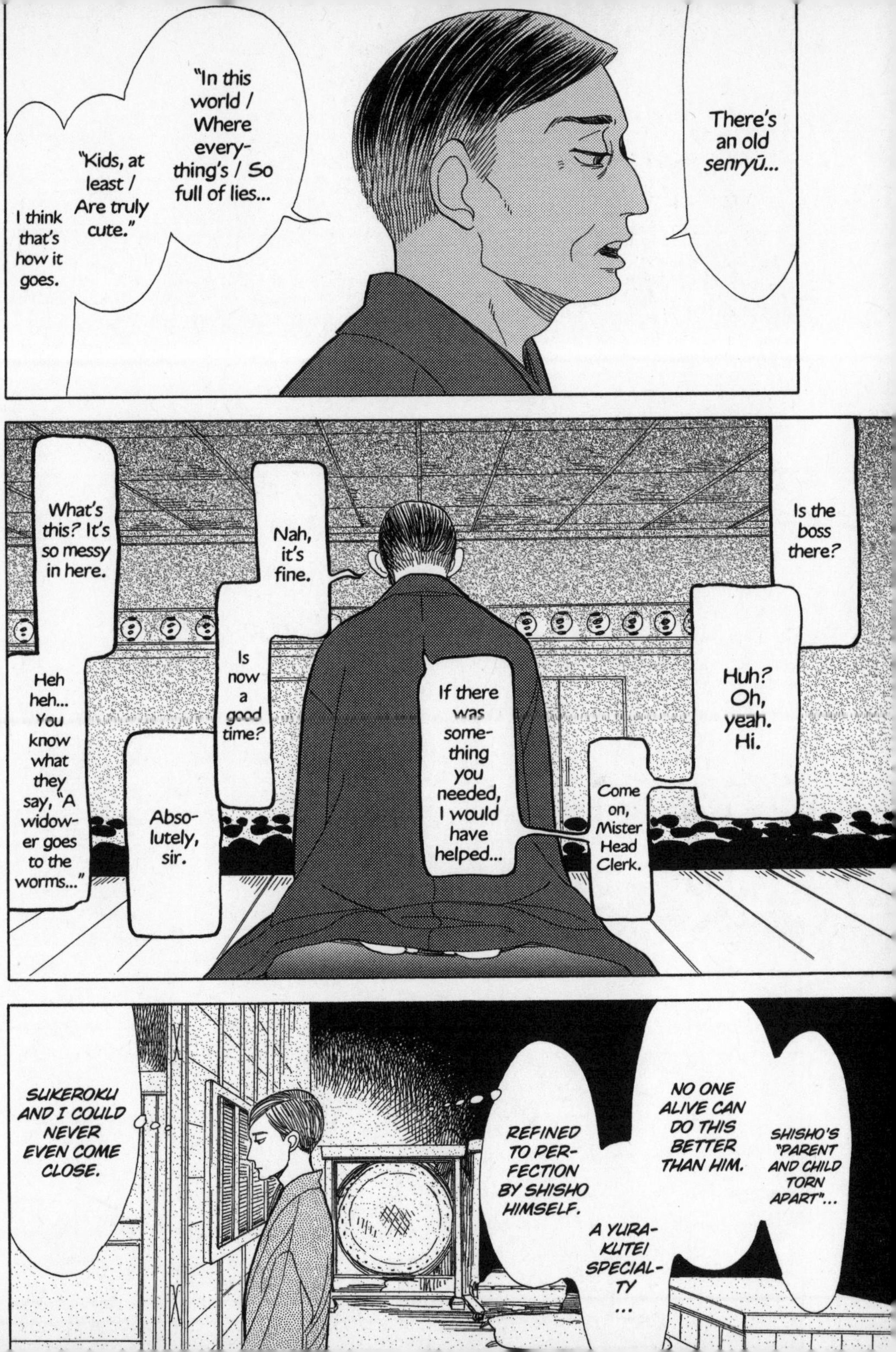
There's an old senryū...
"In this world / Where every-thing's / So full of lies...
"Kids, at least / Are truly cute."
I think that's how it goes.
Is the boss there?
Huh? Oh, yeah. Hi.
Come on, Mister Head Clerk.
If there was some-thing you needed, I would have helped...
Nah, it's fine.
Is now a good time?
Absolutely, sir.
What's this? It's so messy in here.
Heh heh... You know what they say, "A widow-er goes to the worms..."
SHISHO'S "PARENT AND CHILD TORN APART"...
NO ONE ALIVE CAN DO THIS BETTER THAN HIM.
REFINED TO PER-FECTION BY SHISHO HIMSELF.
A YURA-KUTEI SPECIAL-TY ...
SUKEROKU AND I COULD NEVER EVEN COME CLOSE.

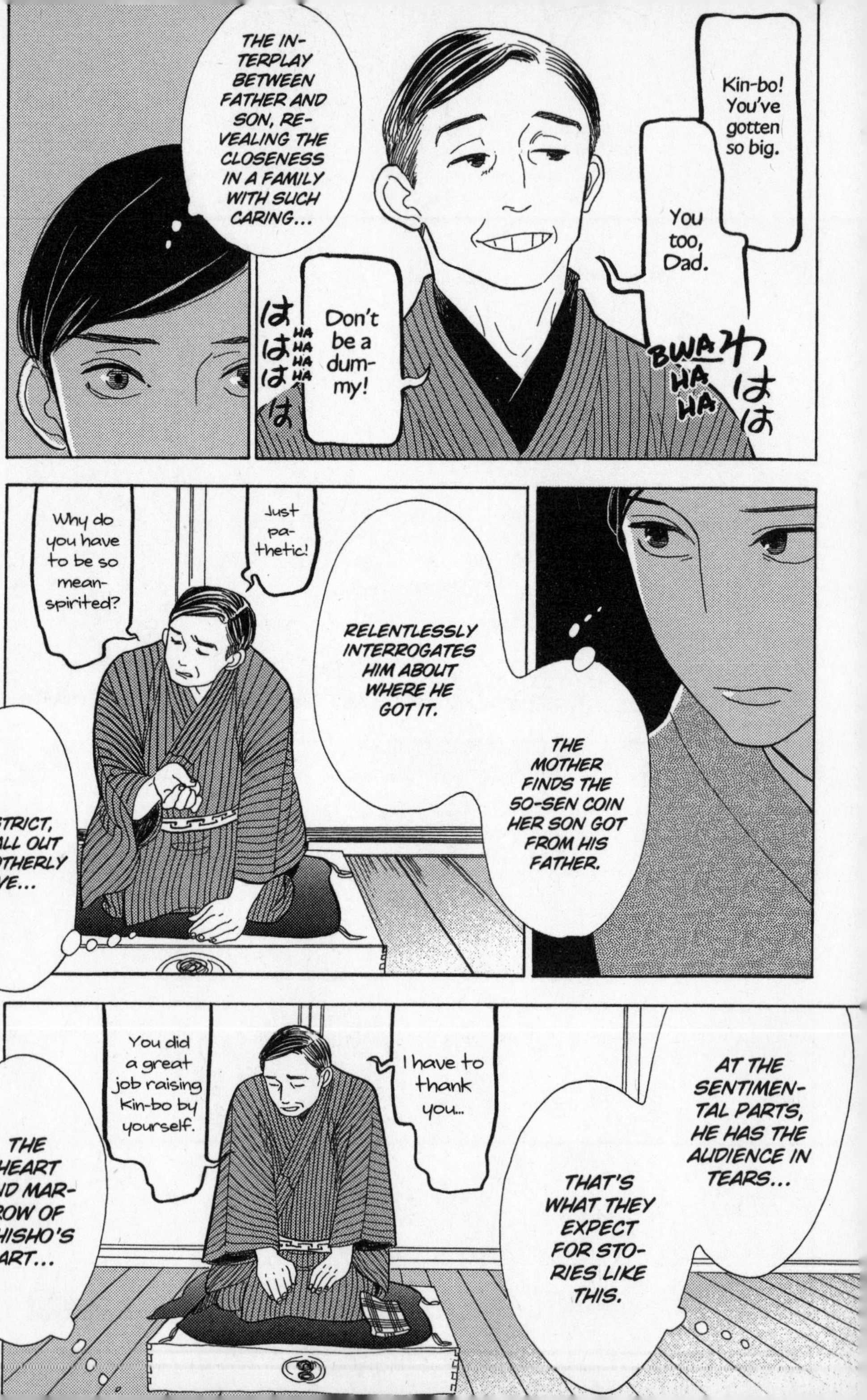
Kin-bo! You've gotten so big.
You too, Dad.
BWA HA HA わはは
Don't be a dum-my!
HA HA HA HA はははは
THE IN-TERPLAY BETWEEN FATHER AND SON, RE-VEALING THE CLOSENESS IN A FAMILY WITH SUCH CARING...
THE MOTHER FINDS THE SO-SEN COIN HER SON GOT FROM HIS FATHER.
RELENTLESSLY INTERROGATES HIM ABOUT WHERE HE GOT IT.
Just pa-thetic!
Why do you have to be so mean-spirited?
SO STRICT, BUT ALL OUT OF MOTHERLY LOVE...
AT THE SENTIMEN-TAL PARTS, HE HAS THE AUDIENCE IN TEARS...
THAT'S WHAT THEY EXPECT FOR STO-RIES LIKE THIS.
I have to thank you...
You did a great job raising Kin-bo by yourself.
THE HEART AND MAR-ROW OF SHISHO'S ART...

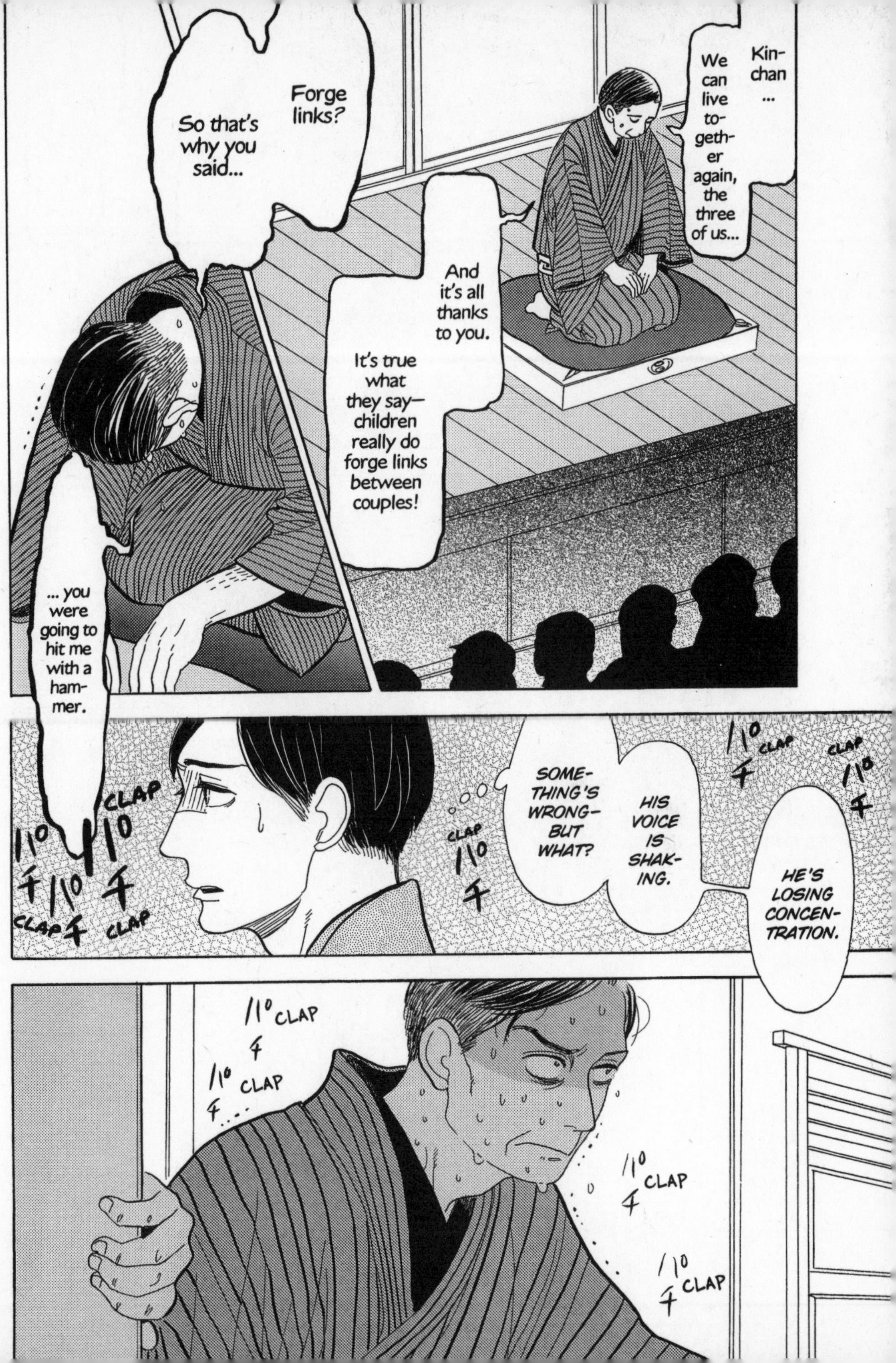
Kin-chan...
We can live together again, the three of us...
And it's all thanks to you.
It's true what they say—children really do forge links between couples!
Forge links?
So that's why you said...
... you were going to hit me with a hammer.
CLAP CLAP
CLAP CLAP
HE'S LOSING CONCENTRATION.
HIS VOICE IS SHAKING.
SOMETHING'S WRONG—BUT WHAT?
CLAP
CLAP CLAP CLAP
CLAP
CLAP
CLAP
CLAP...

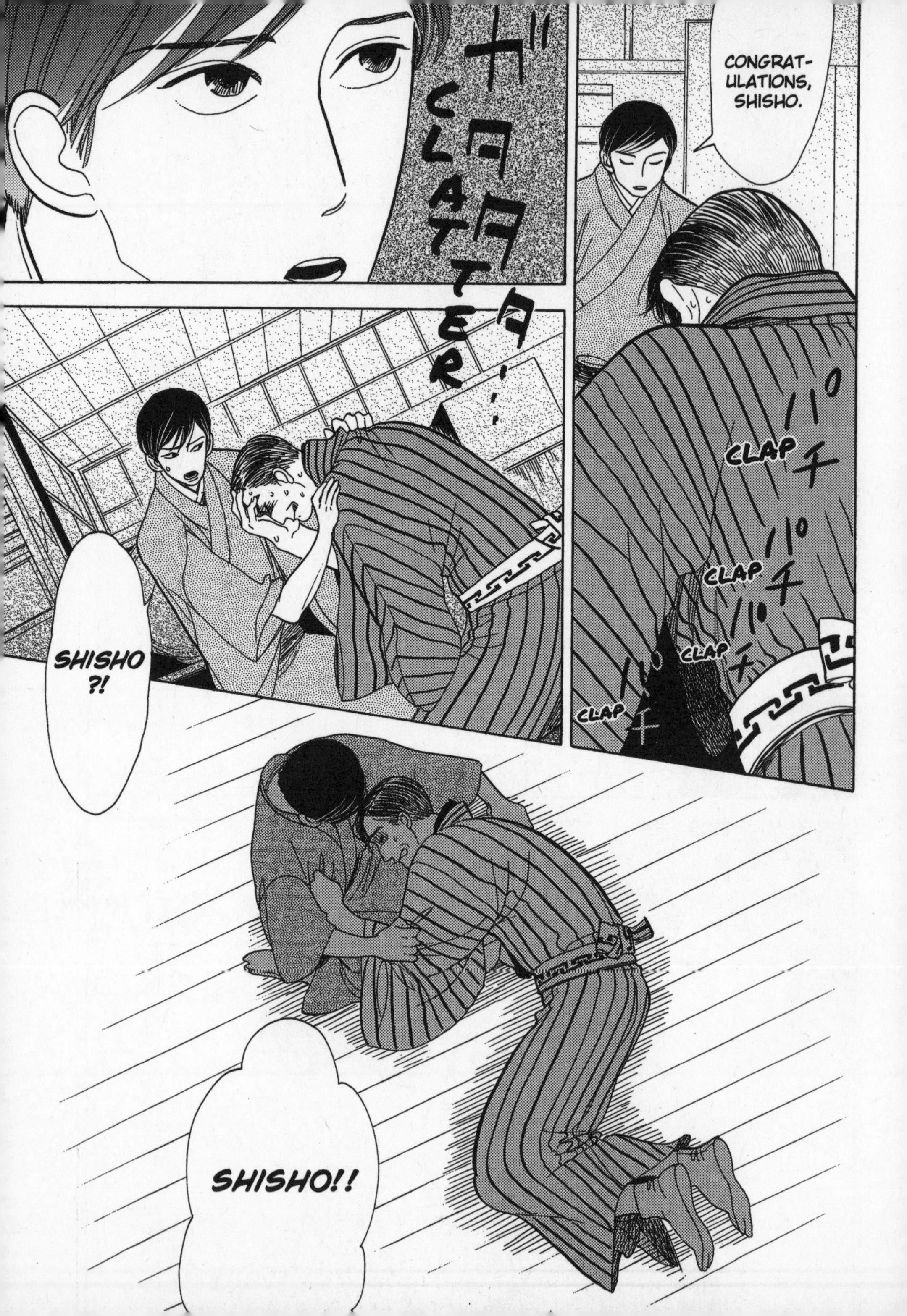
CONGRAT-ULATIONS, SHISHO.
CLAP
CLAP
CLAP
CLAP
CLATTER
SHISHO?!
SHISHO!!

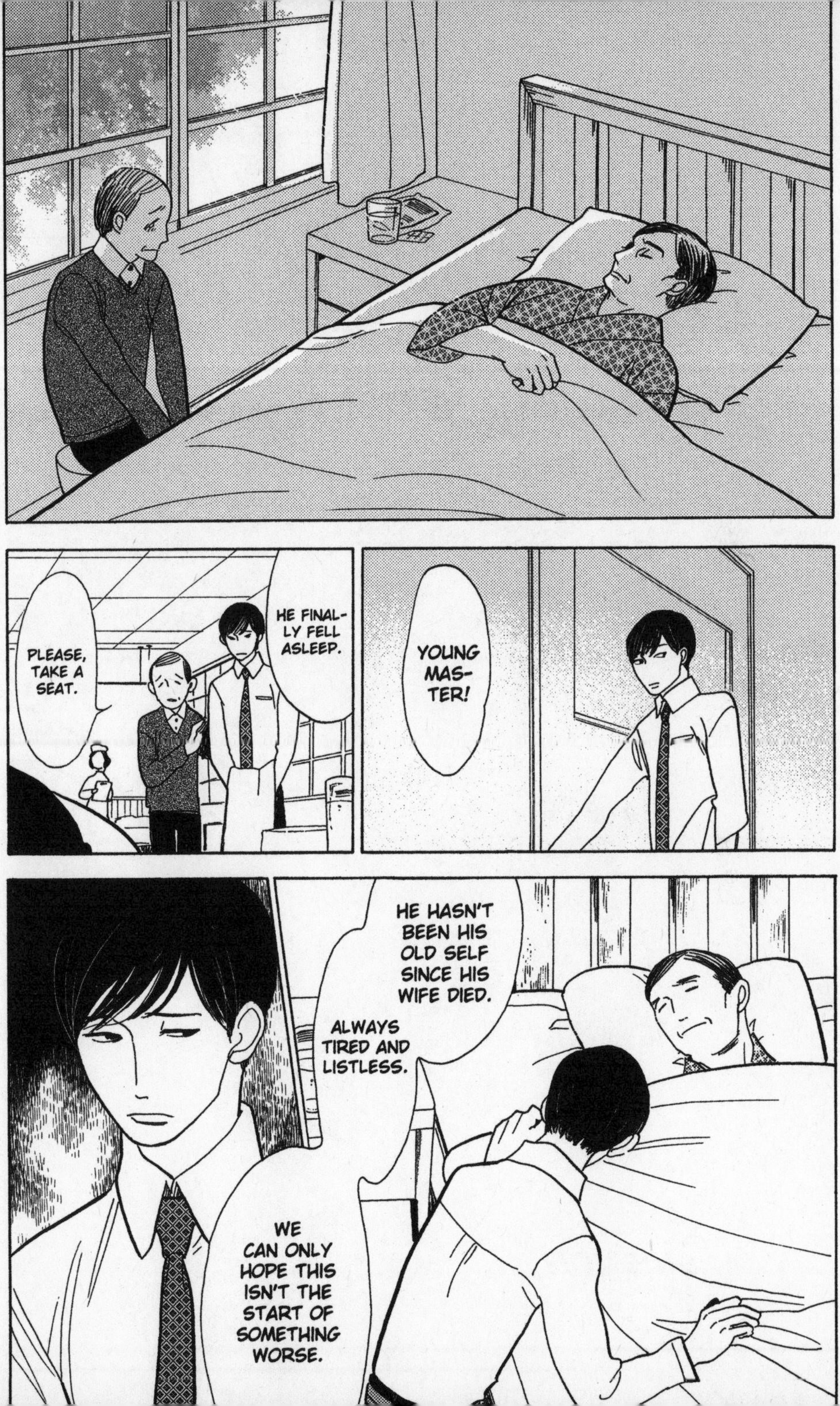
YOUNG MASTER!
HE FINALLY FELL ASLEEP.
PLEASE, TAKE A SEAT.
HE HASN'T BEEN HIS OLD SELF SINCE HIS WIFE DIED.
ALWAYS TIRED AND LISTLESS.
WE CAN ONLY HOPE THIS ISN'T THE START OF SOMETHING WORSE.

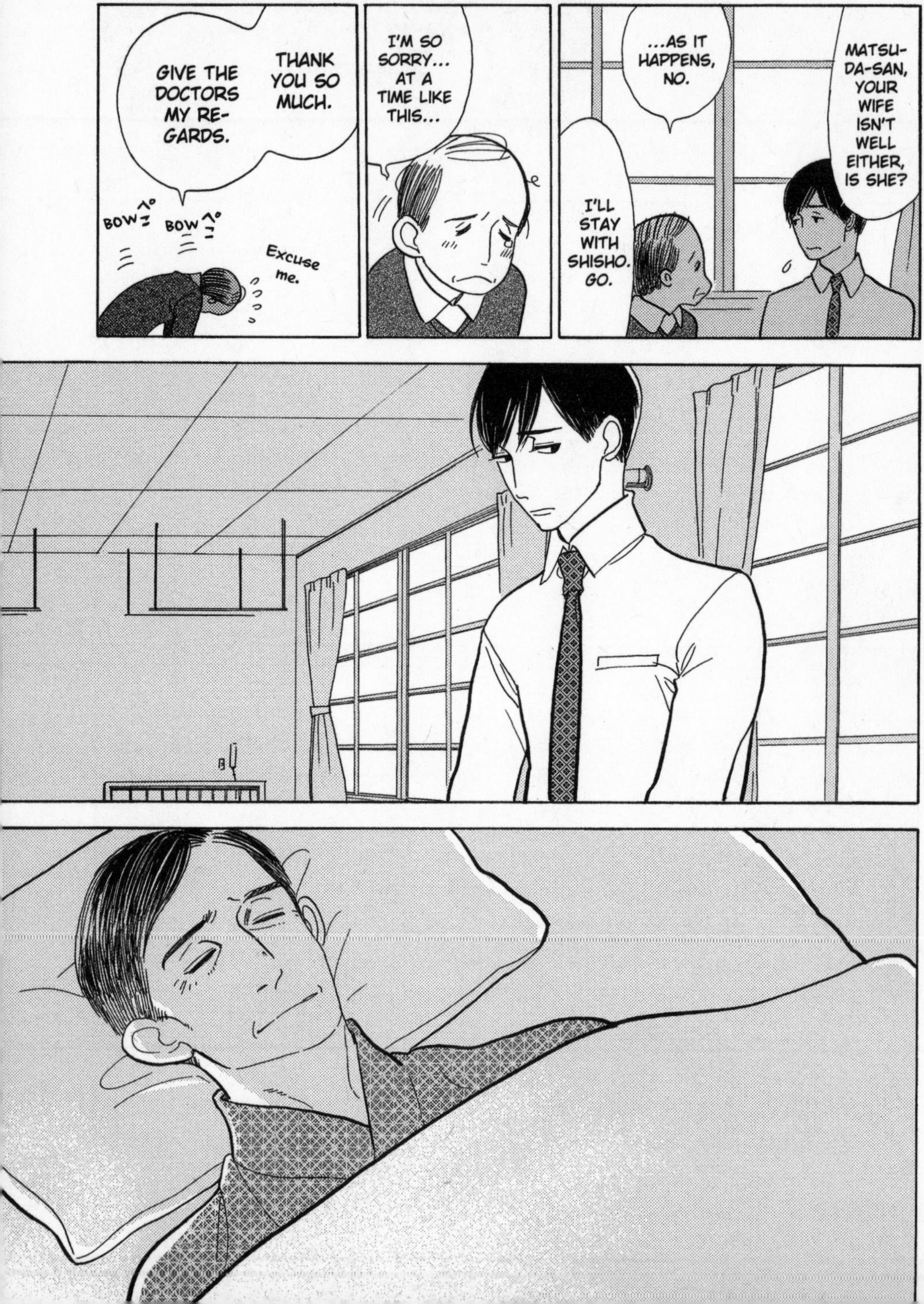
MATSU-DA-SAN, YOUR WIFE ISN'T WELL EITHER, IS SHE?
...AS IT HAPPENS, NO.
I'LL STAY WITH SHISHO. GO.
I'M SO SORRY... AT A TIME LIKE THIS...
THANK YOU SO MUCH.
GIVE THE DOCTORS MY RE-GARDS.
BOW
BOW
Excuse me.

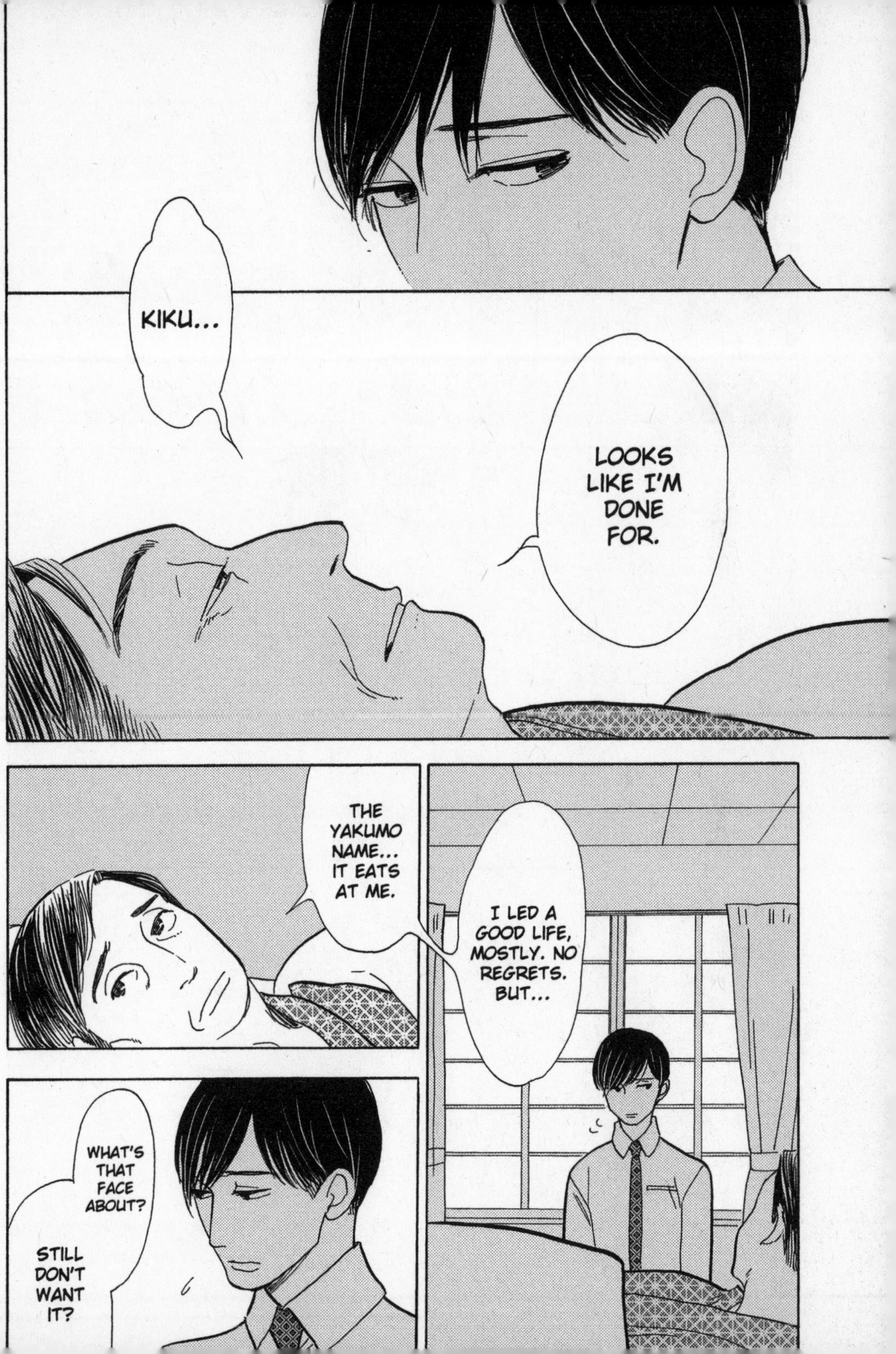
KIKU...
LOOKS LIKE I'M DONE FOR.
I LED A GOOD LIFE, MOSTLY. NO REGRETS. BUT...
THE YAKUMO NAME... IT EATS AT ME.
WHAT'S THAT FACE ABOUT?
STILL DON'T WANT IT?

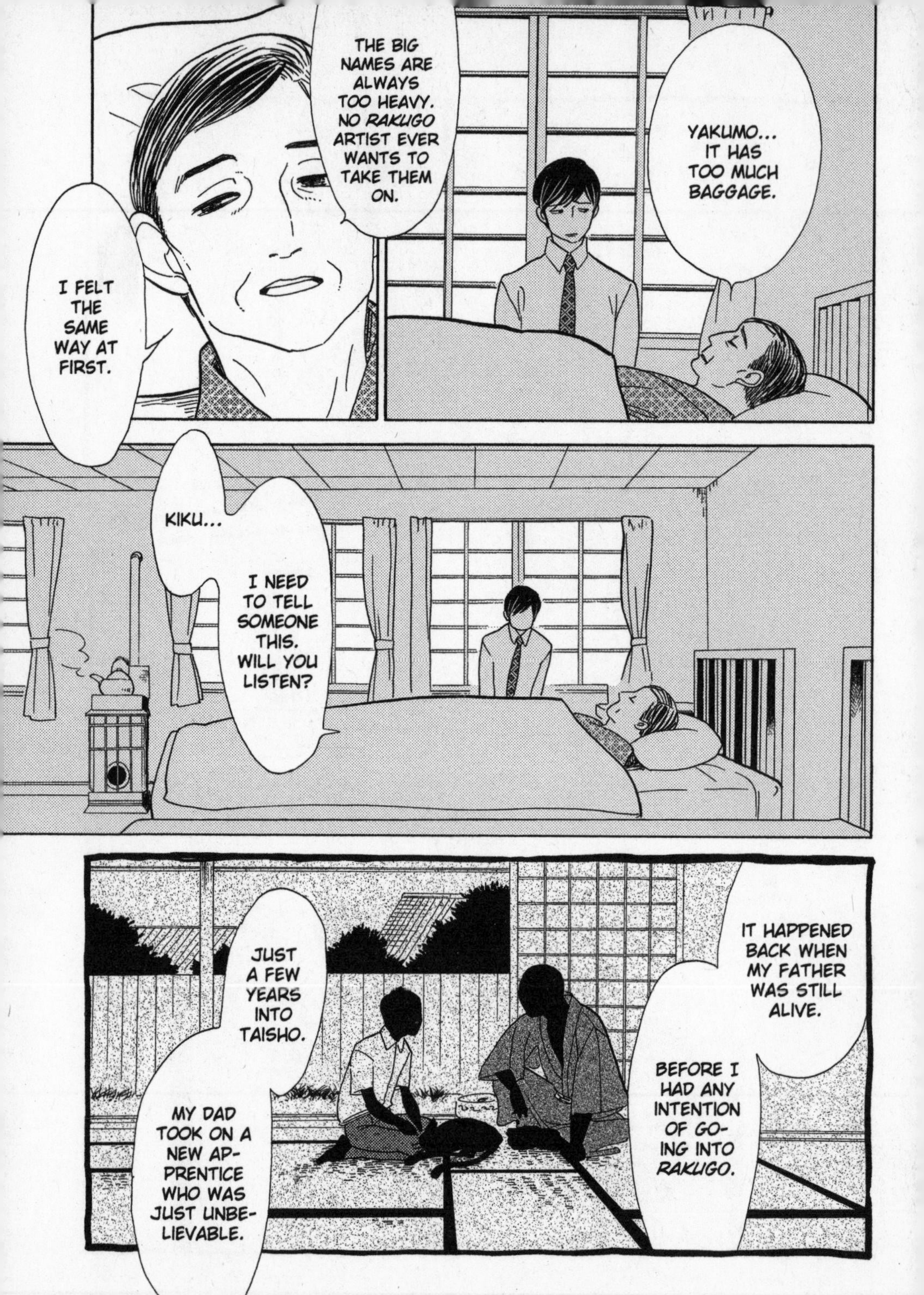
YAKUMO... IT HAS TOO MUCH BAGGAGE.
THE BIG NAMES ARE ALWAYS TOO HEAVY. NO *RAKUGO* ARTIST EVER WANTS TO TAKE THEM ON.
I FELT THE SAME WAY AT FIRST.
KIKU...
I NEED TO TELL SOMEONE THIS. WILL YOU LISTEN?
IT HAPPENED BACK WHEN MY FATHER WAS STILL ALIVE.
BEFORE I HAD ANY INTENTION OF GO-ING INTO *RAKUGO*.
JUST A FEW YEARS INTO TAISHO.
MY DAD TOOK ON A NEW AP-PRENTICE WHO WAS JUST UNBE-LIEVABLE.

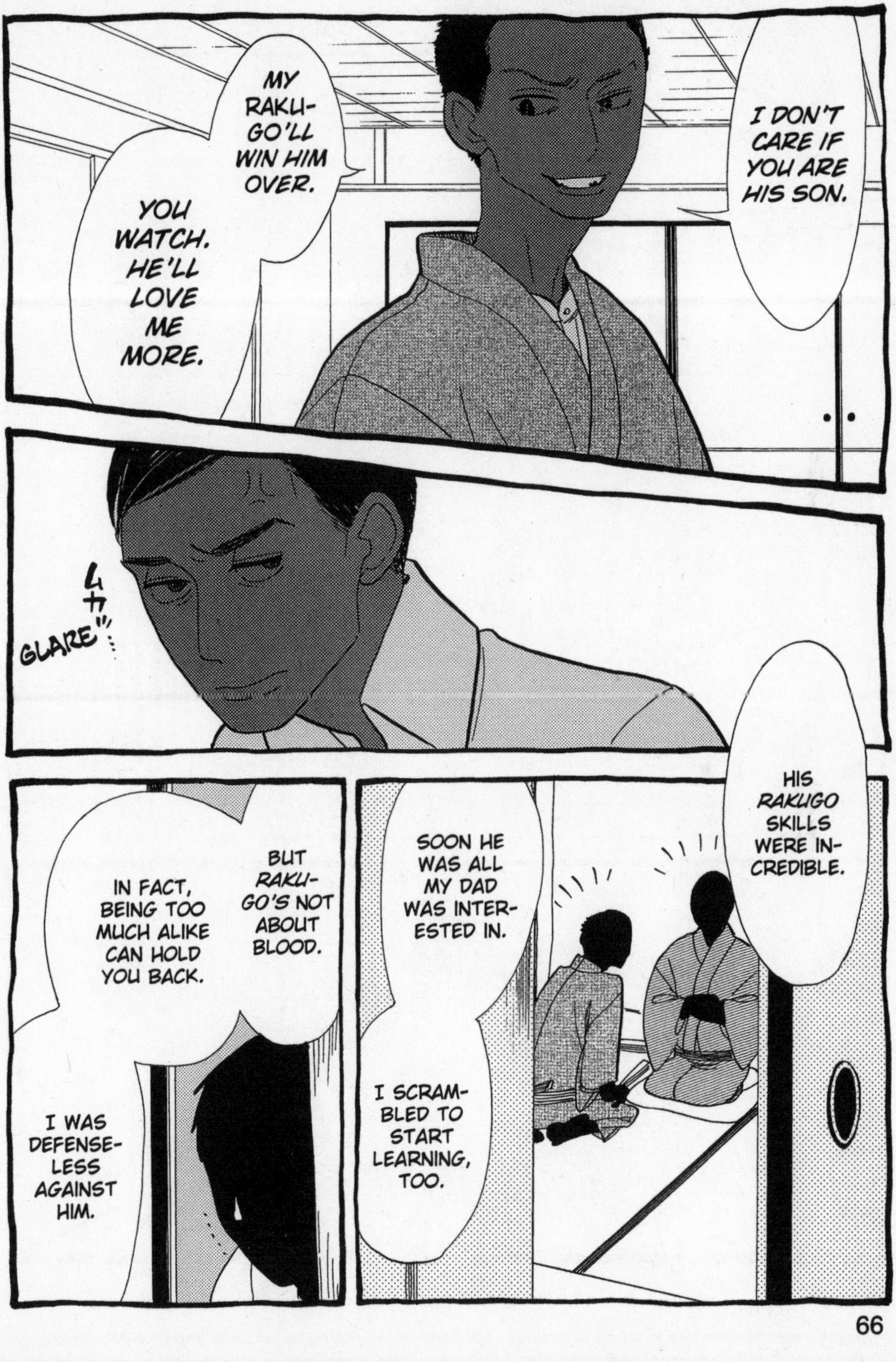
I DON'T CARE IF YOU ARE HIS SON.
MY RAKUGO'LL WIN HIM OVER.
YOU WATCH. HE'LL LOVE ME MORE.
GLARE
HIS RAKUGO SKILLS WERE INCREDIBLE.
SOON HE WAS ALL MY DAD WAS INTERESTED IN.
I SCRAMBLED TO START LEARNING, TOO.
BUT RAKUGO'S NOT ABOUT BLOOD.
IN FACT, BEING TOO MUCH ALIKE CAN HOLD YOU BACK.
I WAS DEFENSELESS AGAINST HIM.

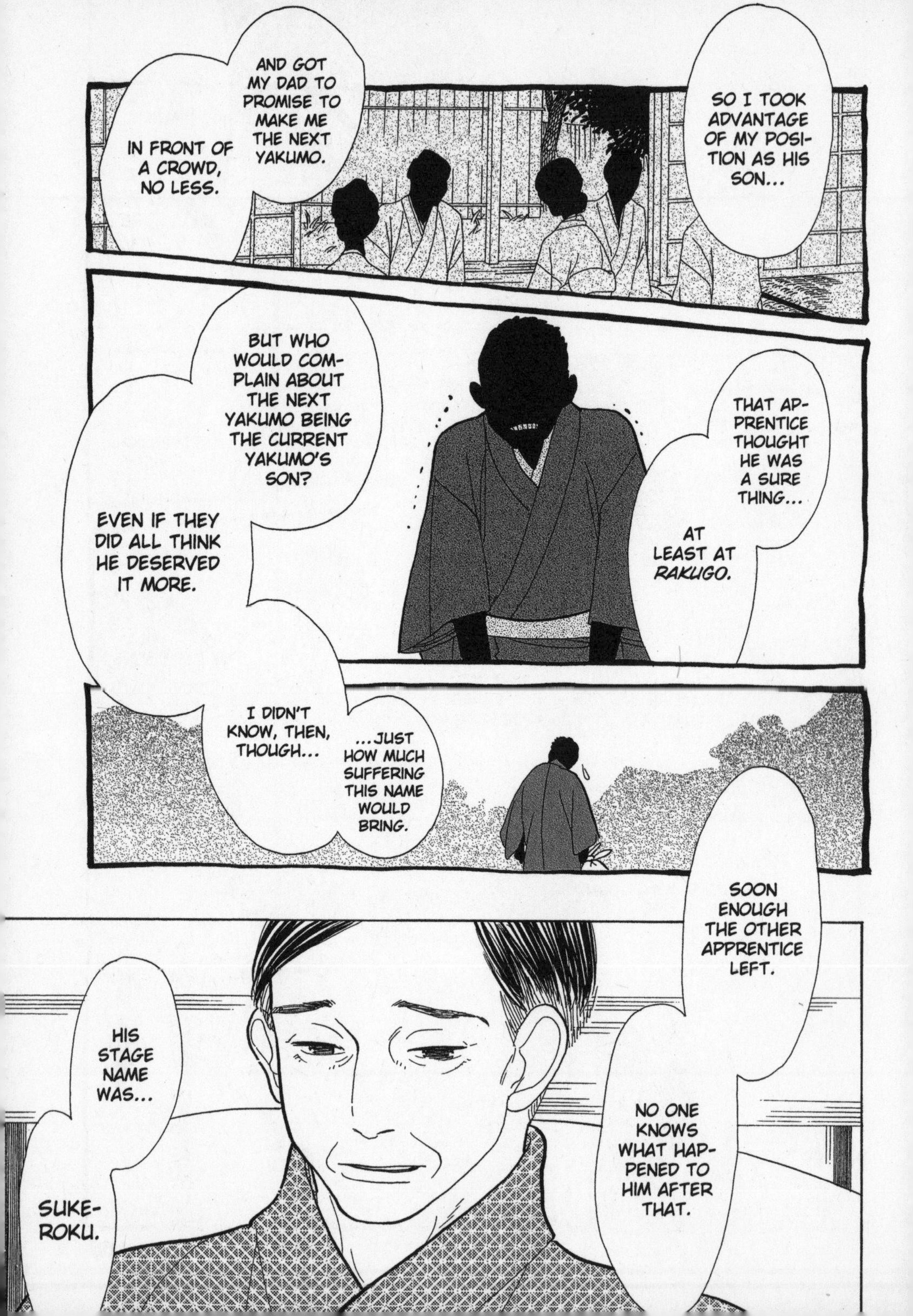
SO I TOOK ADVANTAGE OF MY POSITION AS HIS SON...
AND GOT MY DAD TO PROMISE TO MAKE ME THE NEXT YAKUMO.
IN FRONT OF A CROWD, NO LESS.
THAT APPRENTICE THOUGHT HE WAS A SURE THING...
AT LEAST AT *RAKUGO*.
BUT WHO WOULD COMPLAIN ABOUT THE NEXT YAKUMO BEING THE CURRENT YAKUMO'S SON?
EVEN IF THEY DID ALL THINK HE DESERVED IT MORE.
I DIDN'T KNOW, THEN, THOUGH...
...JUST HOW MUCH SUFFERING THIS NAME WOULD BRING.
SOON ENOUGH THE OTHER APPRENTICE LEFT.
NO ONE KNOWS WHAT HAPPENED TO HIM AFTER THAT.
HIS STAGE NAME WAS...
SUKE-ROKU.

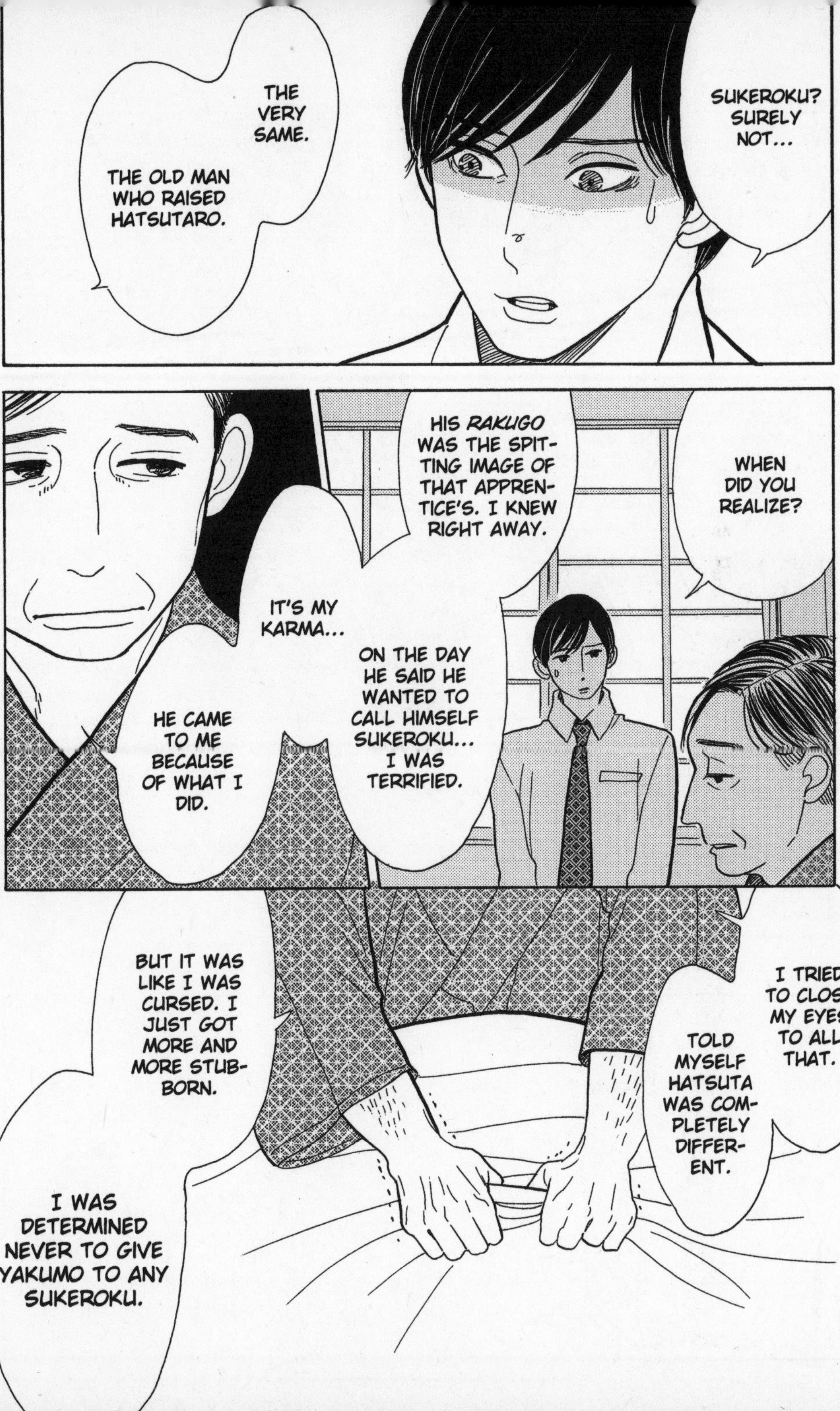
SUKEROKU? SURELY NOT...
THE VERY SAME.
THE OLD MAN WHO RAISED HATSUTARO.
WHEN DID YOU REALIZE?
HIS *RAKUGO* WAS THE SPITTING IMAGE OF THAT APPRENTICE'S. I KNEW RIGHT AWAY.
IT'S MY KARMA...
ON THE DAY HE SAID HE WANTED TO CALL HIMSELF SUKEROKU... I WAS TERRIFIED.
HE CAME TO ME BECAUSE OF WHAT I DID.
I TRIED TO CLOSE MY EYES TO ALL THAT.
TOLD MYSELF HATSUTA WAS COMPLETELY DIFFERENT.
BUT IT WAS LIKE I WAS CURSED. I JUST GOT MORE AND MORE STUBBORN.
I WAS DETERMINED NEVER TO GIVE YAKUMO TO ANY SUKEROKU.

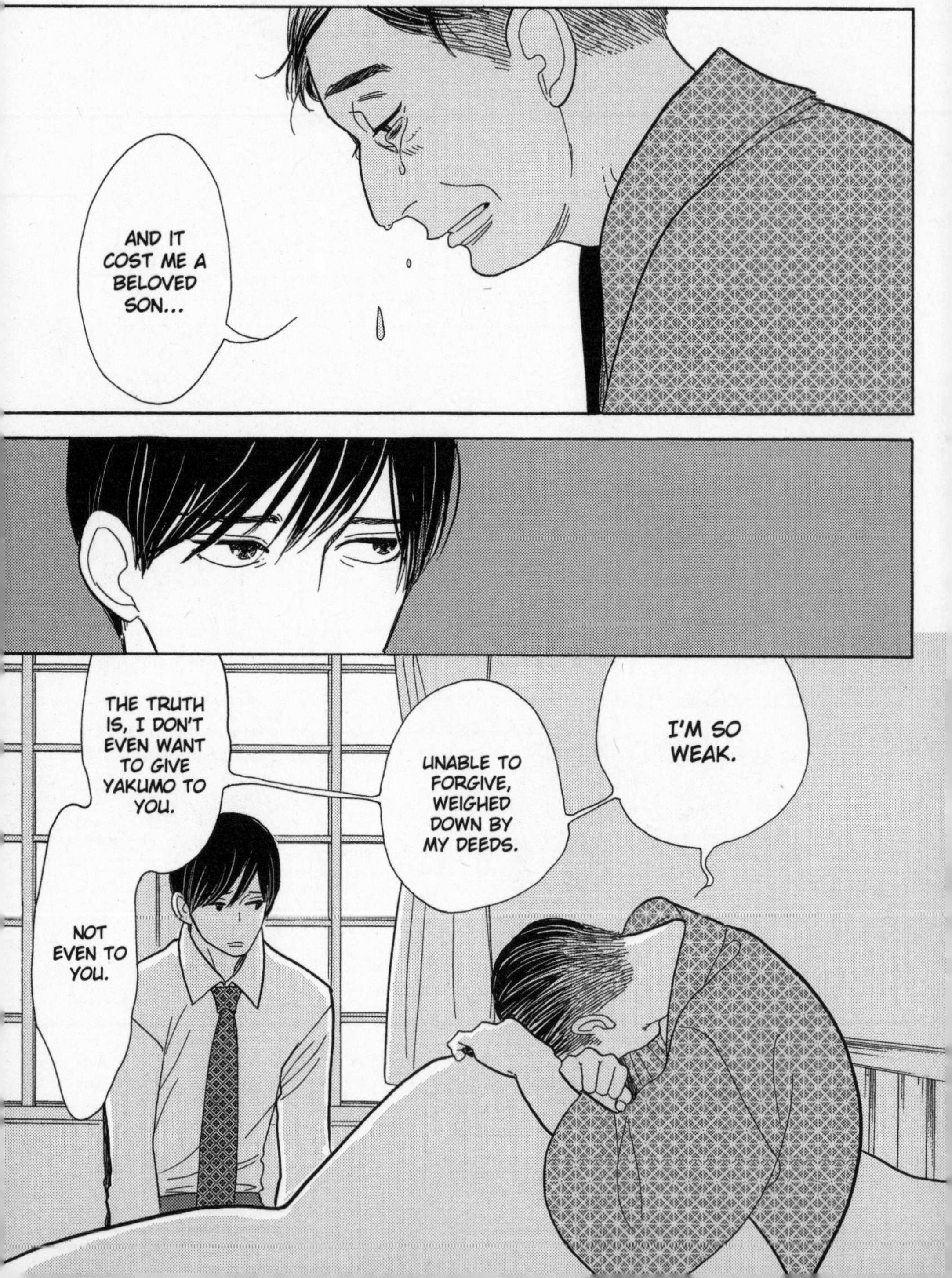
AND IT COST ME A BELOVED SON...
I'M SO WEAK.
UNABLE TO FORGIVE, WEIGHED DOWN BY MY DEEDS.
THE TRUTH IS, I DON'T EVEN WANT TO GIVE YAKUMO TO YOU.
NOT EVEN TO YOU.

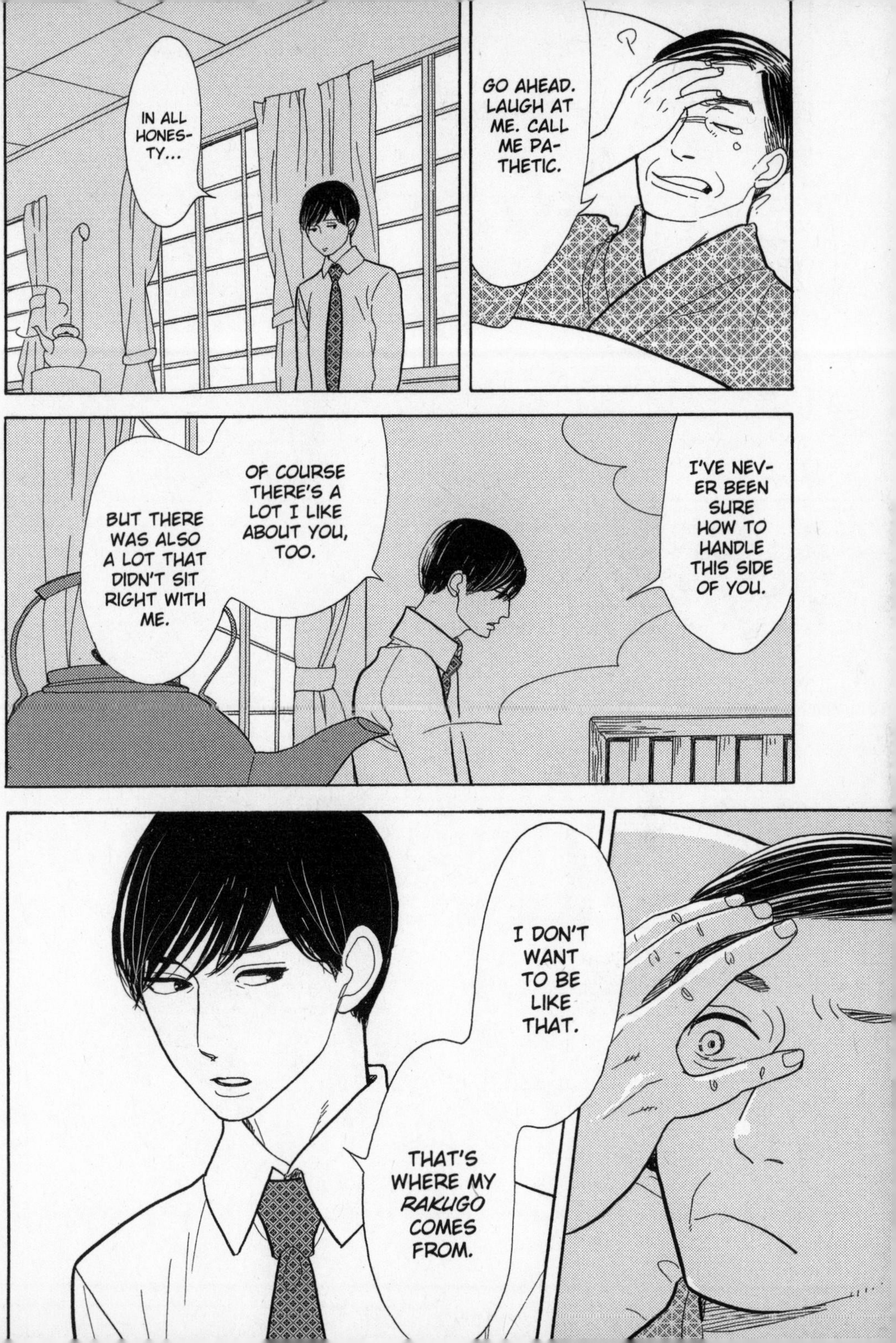
GO AHEAD. LAUGH AT ME. CALL ME PATHETIC.
IN ALL HONESTY...
I'VE NEVER BEEN SURE HOW TO HANDLE THIS SIDE OF YOU.
OF COURSE THERE'S A LOT I LIKE ABOUT YOU, TOO.
BUT THERE WAS ALSO A LOT THAT DIDN'T SIT RIGHT WITH ME.
I DON'T WANT TO BE LIKE THAT.
THAT'S WHERE MY *RAKUGO* COMES FROM.

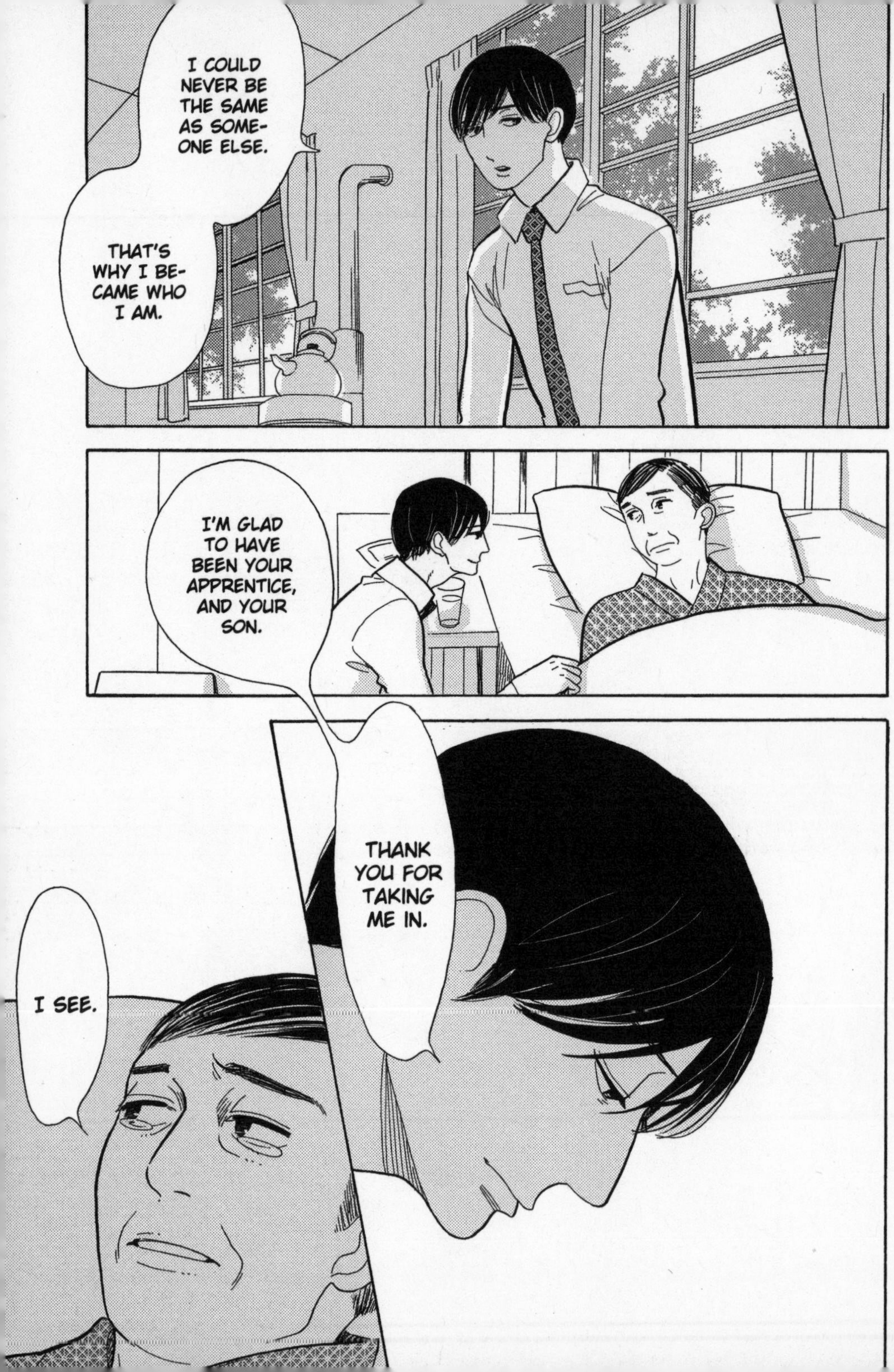
I COULD NEVER BE THE SAME AS SOME-ONE ELSE.
THAT'S WHY I BE-CAME WHO I AM.
I'M GLAD TO HAVE BEEN YOUR APPRENTICE, AND YOUR SON.
THANK YOU FOR TAKING ME IN.
I SEE.

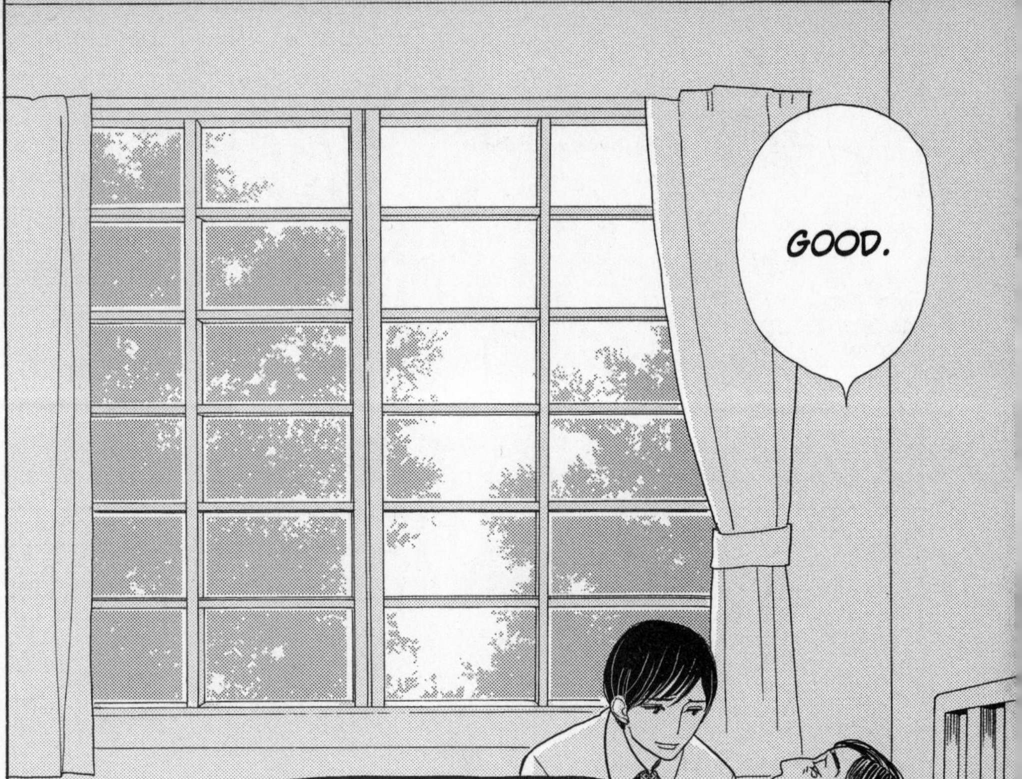
GOOD.

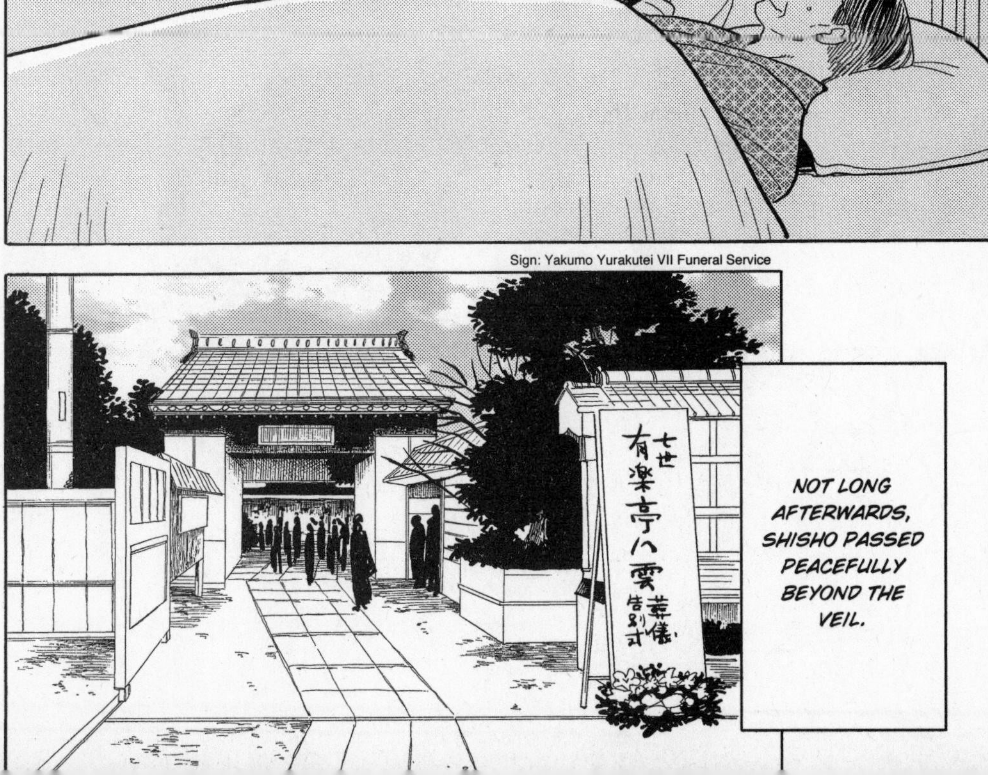
七世
有楽亭八雲
葬儀
告別式
NOT LONG AFTERWARDS, SHISHO PASSED PEACEFULLY BEYOND THE VEIL.
Sign: Yakumo Yurakutei VII Funeral Service

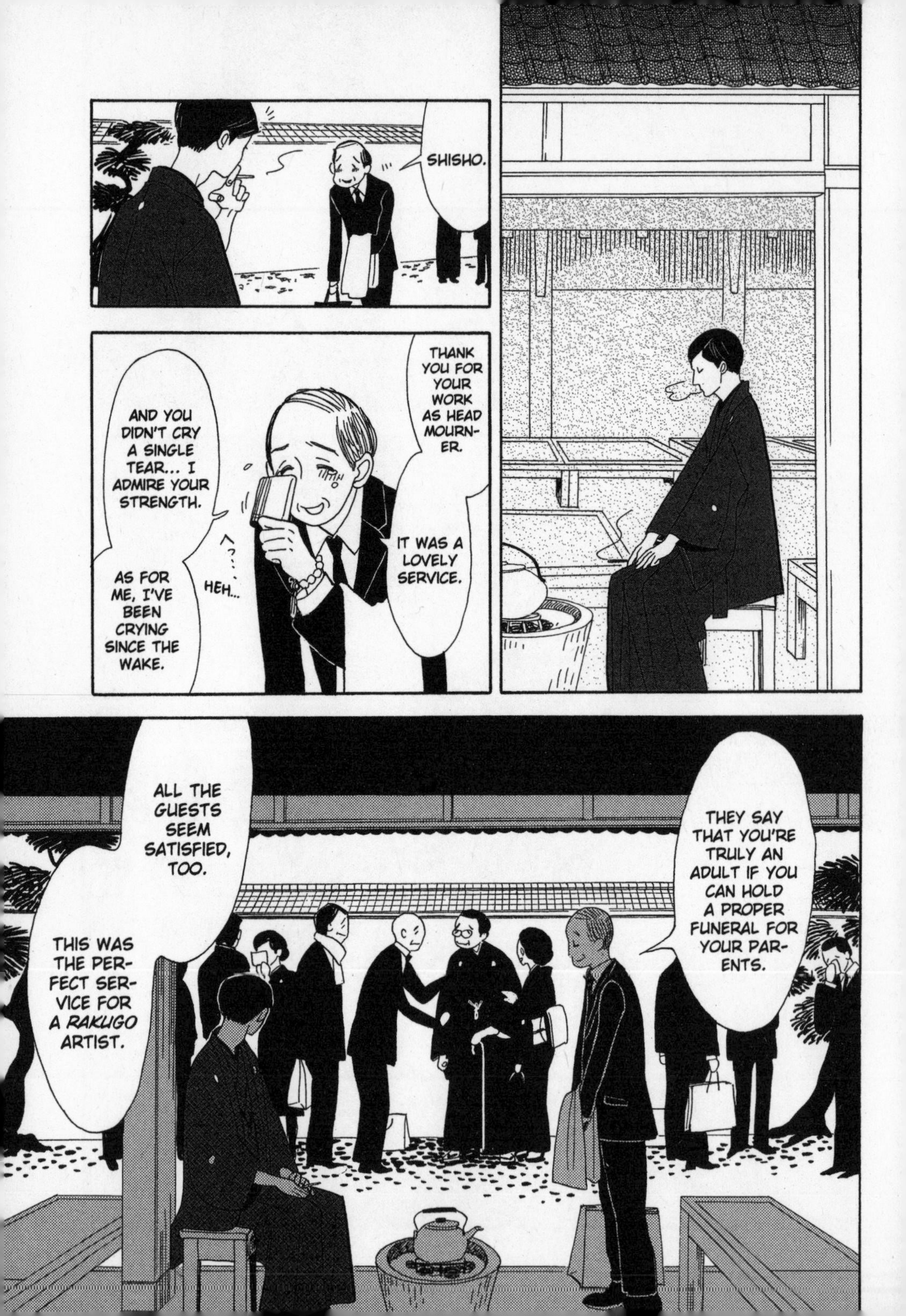
SHISHO.
THANK YOU FOR YOUR WORK AS HEAD MOURNER.
IT WAS A LOVELY SERVICE.
AND YOU DIDN'T CRY A SINGLE TEAR... I ADMIRE YOUR STRENGTH.
HEH...
AS FOR ME, I'VE BEEN CRYING SINCE THE WAKE.
THEY SAY THAT YOU'RE TRULY AN ADULT IF YOU CAN HOLD A PROPER FUNERAL FOR YOUR PARENTS.
ALL THE GUESTS SEEM SATISFIED, TOO.
THIS WAS THE PERFECT SERVICE FOR A *RAKUGO* ARTIST.

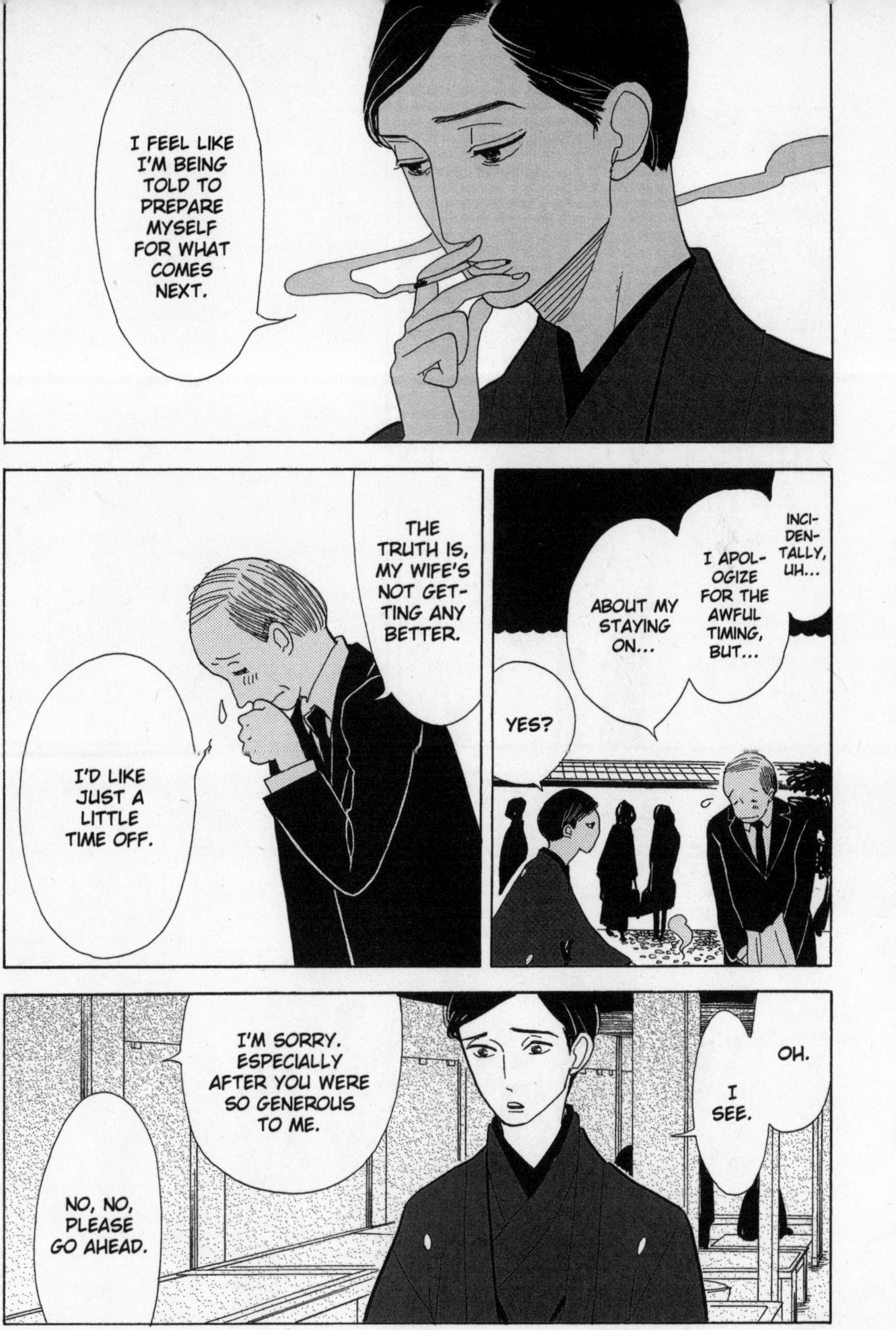
I FEEL LIKE I'M BEING TOLD TO PREPARE MYSELF FOR WHAT COMES NEXT.
INCIDENTALLY, UH...
I APOLOGIZE FOR THE AWFUL TIMING, BUT...
ABOUT MY STAYING ON...
YES?
THE TRUTH IS, MY WIFE'S NOT GETTING ANY BETTER.
I'D LIKE JUST A LITTLE TIME OFF.
OH.
I SEE.
I'M SORRY. ESPECIALLY AFTER YOU WERE SO GENEROUS TO ME.
NO, NO, PLEASE GO AHEAD.

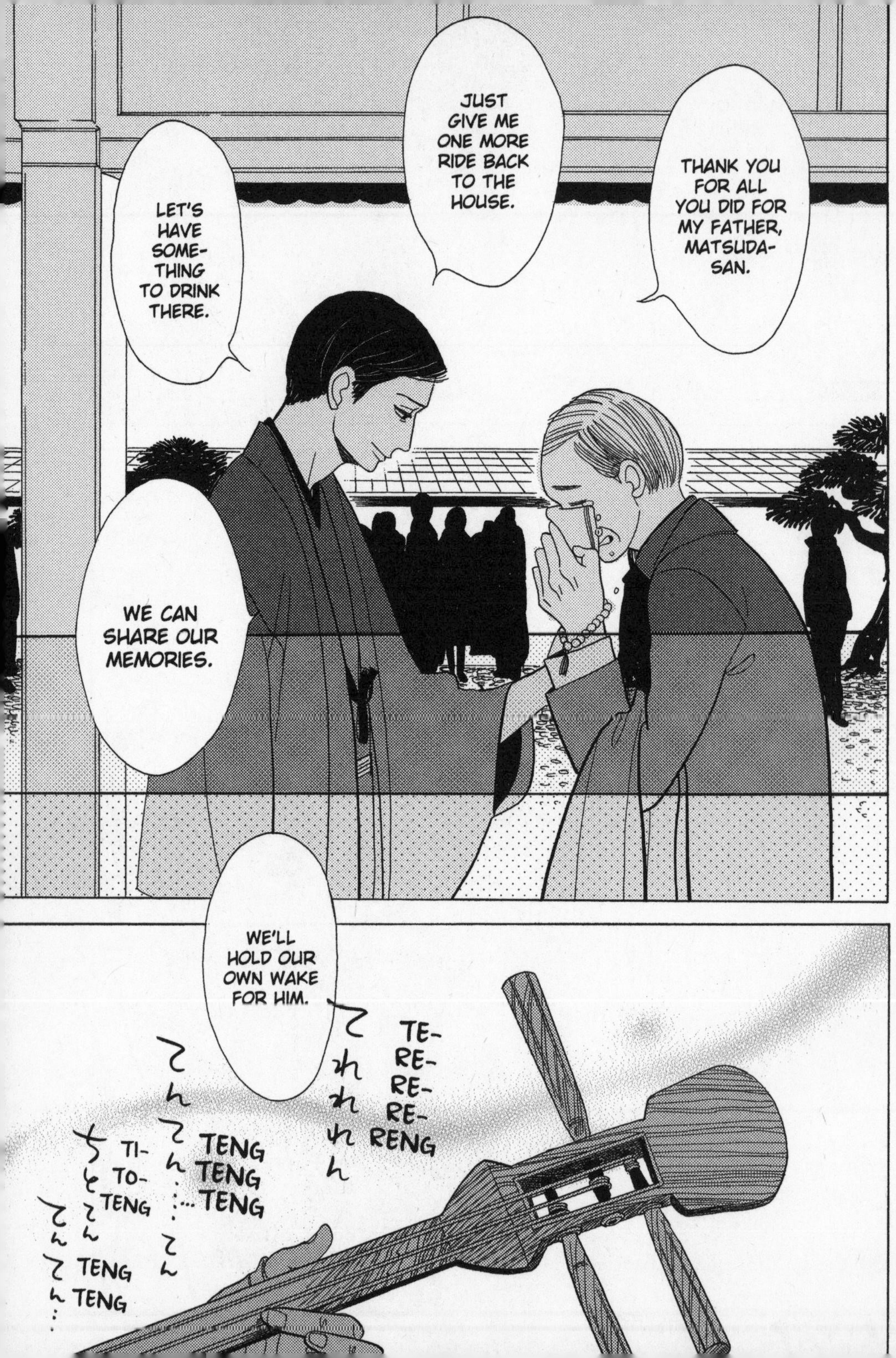
THANK YOU FOR ALL YOU DID FOR MY FATHER, MATSUDA-SAN.
JUST GIVE ME ONE MORE RIDE BACK TO THE HOUSE.
LET'S HAVE SOME-THING TO DRINK THERE.
WE CAN SHARE OUR MEMORIES.
WE'LL HOLD OUR OWN WAKE FOR HIM.
てれれれん
TE-RE-RE-RE-RENG
てんてん…てん
TENG TENG TENG
ちとてん
TI-TO-TENG
てんてん…
TENG TENG

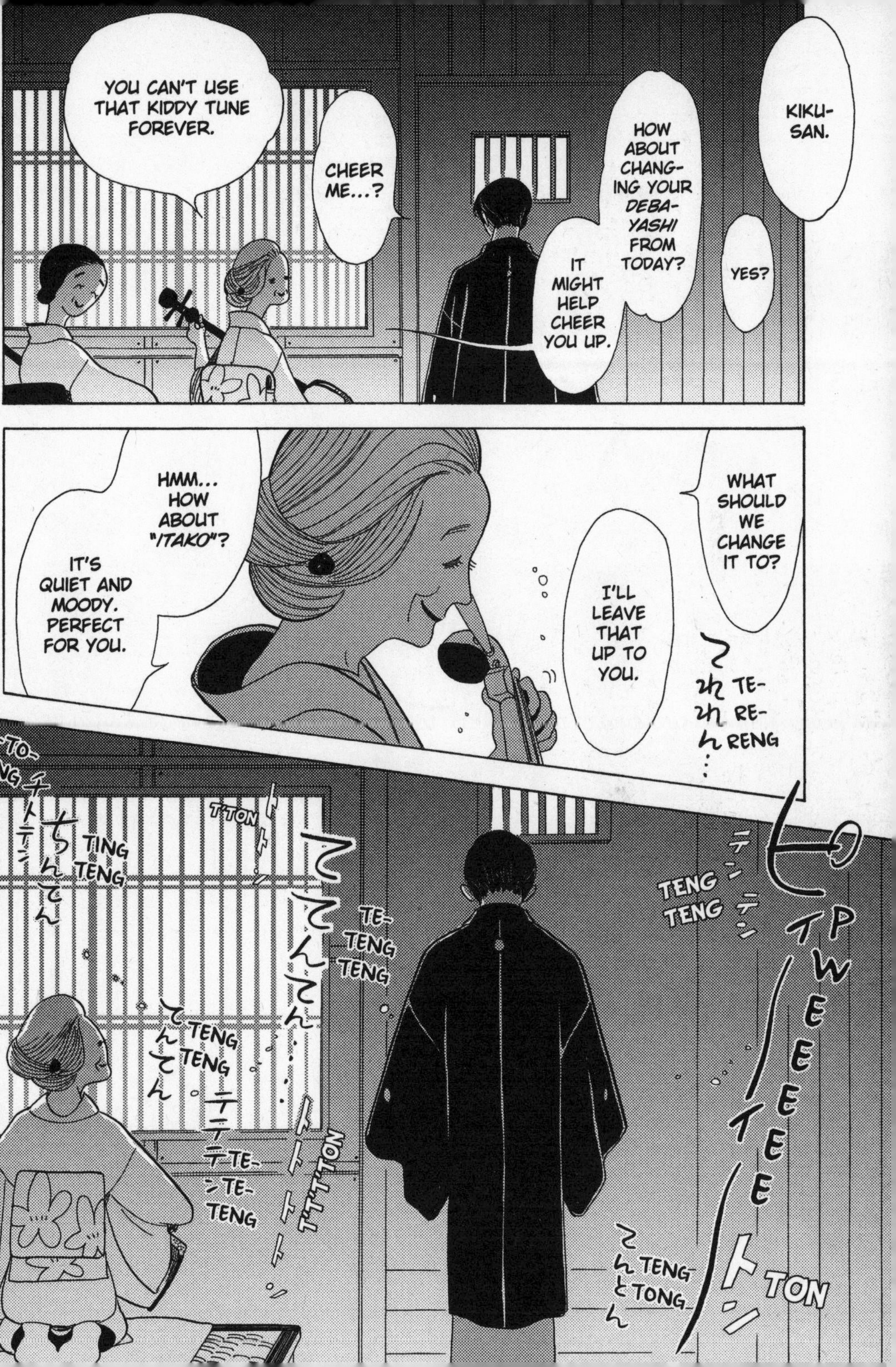
KIKU-SAN.
YES?
HOW ABOUT CHANGING YOUR *DEBAYASHI* FROM TODAY?
IT MIGHT HELP CHEER YOU UP.
CHEER ME...?
YOU CAN'T USE THAT KIDDY TUNE FOREVER.
WHAT SHOULD WE CHANGE IT TO?
I'LL LEAVE THAT UP TO YOU.
TE-RE-RENG
HMM... HOW ABOUT "*ITAKO*"?
IT'S QUIET AND MOODY. PERFECT FOR YOU.
PWEEEEEEE
TON
TENG TENG
TENG TONG
TE-TENG TENG
T'TON
T'T'T'TON
TENG TENG
TE-TE-TENG
TING TENG
TI-TO-TENG

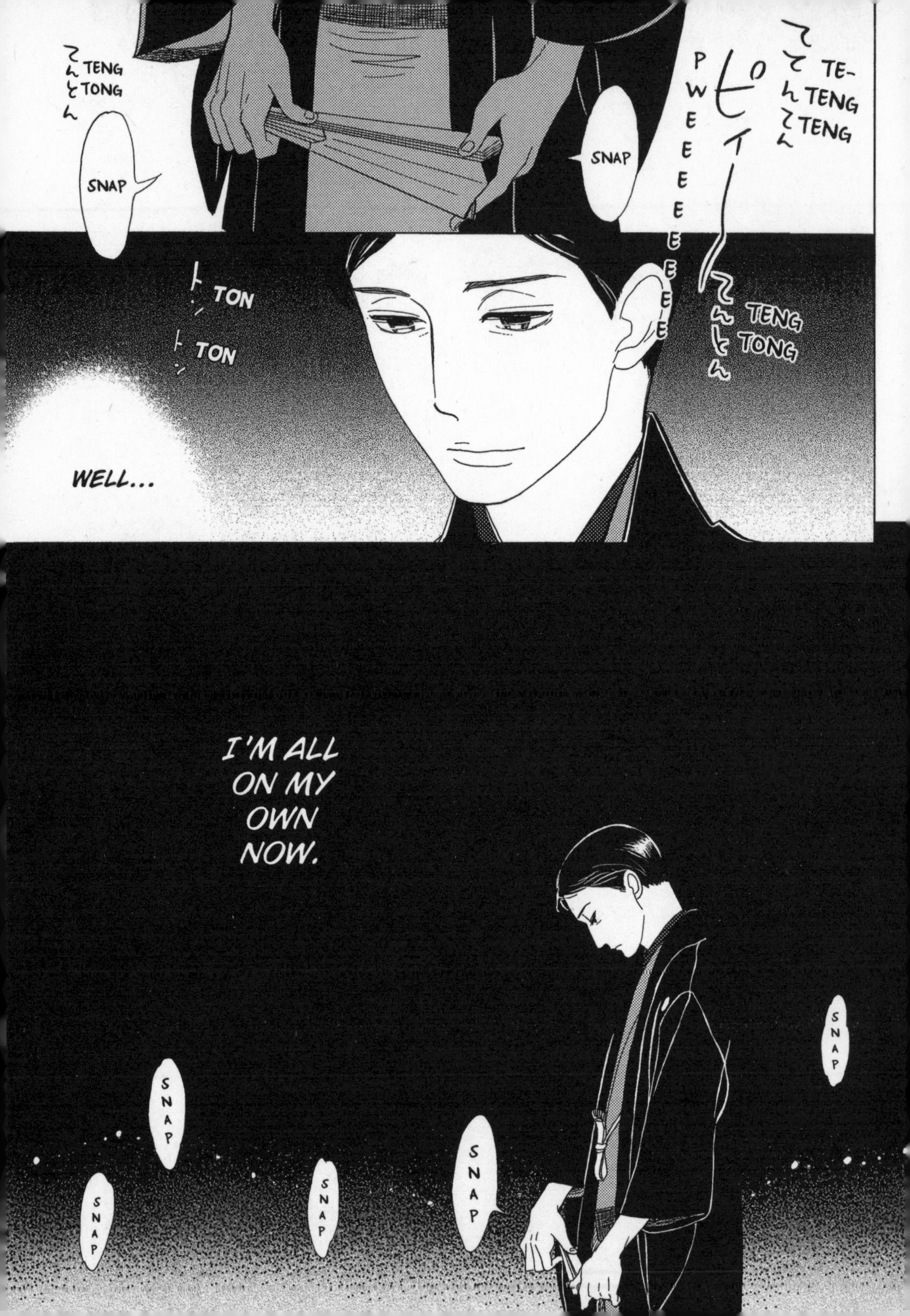
ててんてん TE-TENG TENG
ピイー PWEEEEEEEEE
SNAP
てんとん TENG TONG
SNAP
てんとん TENG TONG
ト TON
ト TON
WELL...
I'M ALL ON MY OWN NOW.
SNAP
SNAP
SNAP
SNAP
SNAP

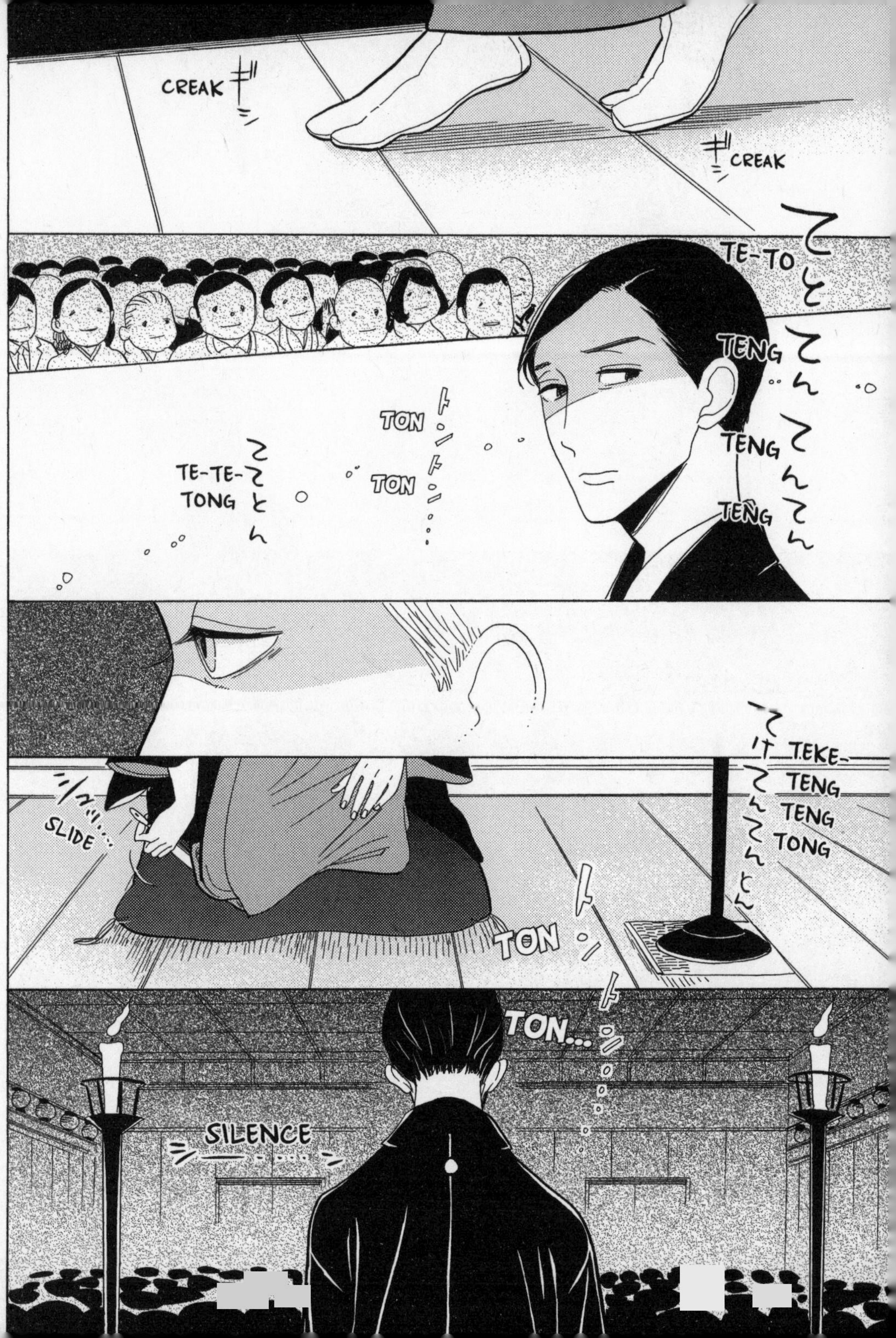
CREAK
CREAK
TE-TO
TENG
TENG
TENG
TON
TON
TE-TE-TONG
TEKE-TENG TENG TONG
SLIDE
TON
TON...
SILENCE

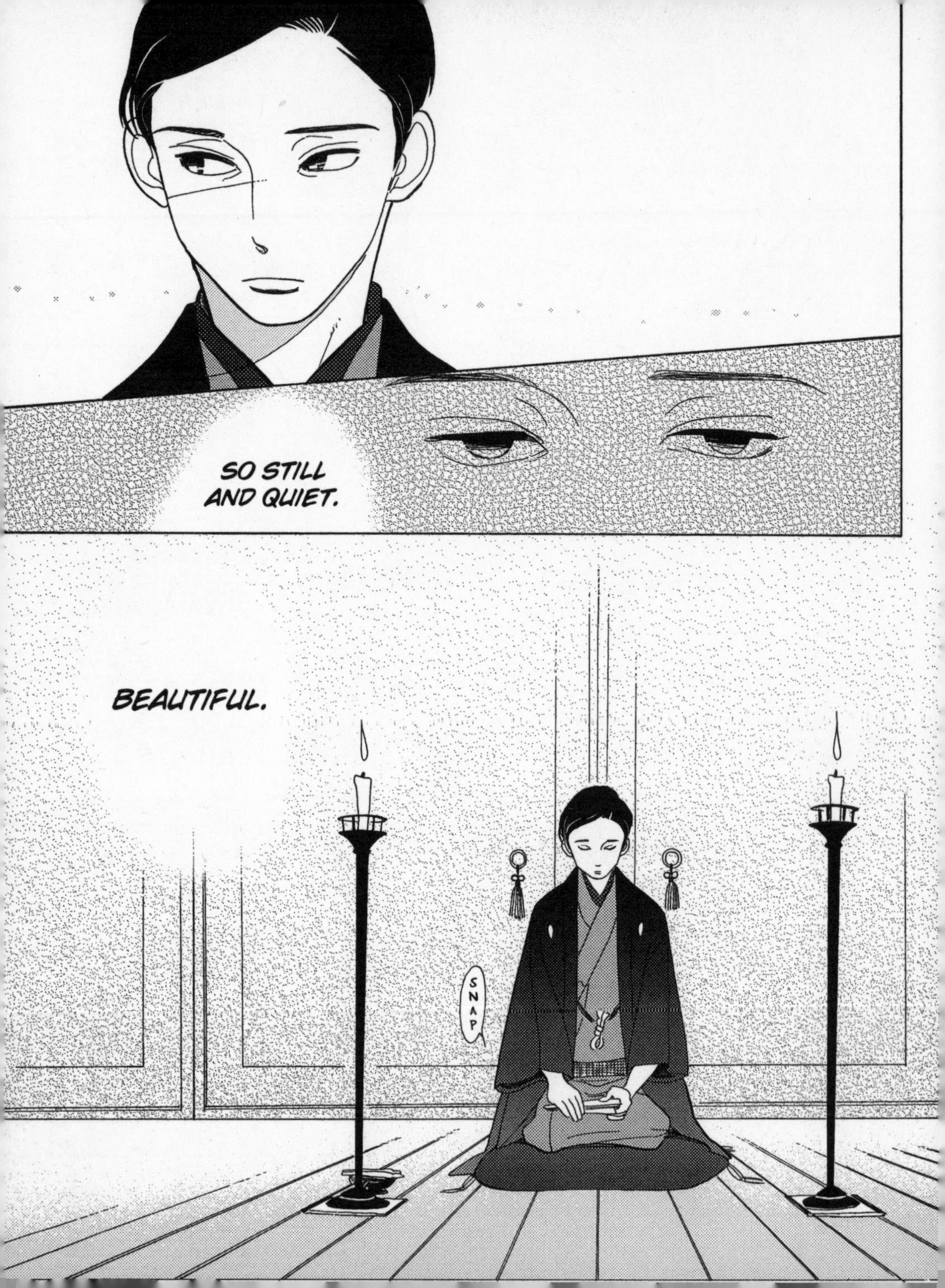
SO STILL AND QUIET.
BEAUTIFUL.
SNAP

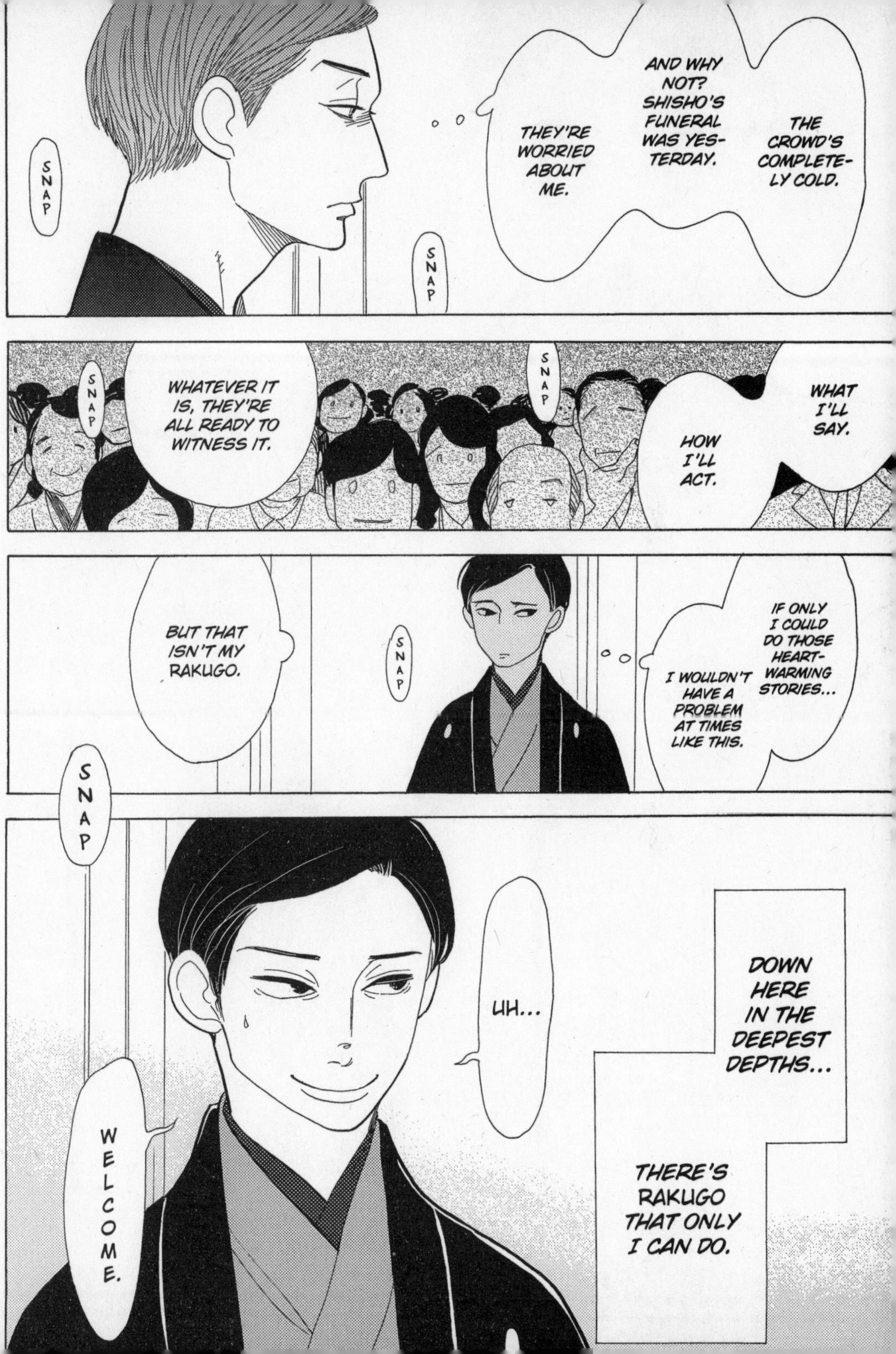
THE CROWD'S COMPLETELY COLD.
AND WHY NOT? SHISHO'S FUNERAL WAS YESTERDAY.
THEY'RE WORRIED ABOUT ME.
SNAP
SNAP
WHAT I'LL SAY.
HOW I'LL ACT.
SNAP
WHATEVER IT IS, THEY'RE ALL READY TO WITNESS IT.
SNAP
IF ONLY I COULD DO THOSE HEART-WARMING STORIES...
I WOULDN'T HAVE A PROBLEM AT TIMES LIKE THIS.
SNAP
BUT THAT ISN'T MY RAKUGO.
SNAP
DOWN HERE IN THE DEEPEST DEPTHS...
THERE'S RAKUGO THAT ONLY I CAN DO.
UH...
WELCOME.

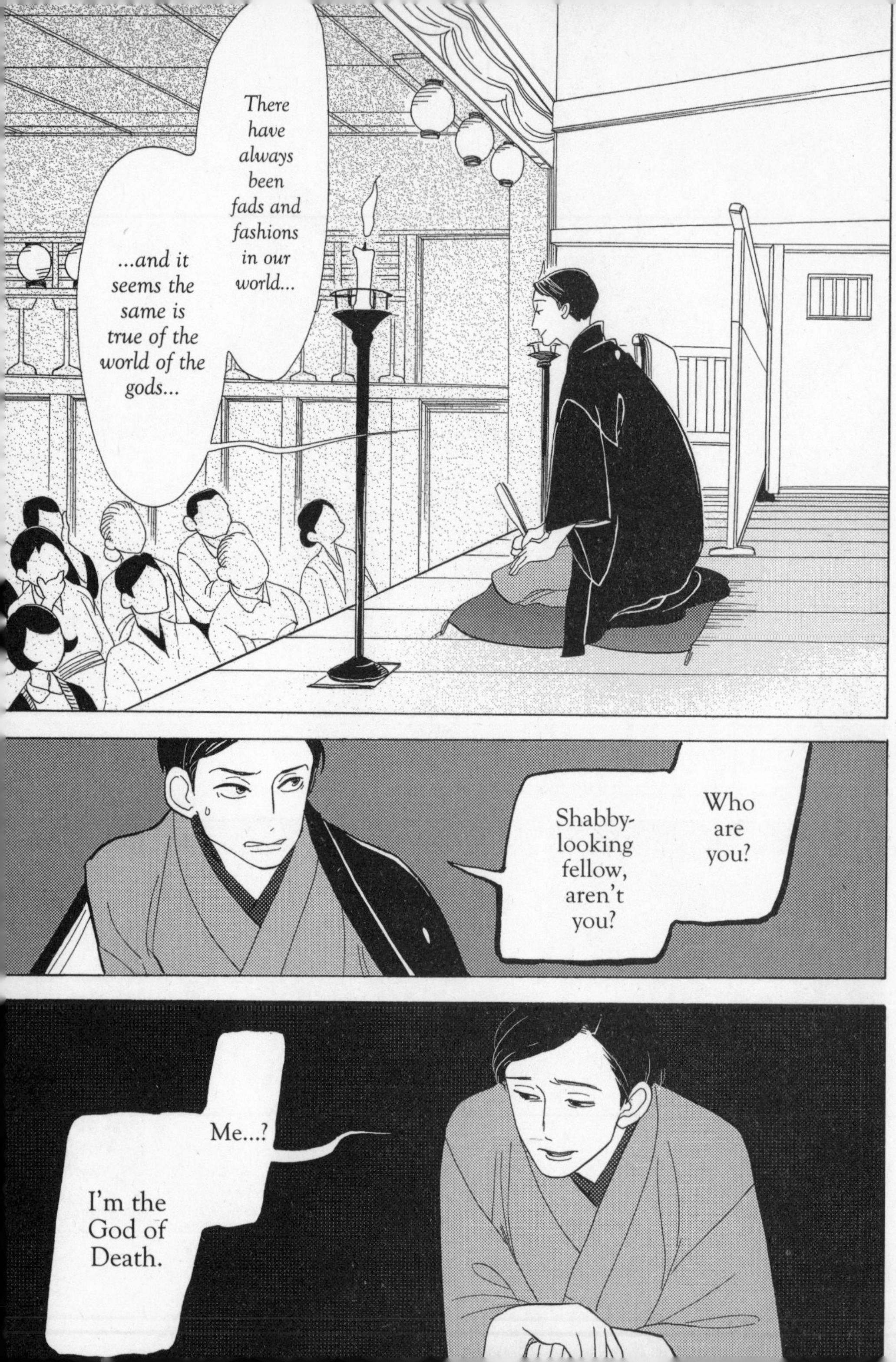
There have always been fads and fashions in our world...
...and it seems the same is true of the world of the gods...
Who are you?
Shabby-looking fellow, aren't you?
Me...?
I'm the God of Death.

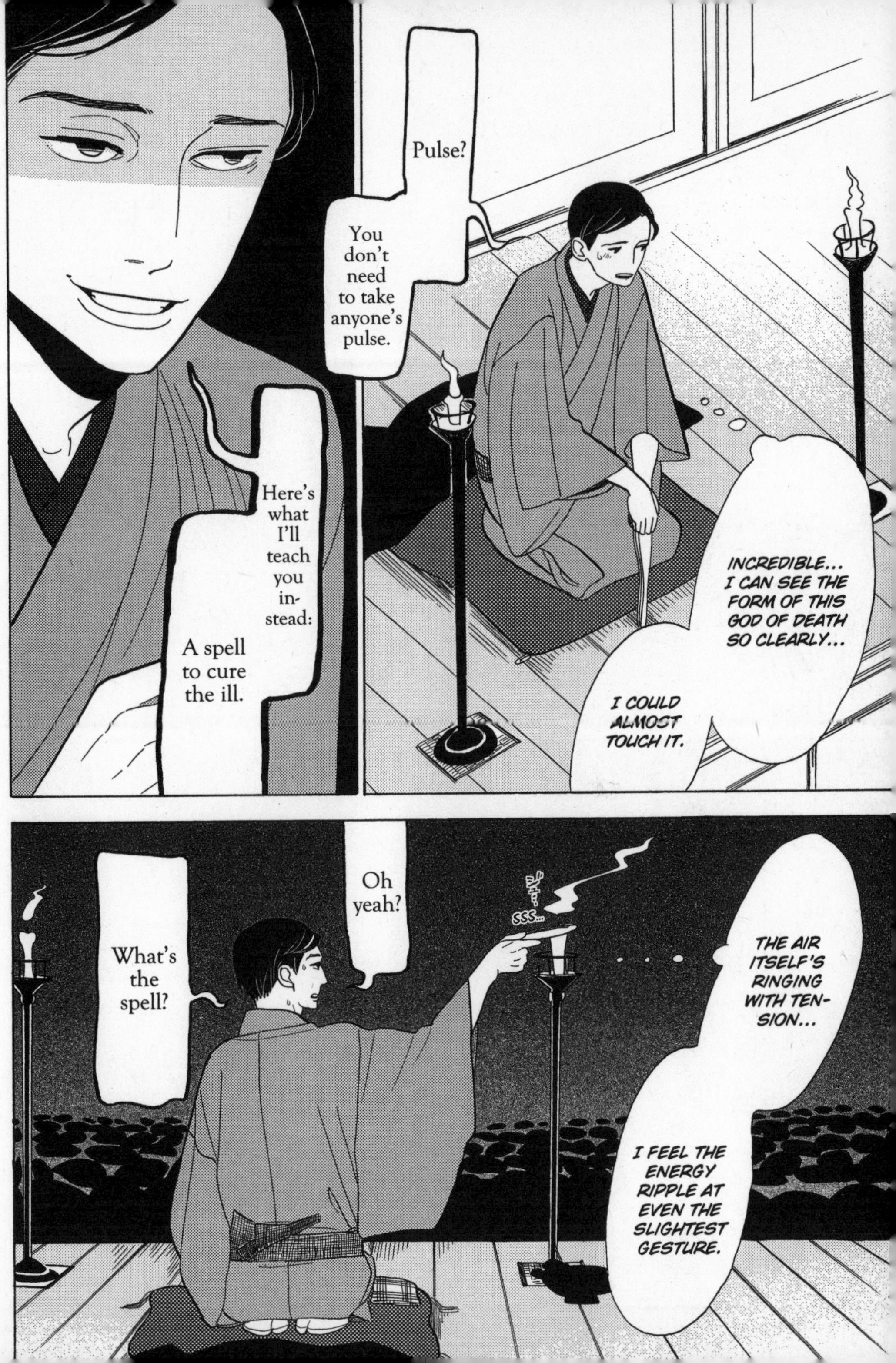
Pulse?
INCREDIBLE... I CAN SEE THE FORM OF THIS GOD OF DEATH SO CLEARLY...
I COULD ALMOST TOUCH IT.
You don't need to take anyone's pulse.
Here's what I'll teach you in-stead:
A spell to cure the ill.
THE AIR ITSELF'S RINGING WITH TEN-SION...
I FEEL THE ENERGY RIPPLE AT EVEN THE SLIGHTEST GESTURE.
SSS...
Oh yeah?
What's the spell?

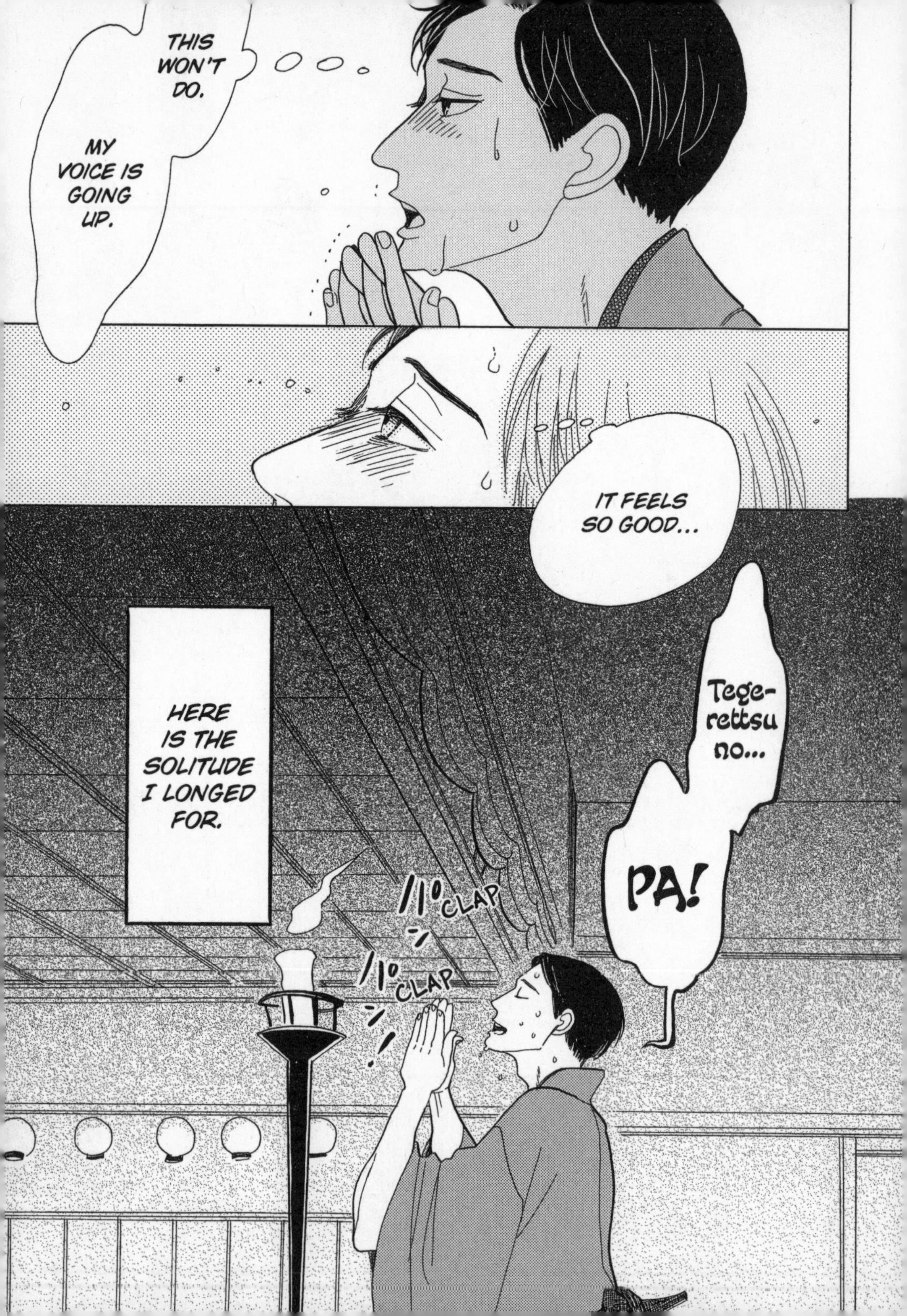
THIS WON'T DO.
MY VOICE IS GOING UP.
IT FEELS SO GOOD...
Tege-rettsu no...
PA!
HERE IS THE SOLITUDE I LONGED FOR.
CLAP
CLAP

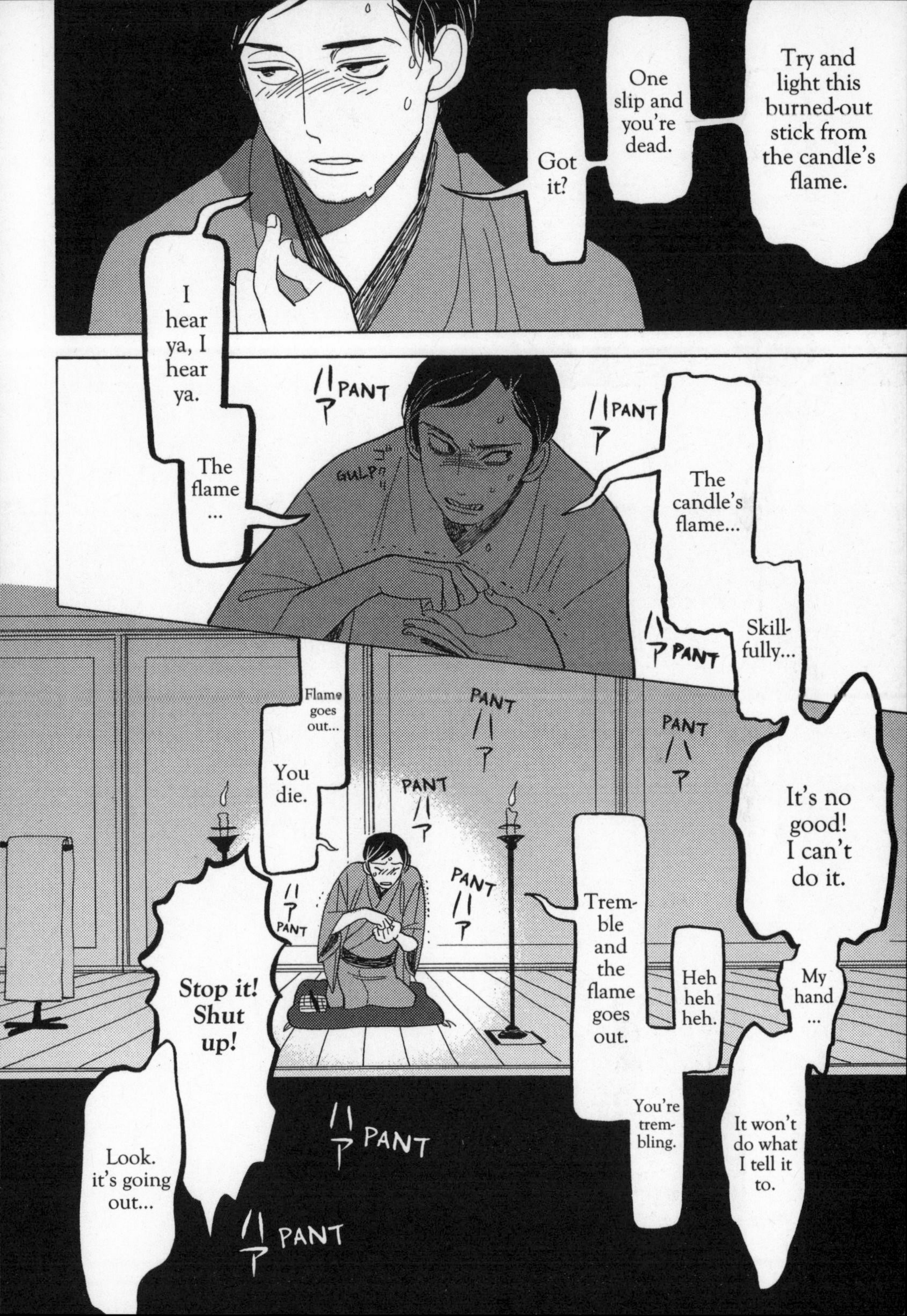
Try and light this burned-out stick from the candle's flame.
One slip and you're dead.
Got it?
I hear ya, I hear ya.
PANT
PANT
The candle's flame...
Skill-fully...
GULP
The flame ...
PANT
PANT
PANT
It's no good! I can't do it.
My hand ...
It won't do what I tell it to.
Heh heh heh.
Tremble and the flame goes out.
You're trem-bling.
PANT
PANT
PANT
Flame goes out...
You die.
PANT
Stop it! Shut up!
Look. it's going out...
PANT
PANT

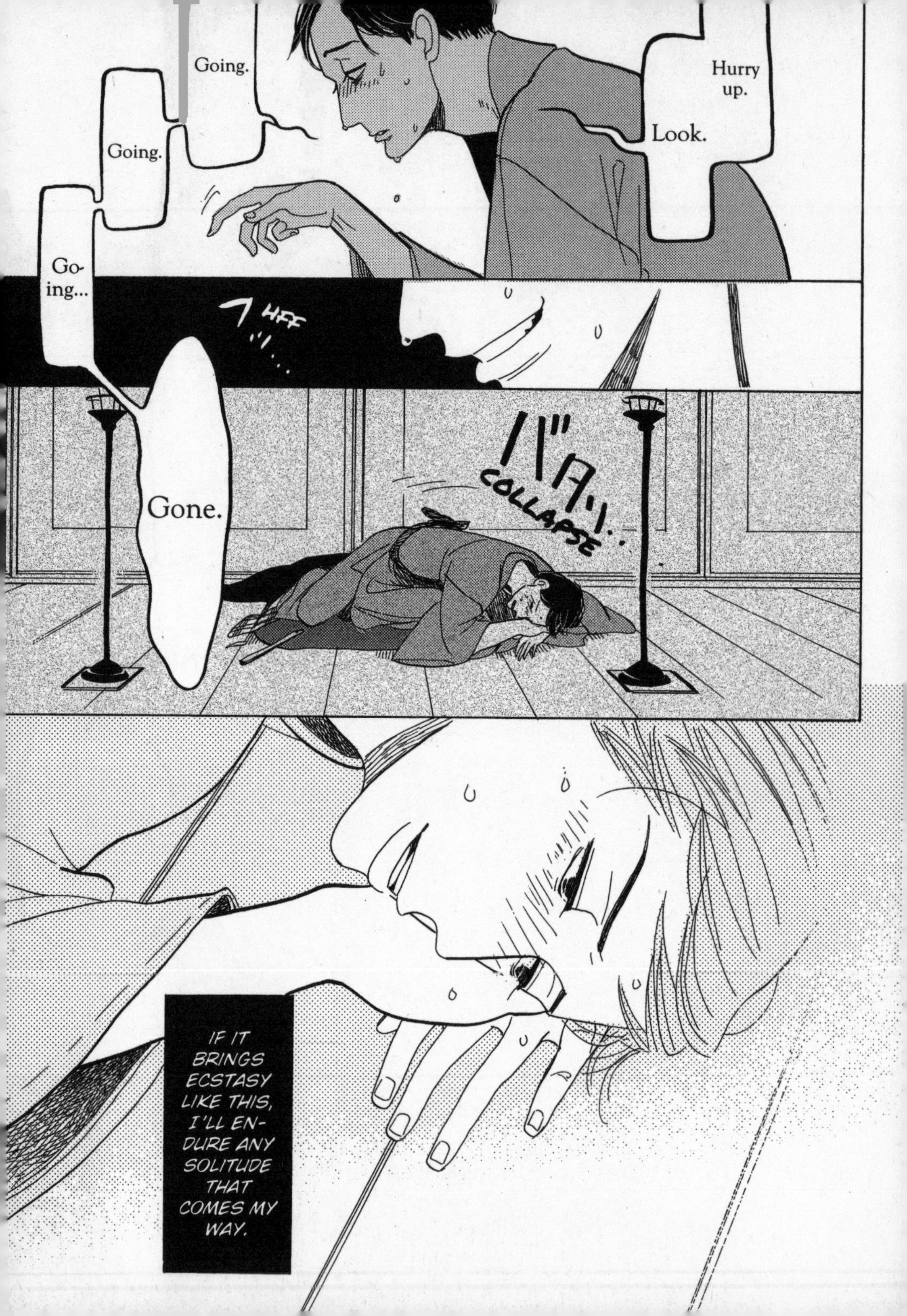
Hurry up.
Look.
Going.
Going.
Go-ing...
HFF
Gone.
バタッ COLLAPSE
IF IT BRINGS ECSTASY LIKE THIS, I'LL ENDURE ANY SOLITUDE THAT COMES MY WAY.

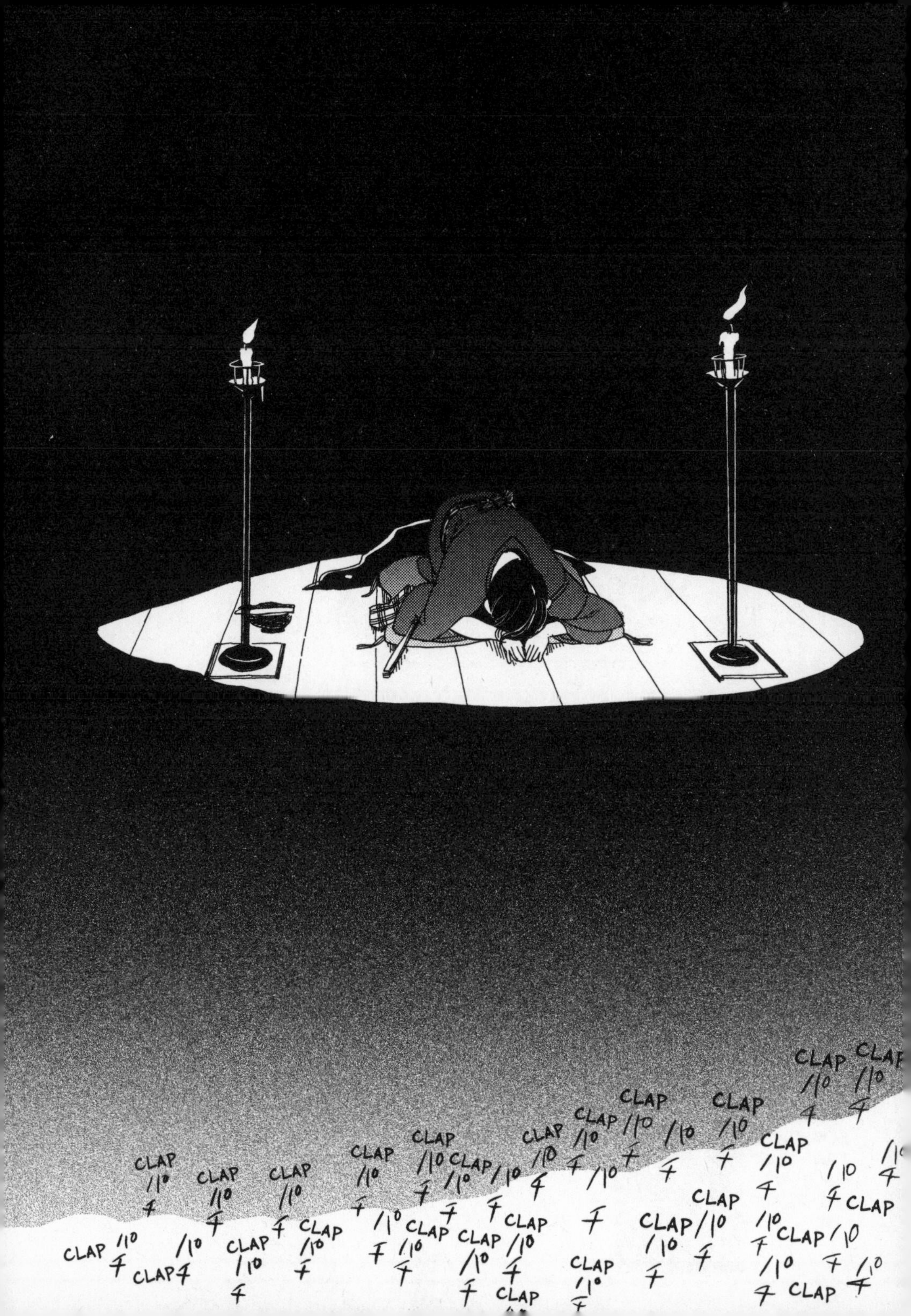
CLAP
CLAP
CLAP
CLAP
CLAP
CLAP
CLAP
CLAP
CLAP
CLAP
CLAP
CLAP
CLAP
CLAP
CLAP
CLAP
CLAP
CLAP
CLAP
CLAP
CLAP
CLAP
CLAP
CLAP
CLAP
CLAP
CLAP

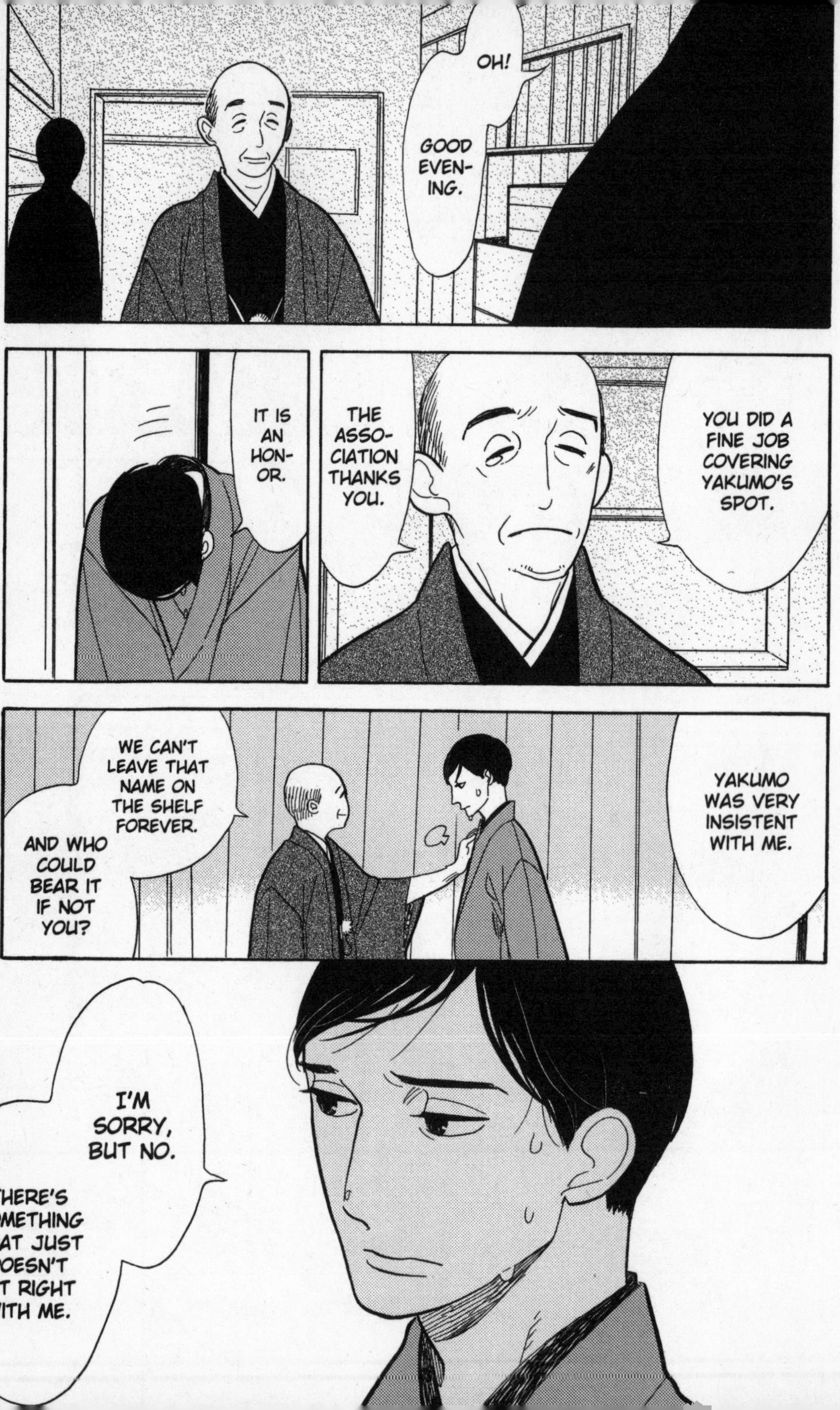
OH!
GOOD EVENING.
YOU DID A FINE JOB COVERING YAKUMO'S SPOT.
THE ASSOCIATION THANKS YOU.
IT IS AN HONOR.
YAKUMO WAS VERY INSISTENT WITH ME.
WE CAN'T LEAVE THAT NAME ON THE SHELF FOREVER.
AND WHO COULD BEAR IT IF NOT YOU?
I'M SORRY, BUT NO.
THERE'S SOMETHING THAT JUST DOESN'T SIT RIGHT WITH ME.

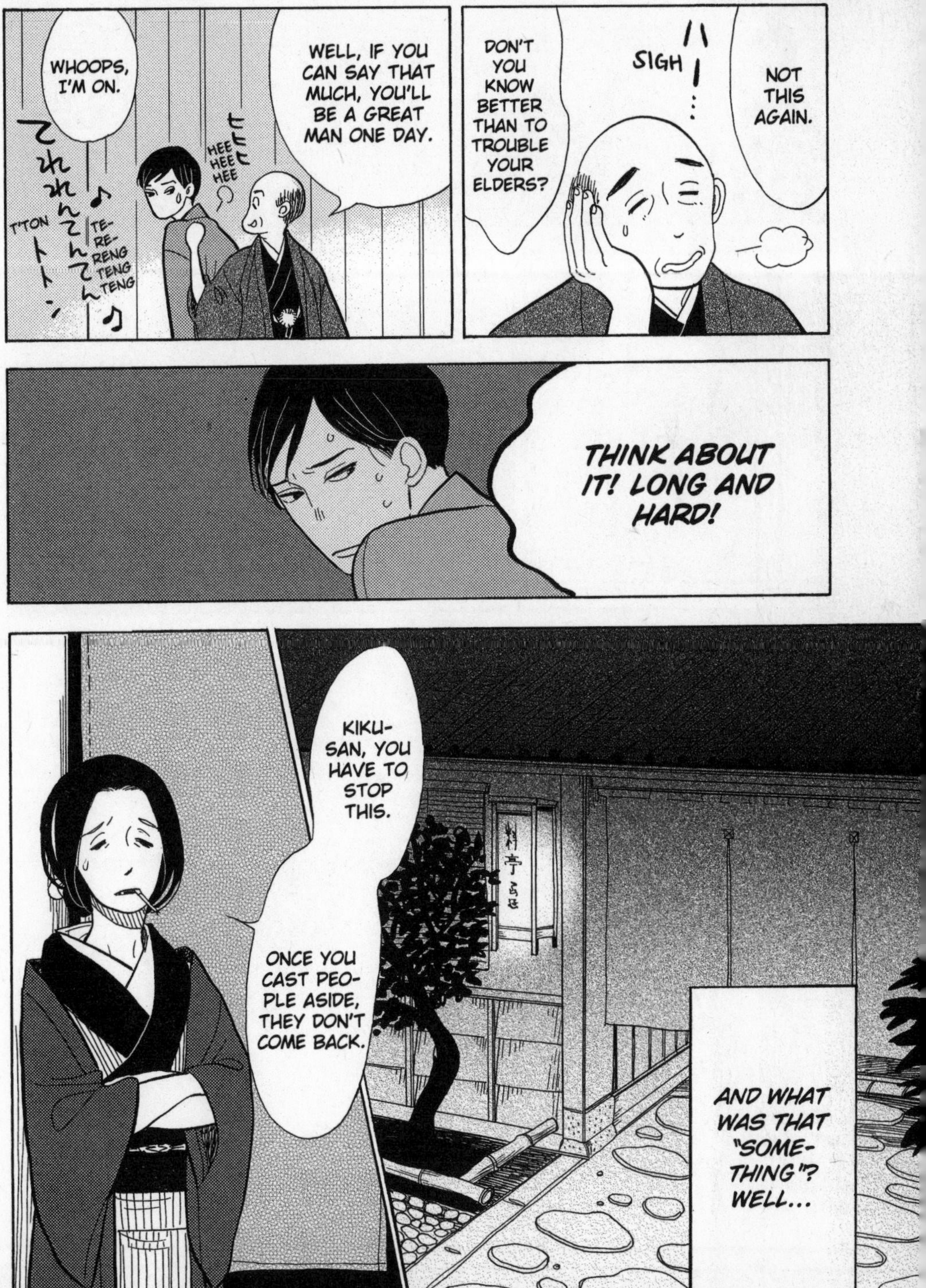
NOT THIS AGAIN.
SIGH
DON'T YOU KNOW BETTER THAN TO TROUBLE YOUR ELDERS?
WELL, IF YOU CAN SAY THAT MUCH, YOU'LL BE A GREAT MAN ONE DAY.
HEE HEE HEE
WHOOPS, I'M ON.
TE-RE-RENG TENG TENG
T'TON
THINK ABOUT IT! LONG AND HARD!
KIKU-SAN, YOU HAVE TO STOP THIS.
ONCE YOU CAST PEO-PLE ASIDE, THEY DON'T COME BACK.
AND WHAT WAS THAT "SOME-THING"? WELL...

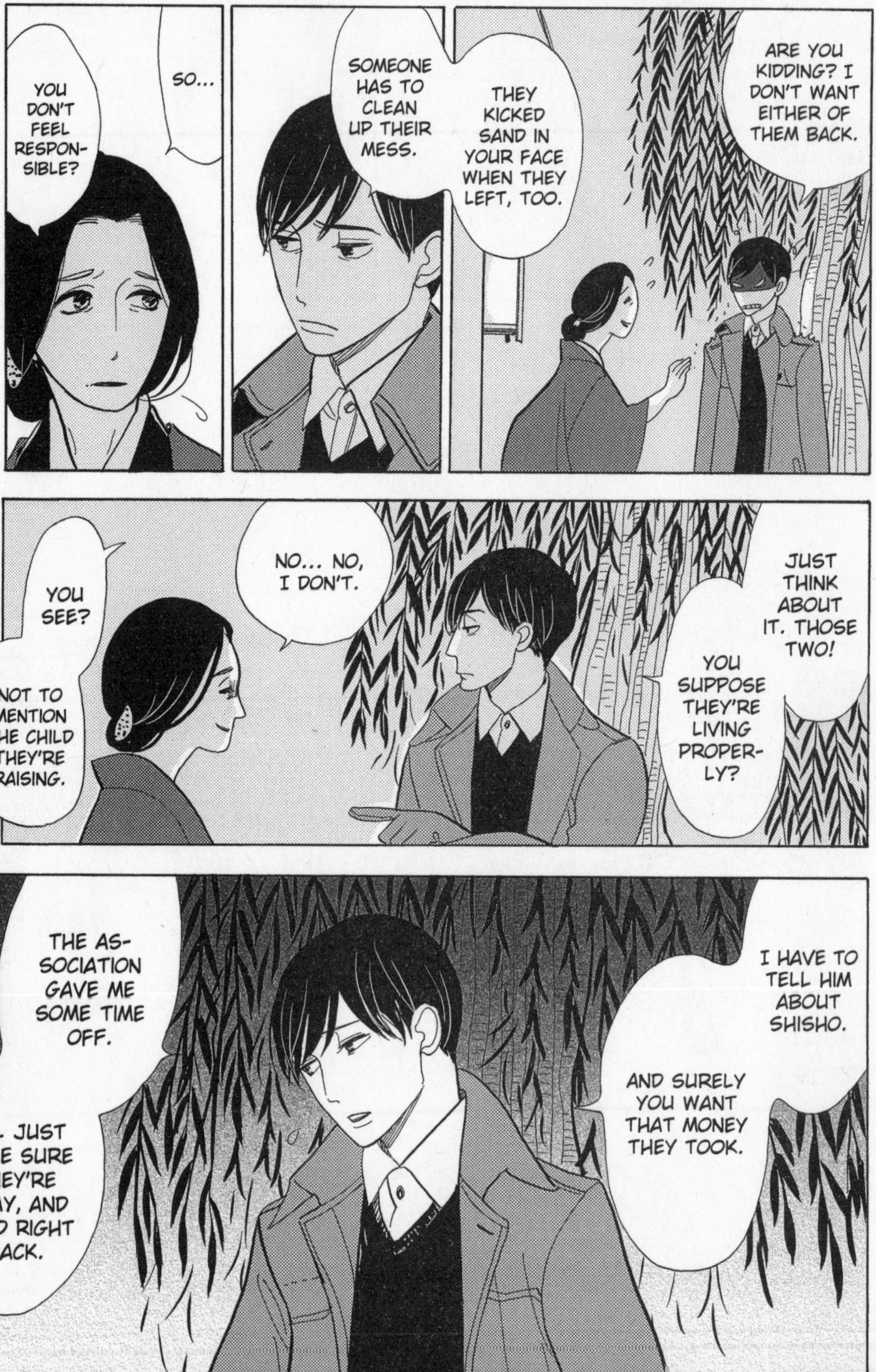
ARE YOU KIDDING? I DON'T WANT EITHER OF THEM BACK.
THEY KICKED SAND IN YOUR FACE WHEN THEY LEFT, TOO.
SOMEONE HAS TO CLEAN UP THEIR MESS.
SO...
YOU DON'T FEEL RESPON-SIBLE?
JUST THINK ABOUT IT. THOSE TWO!
YOU SUPPOSE THEY'RE LIVING PROPER-LY?
NO... NO, I DON'T.
YOU SEE?
NOT TO MENTION THE CHILD THEY'RE RAISING.
I HAVE TO TELL HIM ABOUT SHISHO.
AND SURELY YOU WANT THAT MONEY THEY TOOK.
THE AS-SOCIATION GAVE ME SOME TIME OFF.
I'LL JUST MAKE SURE THEY'RE OKAY, AND HEAD RIGHT BACK.

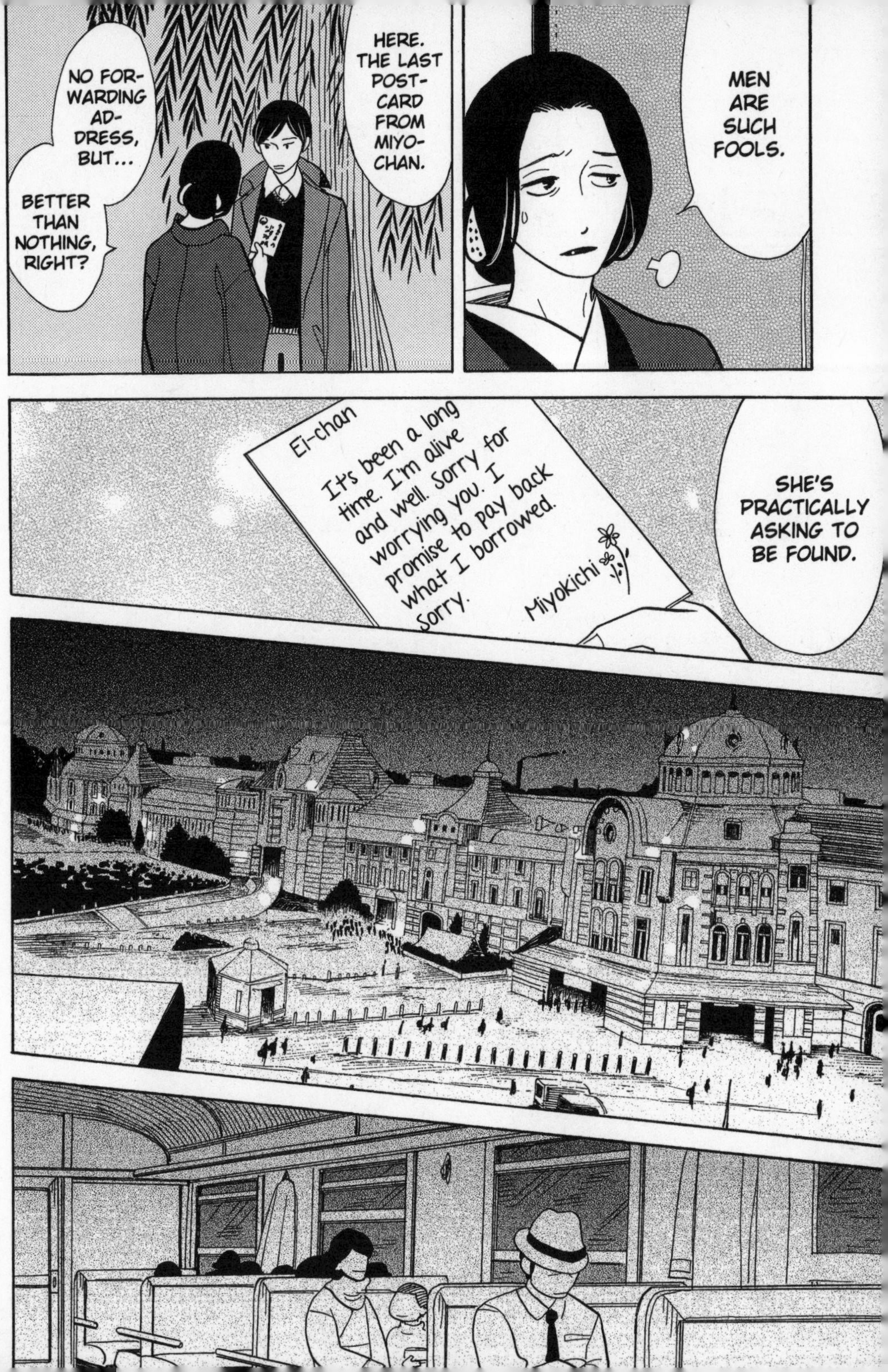
MEN ARE SUCH FOOLS.
HERE. THE LAST POST-CARD FROM MIYO-CHAN.
NO FOR-WARDING AD-DRESS, BUT...
BETTER THAN NOTHING, RIGHT?
SHE'S PRACTICALLY ASKING TO BE FOUND.
Ei-chan
It's been a long time. I'm alive and well. Sorry for worrying you. I promise to pay back what I borrowed. Sorry.
Miyokichi

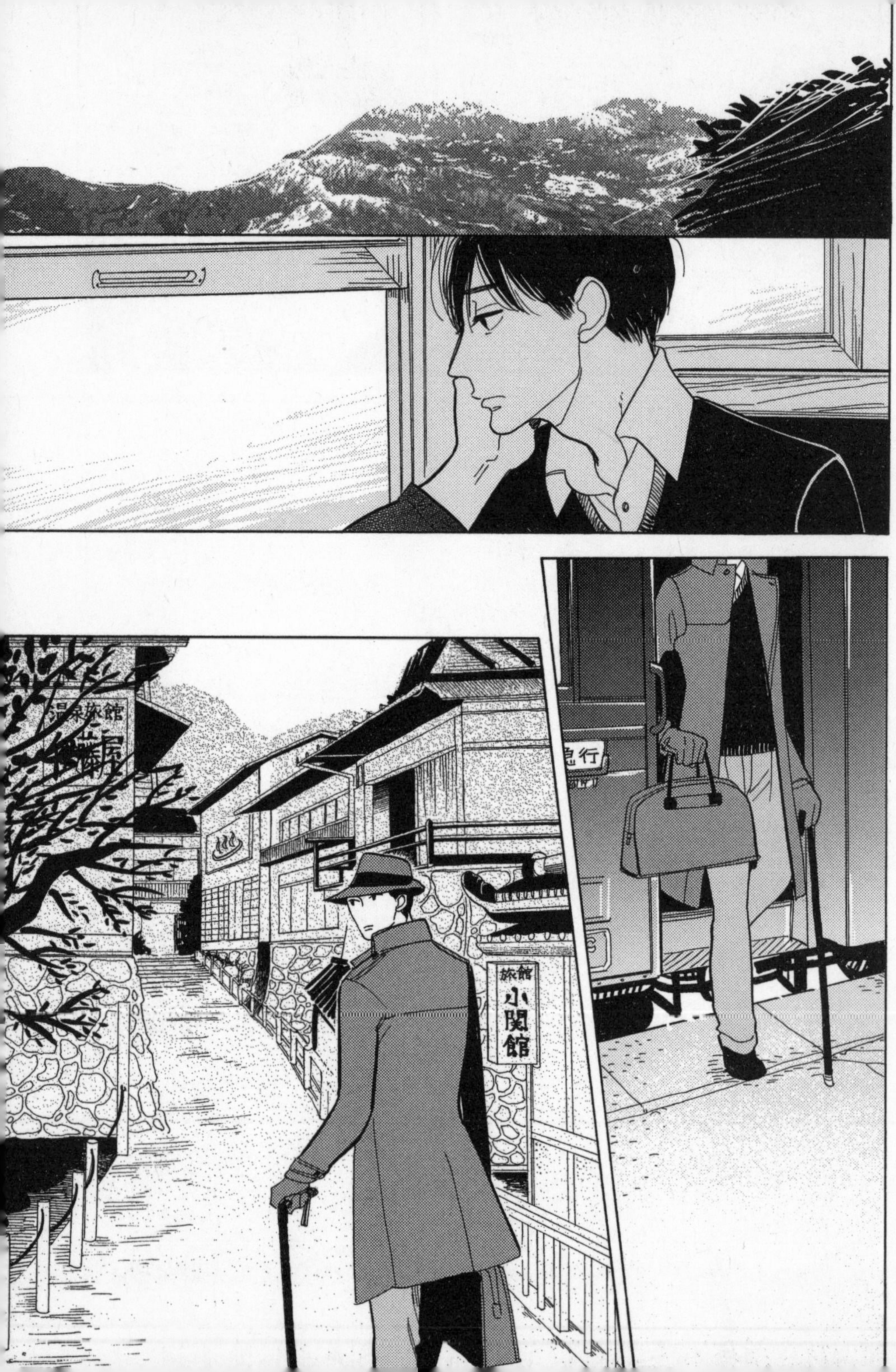
急行
温泉旅館
旅館
小関館

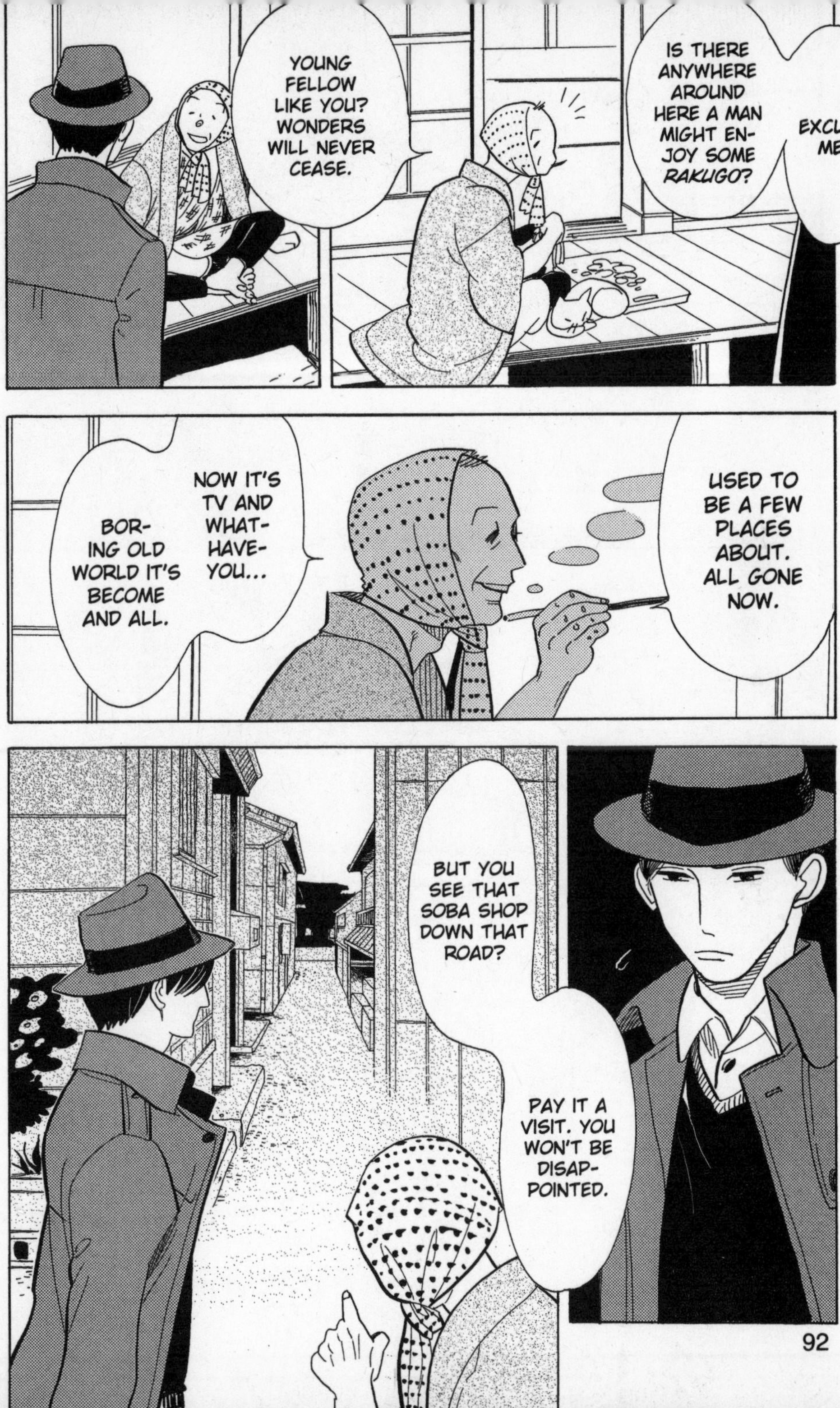
EXCUSE ME.
IS THERE ANYWHERE AROUND HERE A MAN MIGHT ENJOY SOME *RAKUGO*?
YOUNG FELLOW LIKE YOU? WONDERS WILL NEVER CEASE.
USED TO BE A FEW PLACES ABOUT. ALL GONE NOW.
NOW IT'S TV AND WHAT-HAVE-YOU...
BORING OLD WORLD IT'S BECOME AND ALL.
BUT YOU SEE THAT SOBA SHOP DOWN THAT ROAD?
PAY IT A VISIT. YOU WON'T BE DISAPPOINTED.

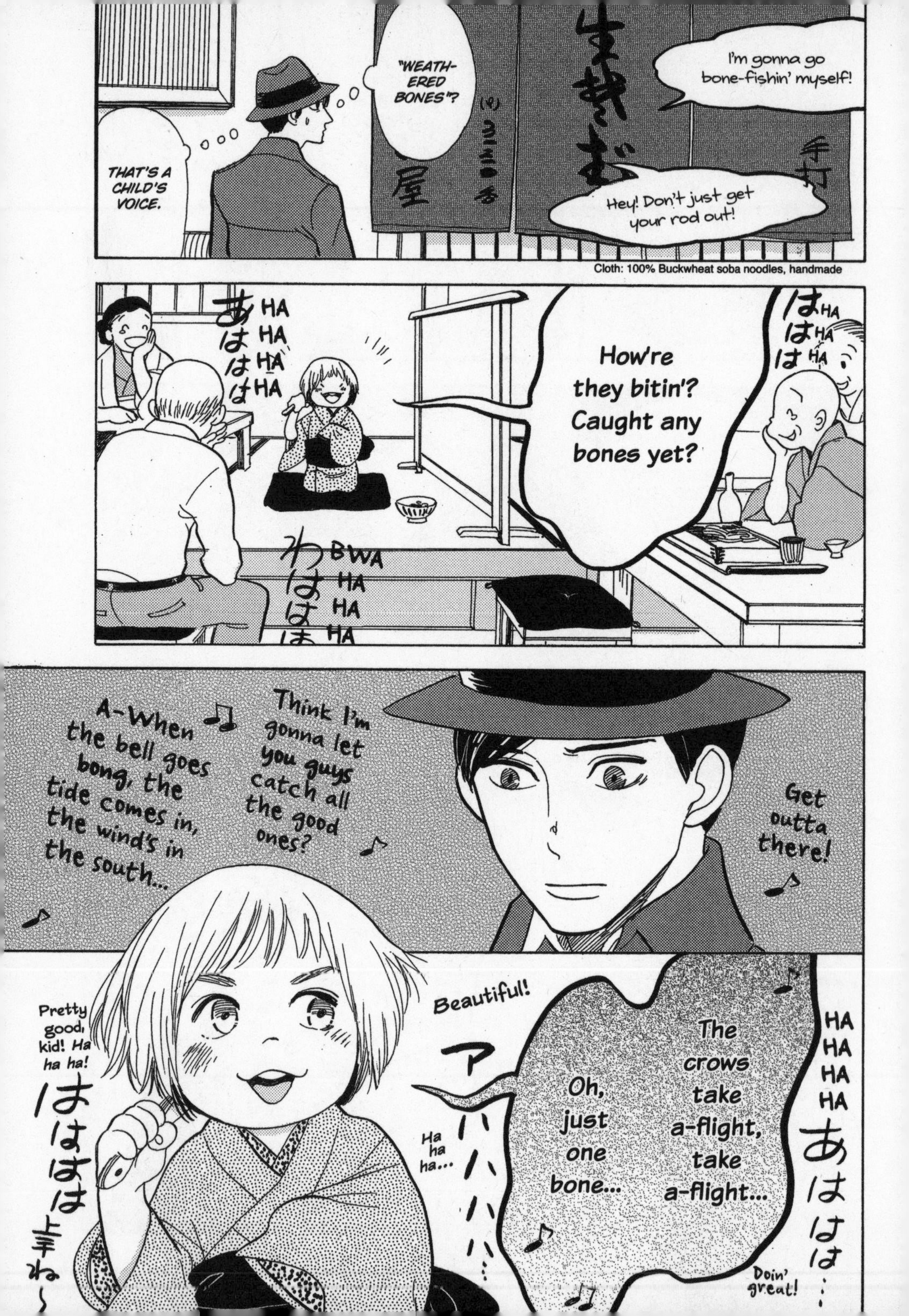
I'm gonna go bone-fishin' myself!
Hey! Don't just get your rod out!
"WEATH-ERED BONES"?
THAT'S A CHILD'S VOICE.
Cloth: 100% Buckwheat soba noodles, handmade
ははは HA HA HA
How're they bitin'? Caught any bones yet?
あははは HA HA HA HA
わははは BWA HA HA HA
Get outta there!
Think I'm gonna let you guys catch all the good ones?
A-When the bell goes bong, the tide comes in, the wind's in the south...
HA HA HA HA
あははは…
Doin' great!
The crows take a-flight, take a-flight...
Oh, just one bone...
Beautiful!
アハハ…
Ha ha ha...
Pretty good, kid! Ha ha ha!
ははは上手ね~

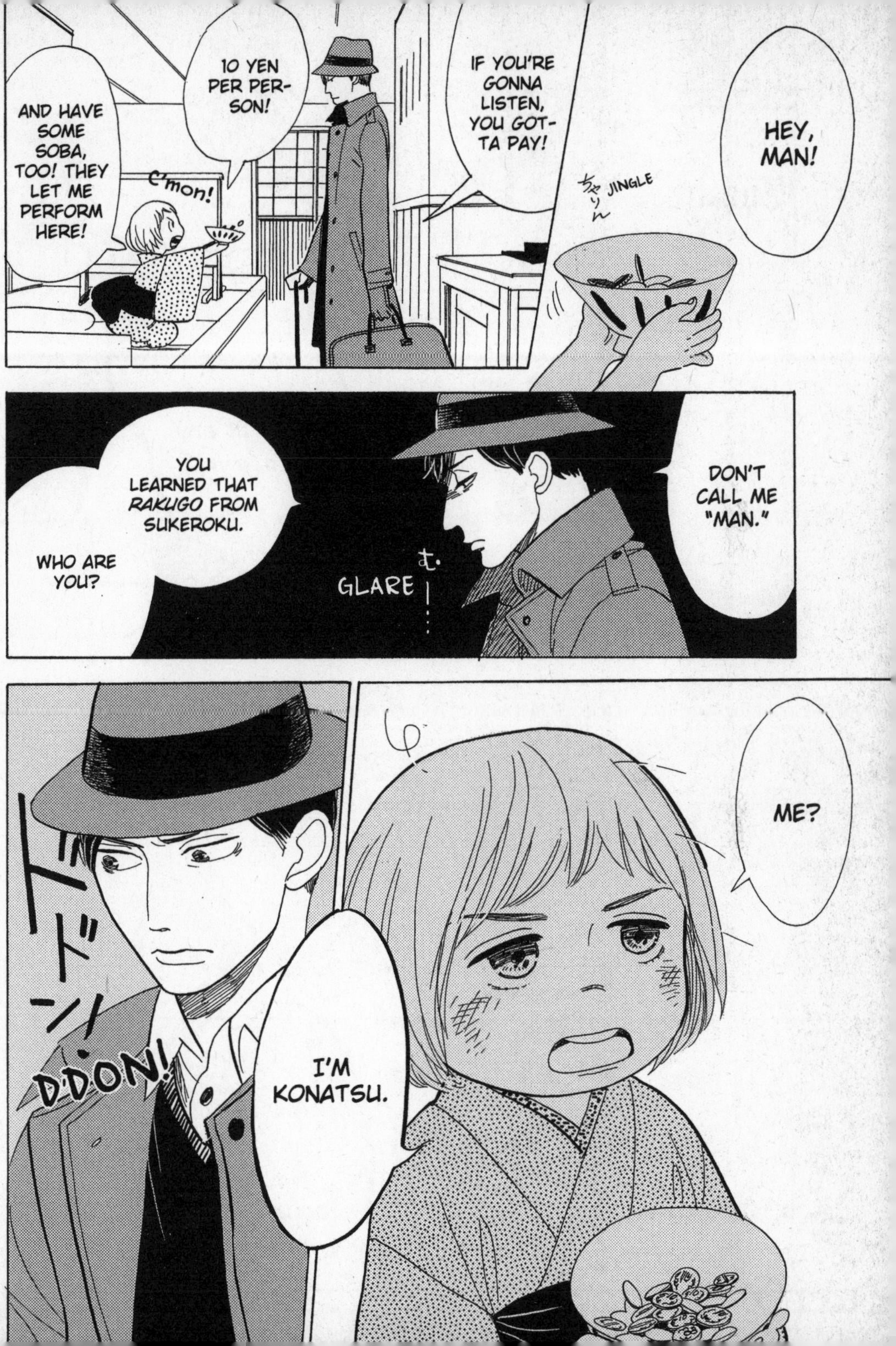
HEY, MAN!
ちゃりん JINGLE
IF YOU'RE GONNA LISTEN, YOU GOTTA PAY!
10 YEN PER PERSON!
C'mon!
AND HAVE SOME SOBA, TOO! THEY LET ME PERFORM HERE!
DON'T CALL ME "MAN."
む… GLARE
YOU LEARNED THAT RAKUGO FROM SUKEROKU.
WHO ARE YOU?
ME?
I'M KONATSU.
ドーン D'DON!

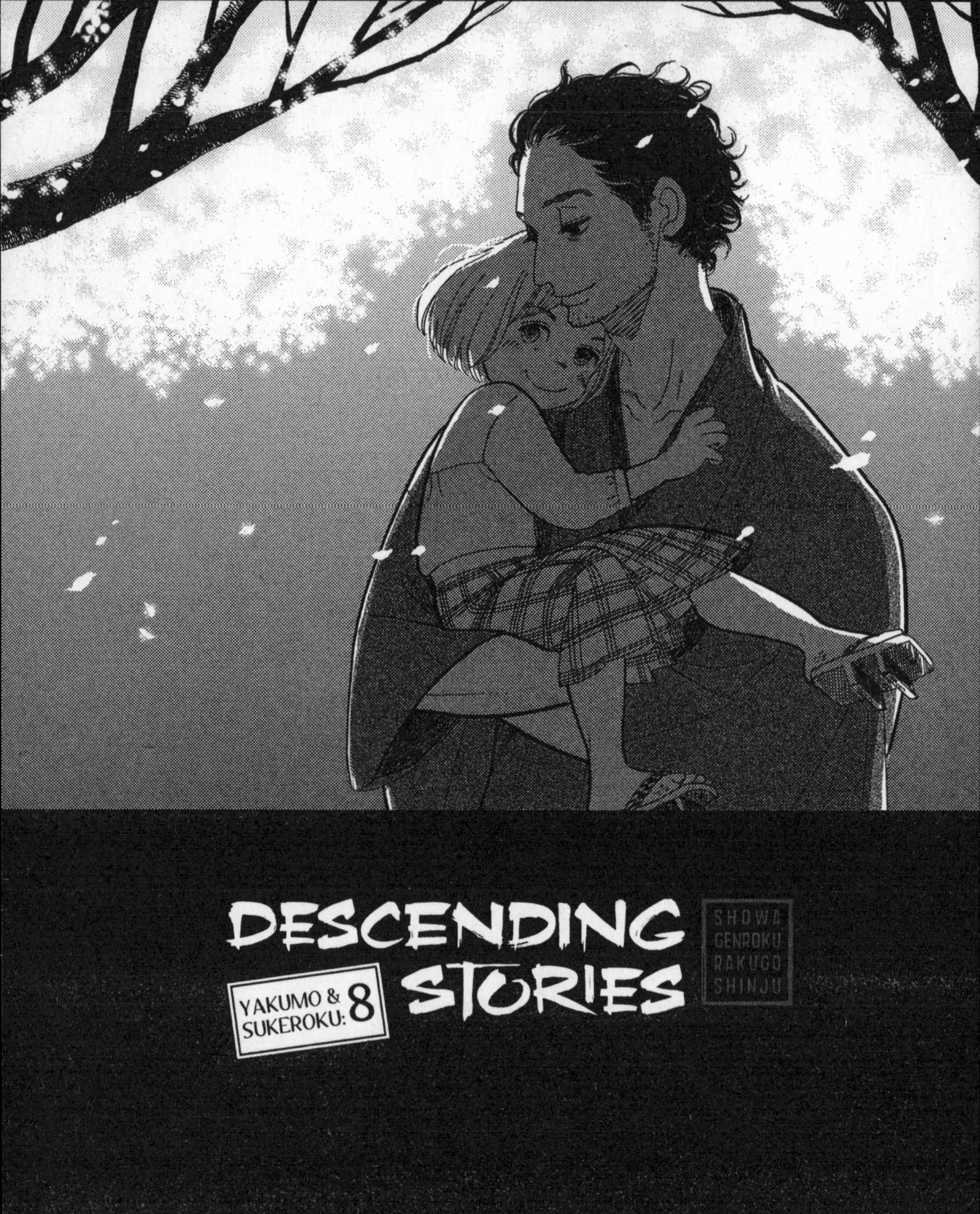

DESCENDING STORIES

YAKUMO & SUKEROKU: 8

SHOWA GENROKU RAKUGO SHINJU

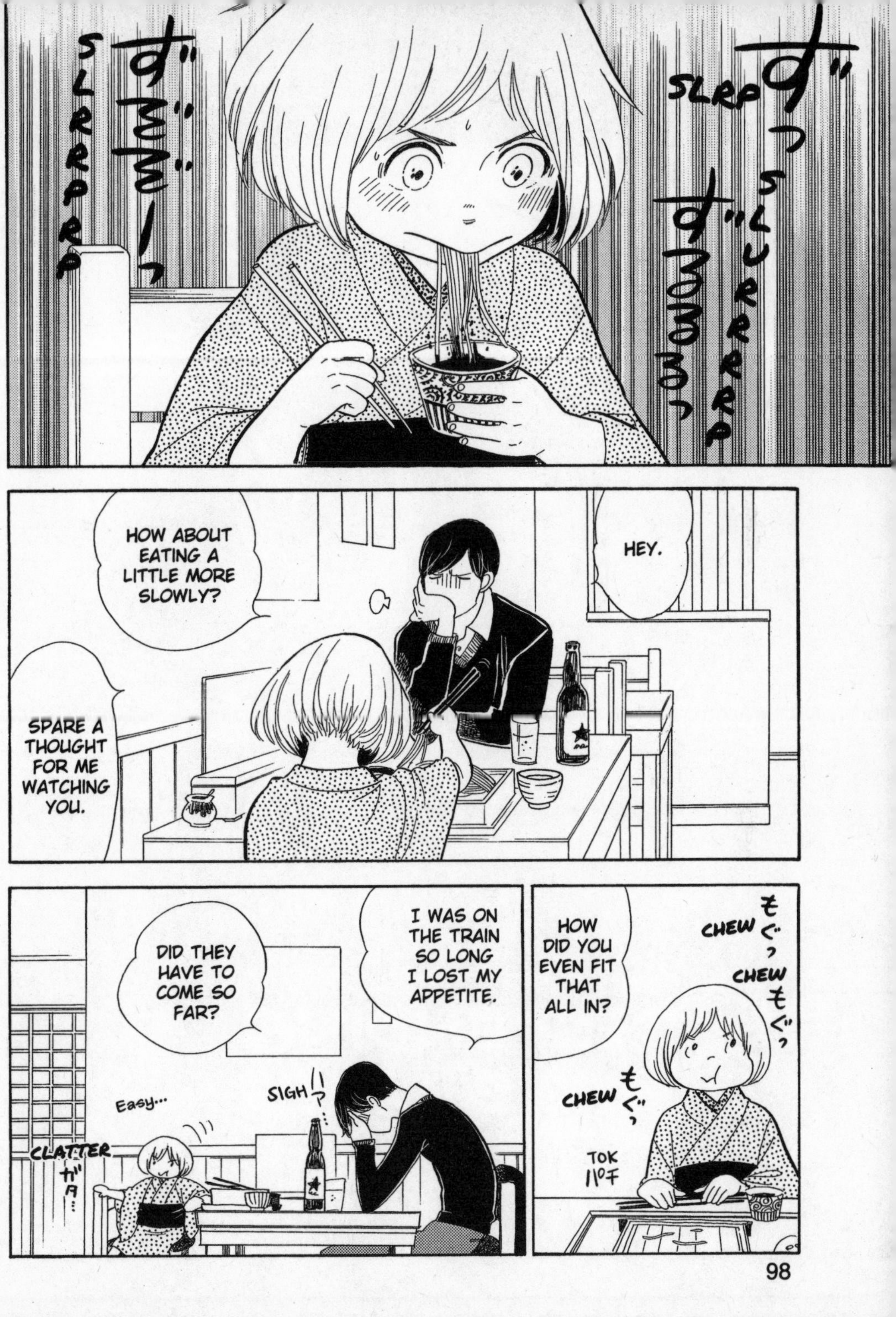
SLRP
ずっ
SLURRRRP
ずるるるっ
SLRRRPRP
ずぞぞーっ
HEY.
HOW ABOUT EATING A LITTLE MORE SLOWLY?
SPARE A THOUGHT FOR ME WATCHING YOU.
CHEW もぐっ
CHEW もぐっ
CHEW もぐっ
HOW DID YOU EVEN FIT THAT ALL IN?
TOK パチ
I WAS ON THE TRAIN SO LONG I LOST MY APPETITE.
DID THEY HAVE TO COME SO FAR?
SIGH ハァ…
Easy...
CLATTER ガタ…

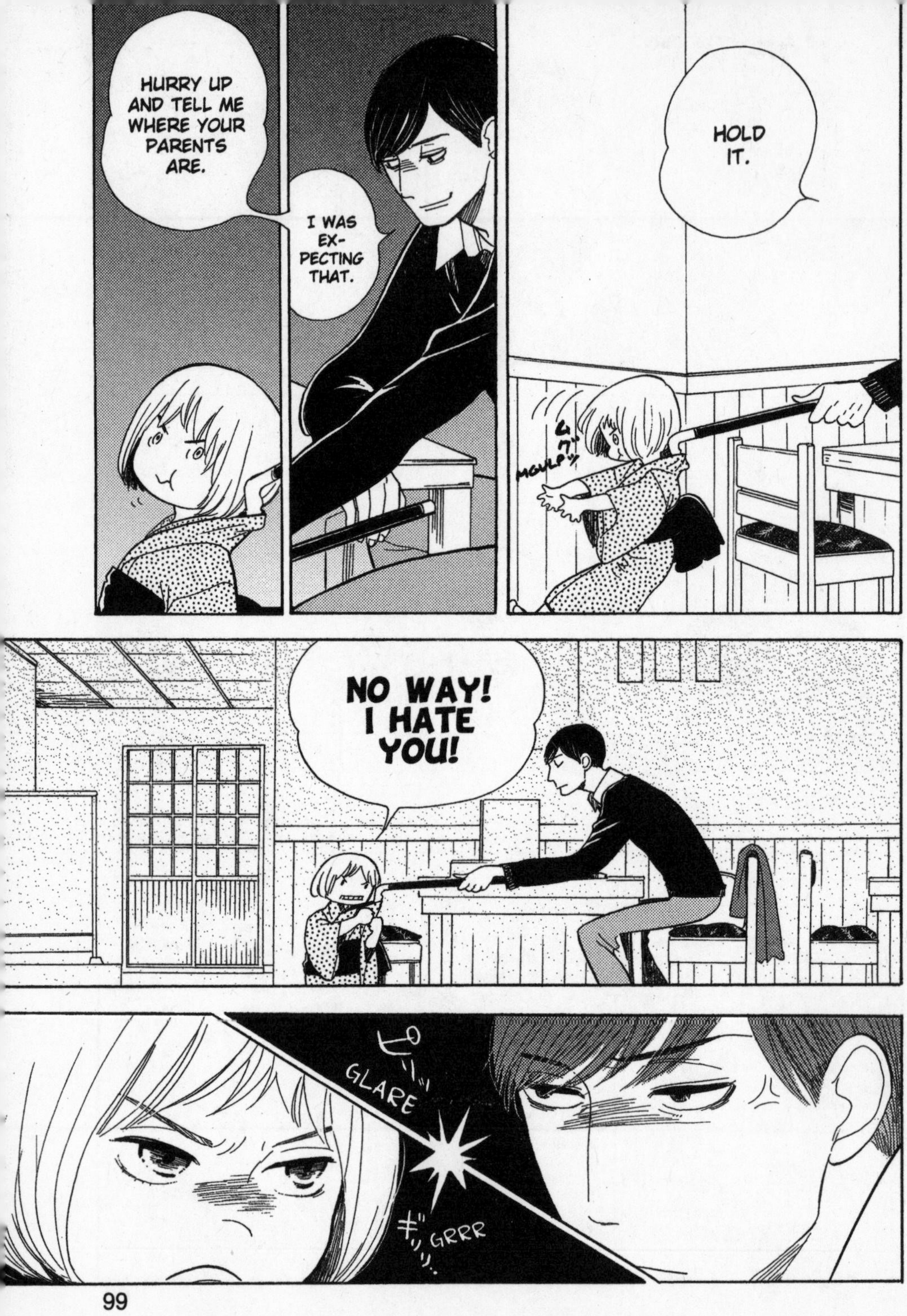
HOLD IT.
MGULP
I WAS EX-PECTING THAT.
HURRY UP AND TELL ME WHERE YOUR PARENTS ARE.
NO WAY! I HATE YOU!
GLARE
GRRR

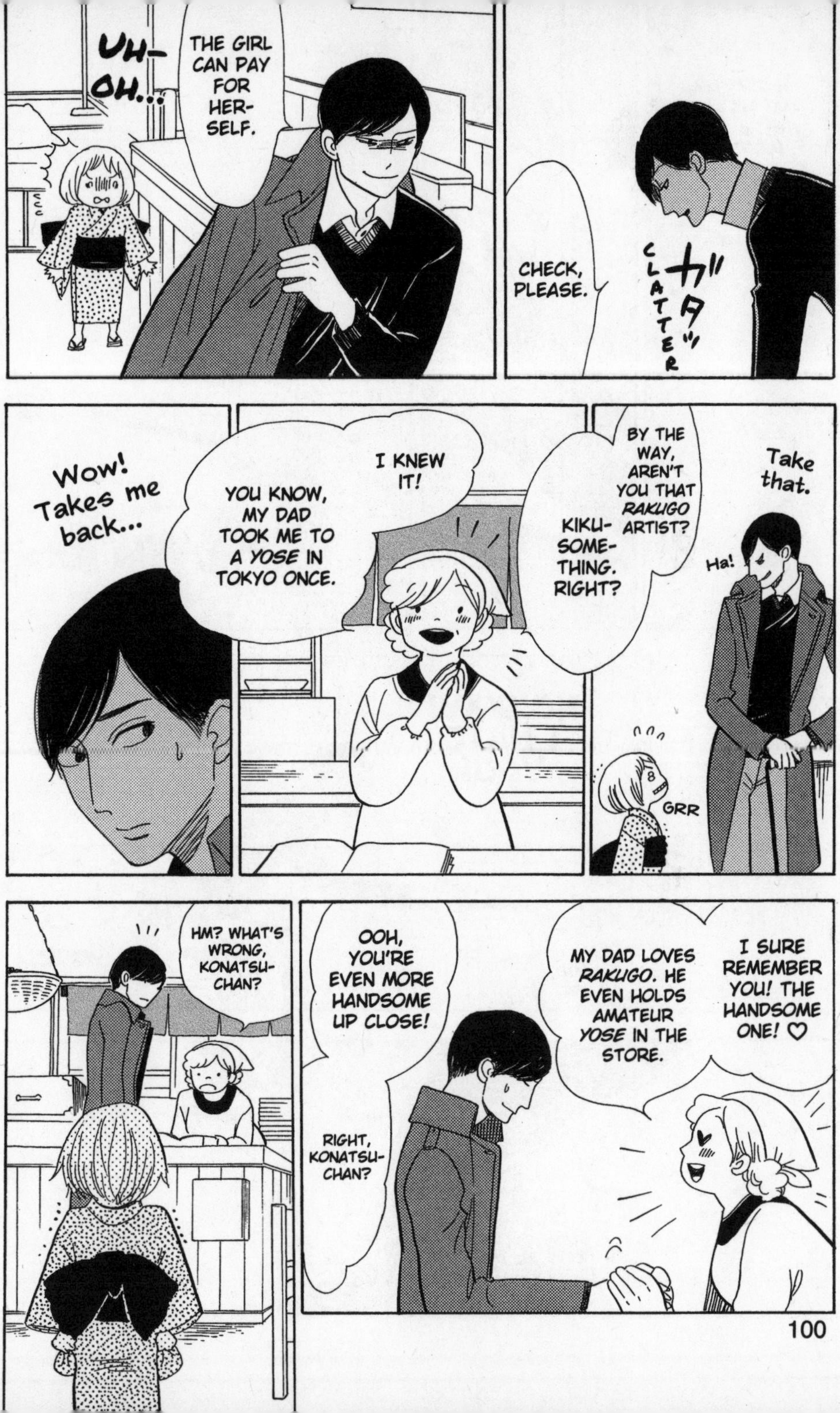
CLATTER
CHECK, PLEASE.
THE GIRL CAN PAY FOR HER-SELF.
UH-OH...
Take that.
Ha!
BY THE WAY, AREN'T YOU THAT *RAKUGO* ARTIST?
KIKU-SOME-THING. RIGHT?
GRR
I KNEW IT!
YOU KNOW, MY DAD TOOK ME TO A *YOSE* IN TOKYO ONCE.
Wow! Takes me back...
I SURE REMEMBER YOU! THE HANDSOME ONE! ♡
MY DAD LOVES *RAKUGO*. HE EVEN HOLDS AMATEUR *YOSE* IN THE STORE.
OOH, YOU'RE EVEN MORE HANDSOME UP CLOSE!
RIGHT, KONATSU-CHAN?
HM? WHAT'S WRONG, KONATSU-CHAN?

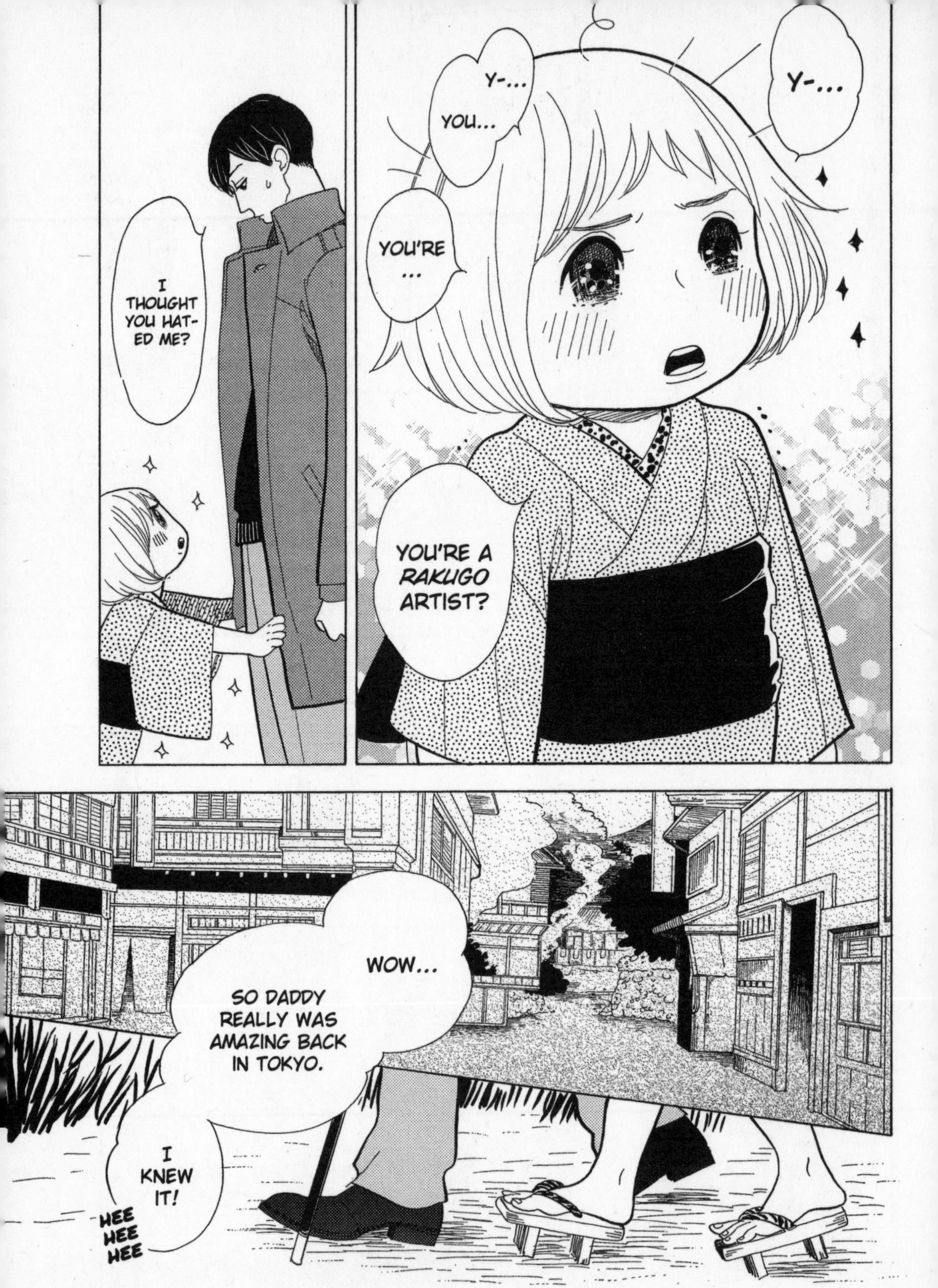
Y-...
Y-... YOU...
YOU'RE ...
YOU'RE A *RAKUGO* ARTIST?
I THOUGHT YOU HAT-ED ME?
WOW... SO DADDY REALLY WAS AMAZING BACK IN TOKYO.
I KNEW IT!
HEE HEE HEE

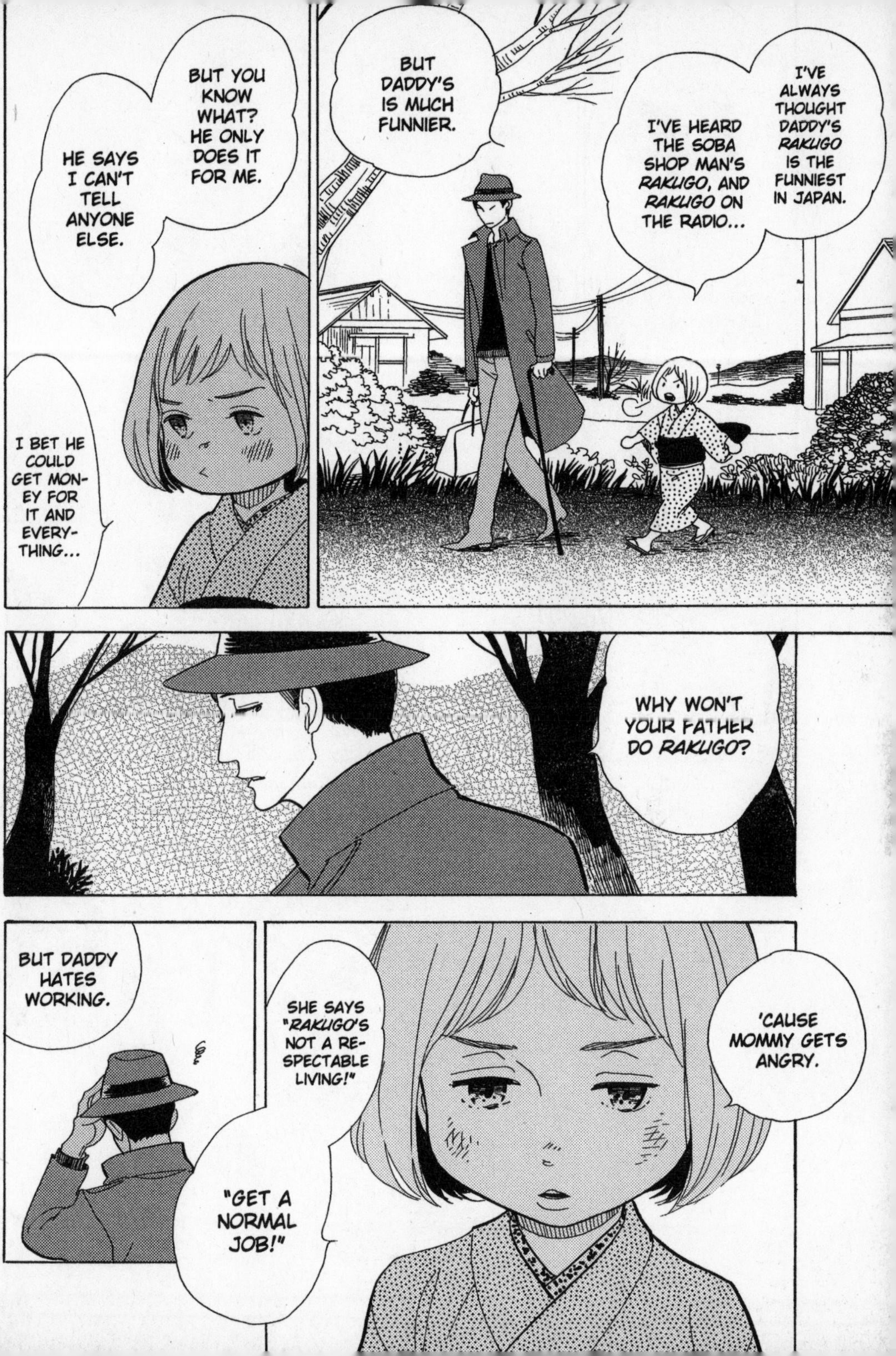
I'VE ALWAYS THOUGHT DADDY'S *RAKUGO* IS THE FUNNIEST IN JAPAN.
I'VE HEARD THE SOBA SHOP MAN'S *RAKUGO*, AND *RAKUGO* ON THE RADIO...
BUT DADDY'S IS MUCH FUNNIER.
BUT YOU KNOW WHAT? HE ONLY DOES IT FOR ME.
HE SAYS I CAN'T TELL ANYONE ELSE.
I BET HE COULD GET MON-EY FOR IT AND EVERY-THING...
WHY WON'T YOUR FATHER DO *RAKUGO*?
'CAUSE MOMMY GETS ANGRY.
SHE SAYS "*RAKUGO*'S NOT A RE-SPECTABLE LIVING!"
"GET A NORMAL JOB!"
BUT DADDY HATES WORKING.

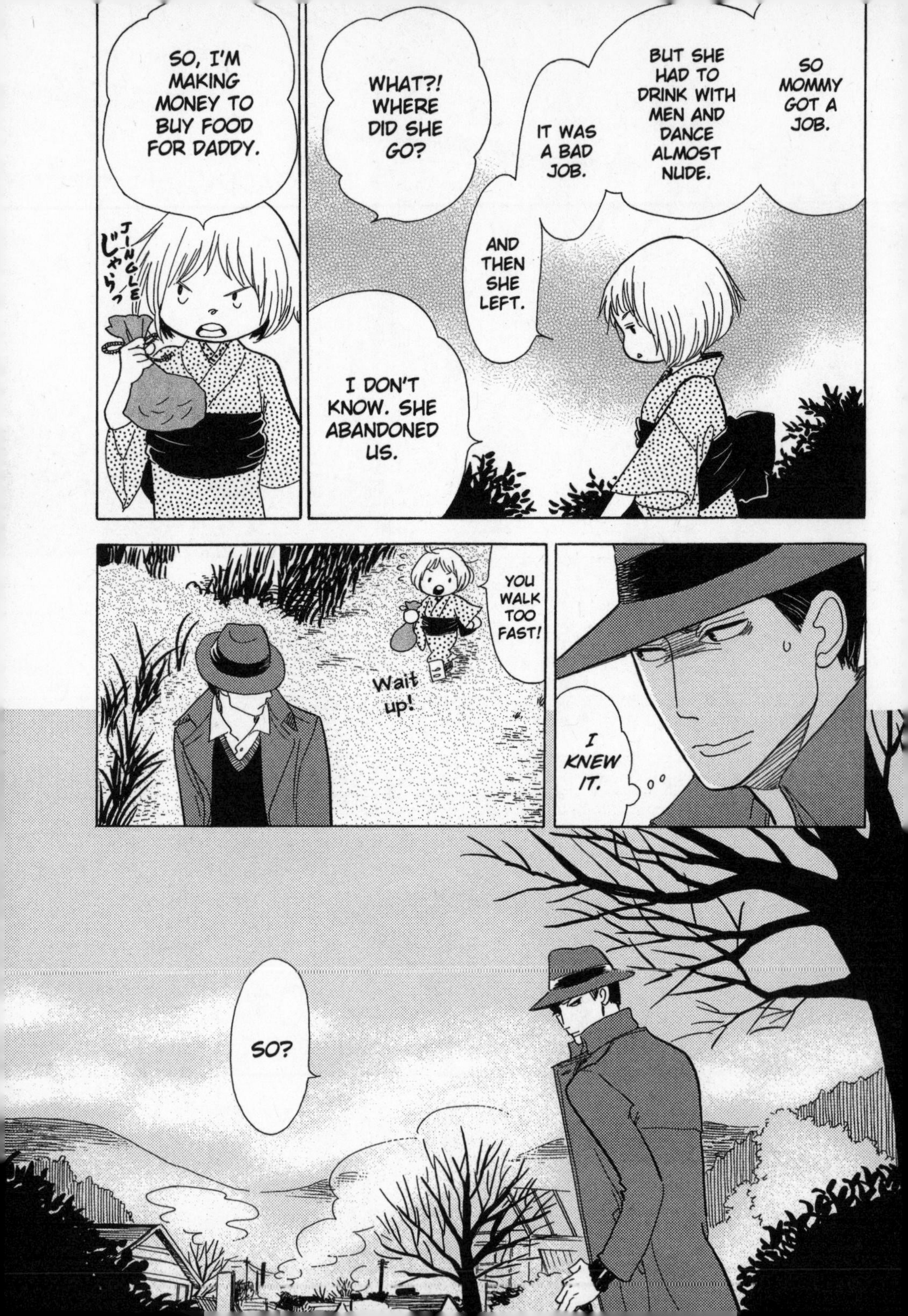
SO MOMMY GOT A JOB.
BUT SHE HAD TO DRINK WITH MEN AND DANCE ALMOST NUDE.
IT WAS A BAD JOB.
AND THEN SHE LEFT.
WHAT?! WHERE DID SHE GO?
I DON'T KNOW. SHE ABANDONED US.
SO, I'M MAKING MONEY TO BUY FOOD FOR DADDY.
JINGLE
じゃらっ
I KNEW IT.
YOU WALK TOO FAST!
Wait up!
SO?

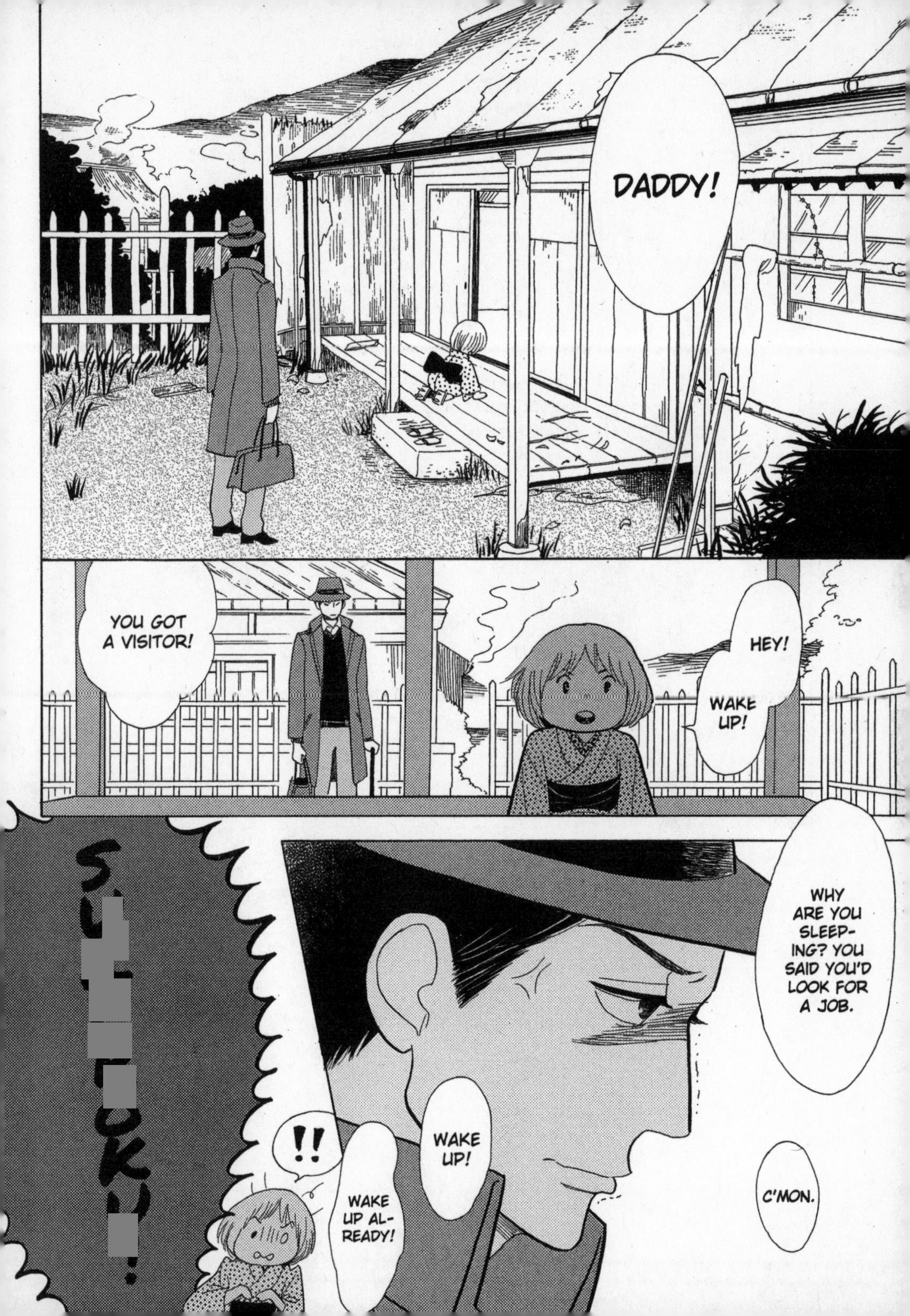
DADDY!
HEY!
WAKE UP!
YOU GOT A VISITOR!
WHY ARE YOU SLEEP-ING? YOU SAID YOU'D LOOK FOR A JOB.
C'MON.
WAKE UP!
WAKE UP AL-READY!
!!

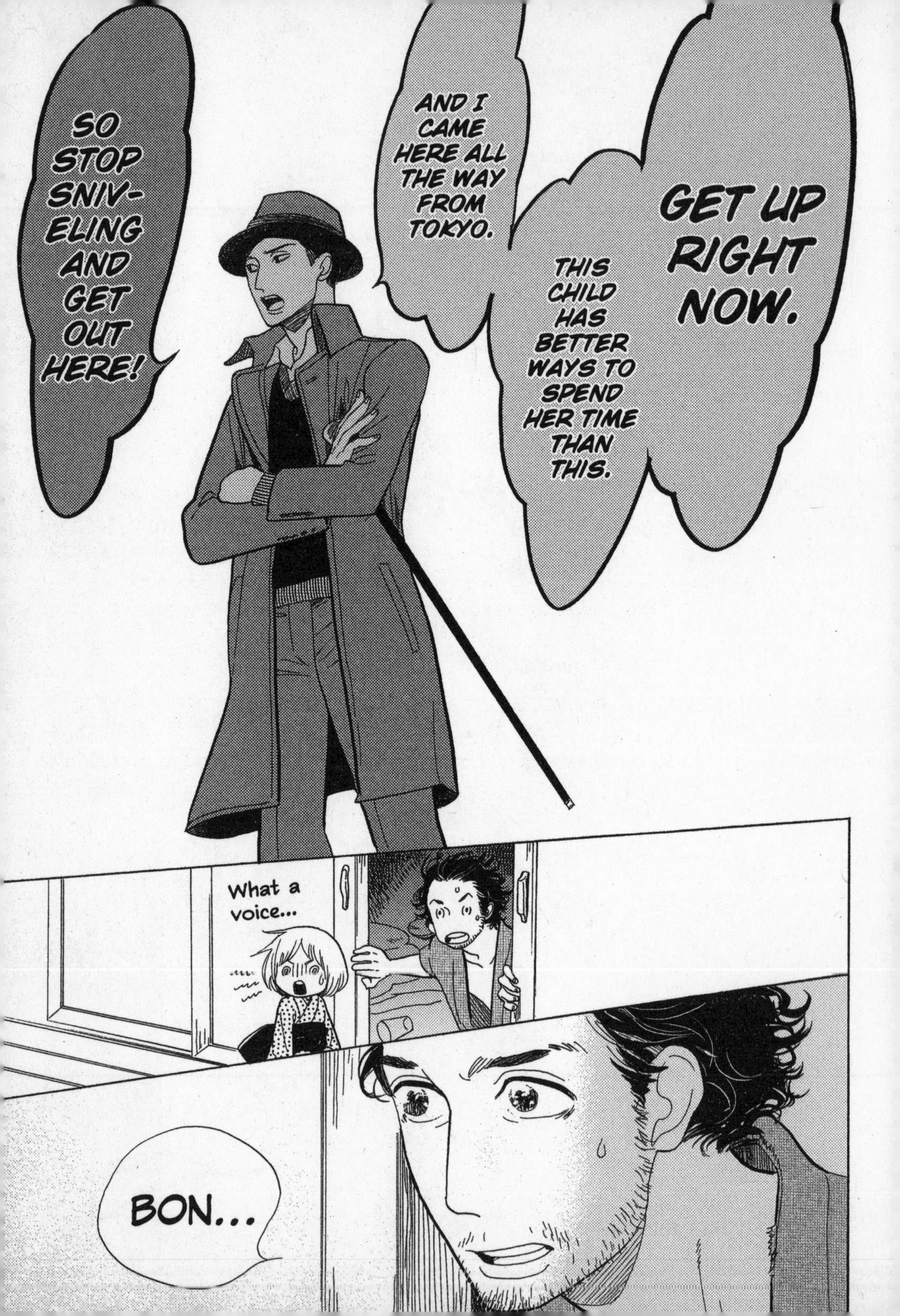
GET UP RIGHT NOW.
THIS CHILD HAS BETTER WAYS TO SPEND HER TIME THAN THIS.
AND I CAME HERE ALL THE WAY FROM TOKYO.
SO STOP SNIV-ELING AND GET OUT HERE!
What a voice...
BON...

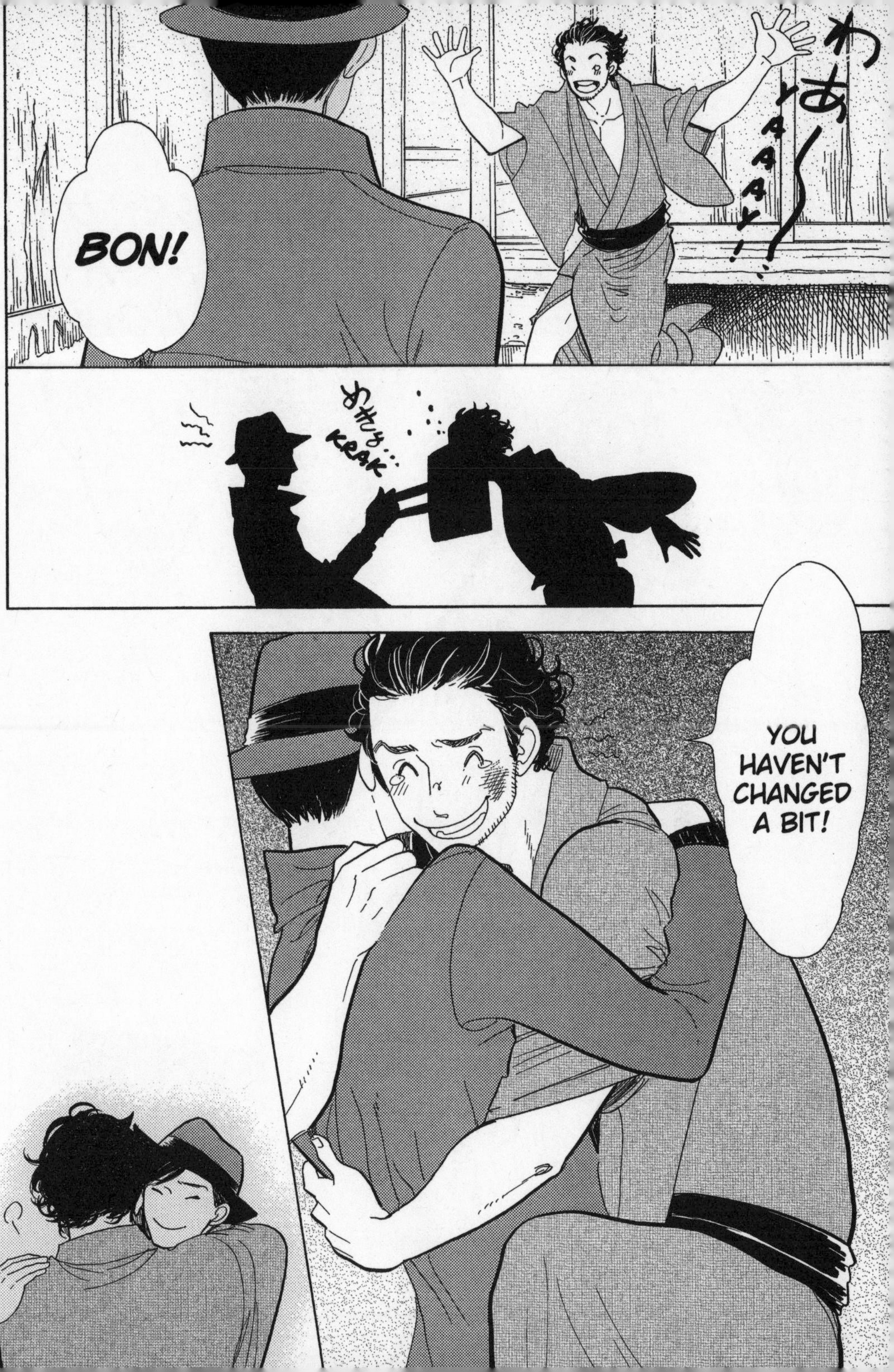
わあ～
YAAAAY!!
BON!
めきょ…
KRAK
YOU HAVEN'T CHANGED A BIT!

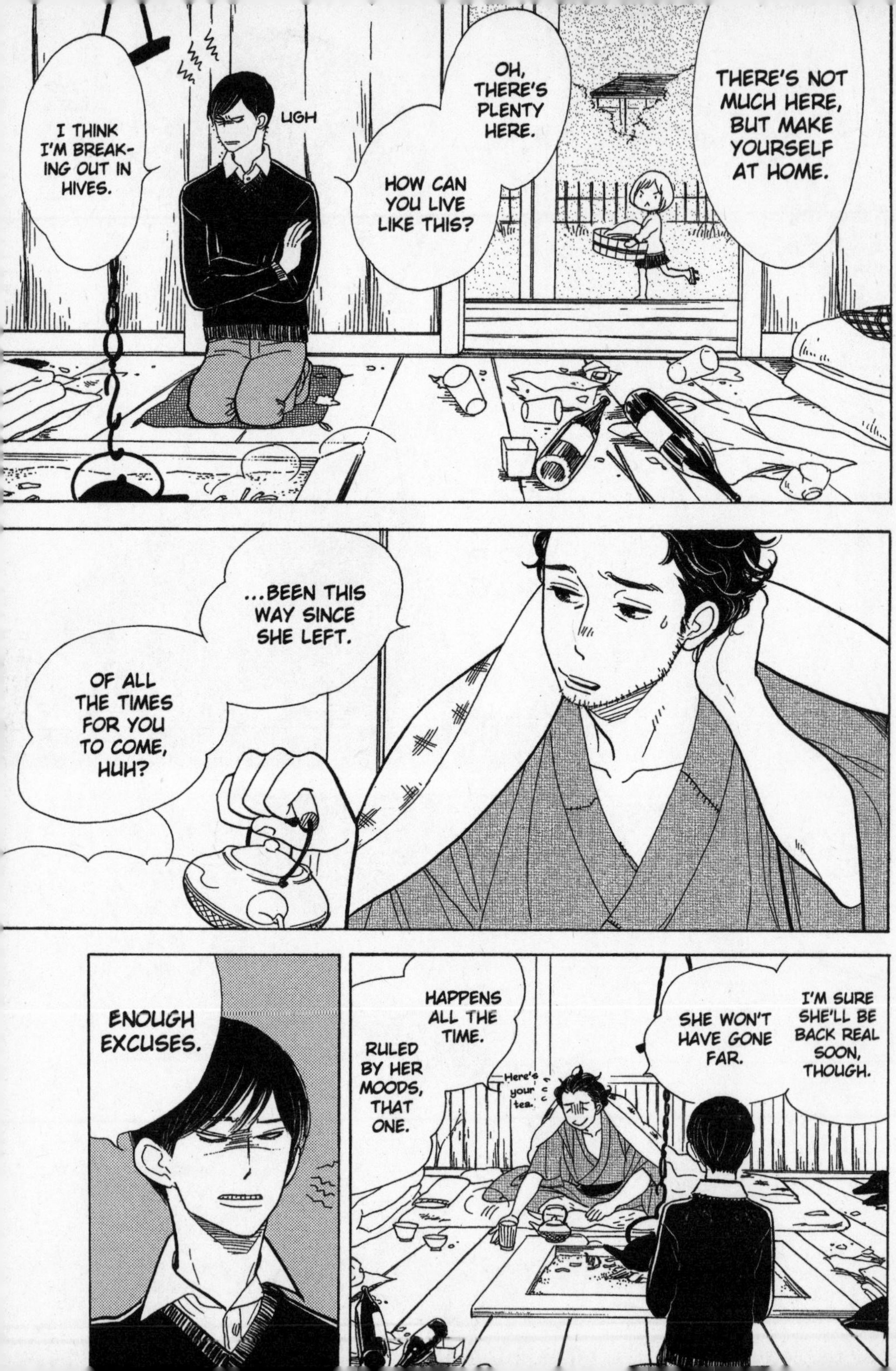
THERE'S NOT MUCH HERE, BUT MAKE YOURSELF AT HOME.
OH, THERE'S PLENTY HERE.
HOW CAN YOU LIVE LIKE THIS?
UGH
I THINK I'M BREAK-ING OUT IN HIVES.
...BEEN THIS WAY SINCE SHE LEFT.
OF ALL THE TIMES FOR YOU TO COME, HUH?
I'M SURE SHE'LL BE BACK REAL SOON, THOUGH.
SHE WON'T HAVE GONE FAR.
HAPPENS ALL THE TIME.
RULED BY HER MOODS, THAT ONE.
Here's your tea.
ENOUGH EXCUSES.

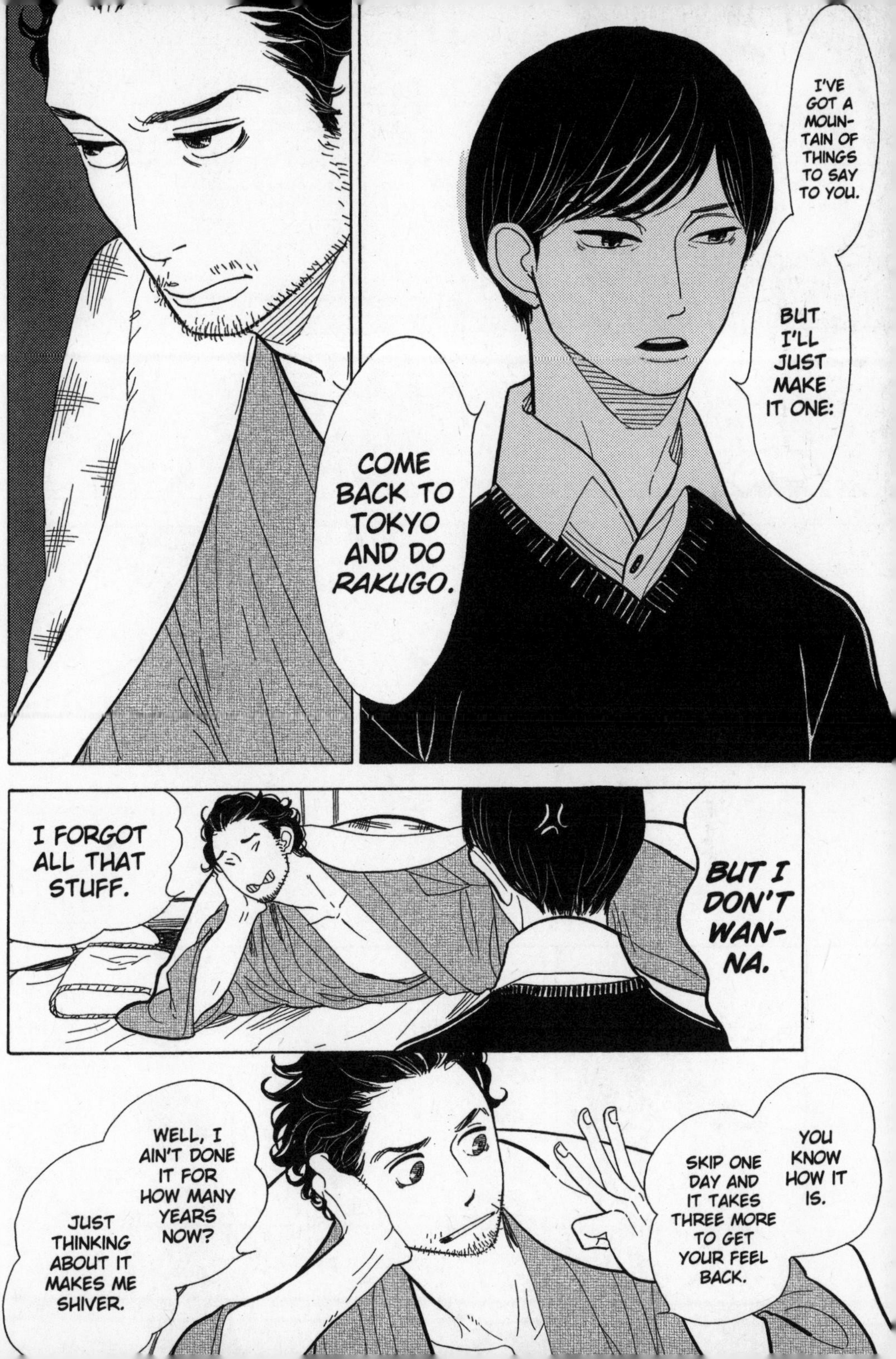
I'VE GOT A MOUNTAIN OF THINGS TO SAY TO YOU.
BUT I'LL JUST MAKE IT ONE:
COME BACK TO TOKYO AND DO *RAKUGO*.
BUT I DON'T WAN-NA.
I FORGOT ALL THAT STUFF.
YOU KNOW HOW IT IS.
SKIP ONE DAY AND IT TAKES THREE MORE TO GET YOUR FEEL BACK.
WELL, I AIN'T DONE IT FOR HOW MANY YEARS NOW?
JUST THINKING ABOUT IT MAKES ME SHIVER.

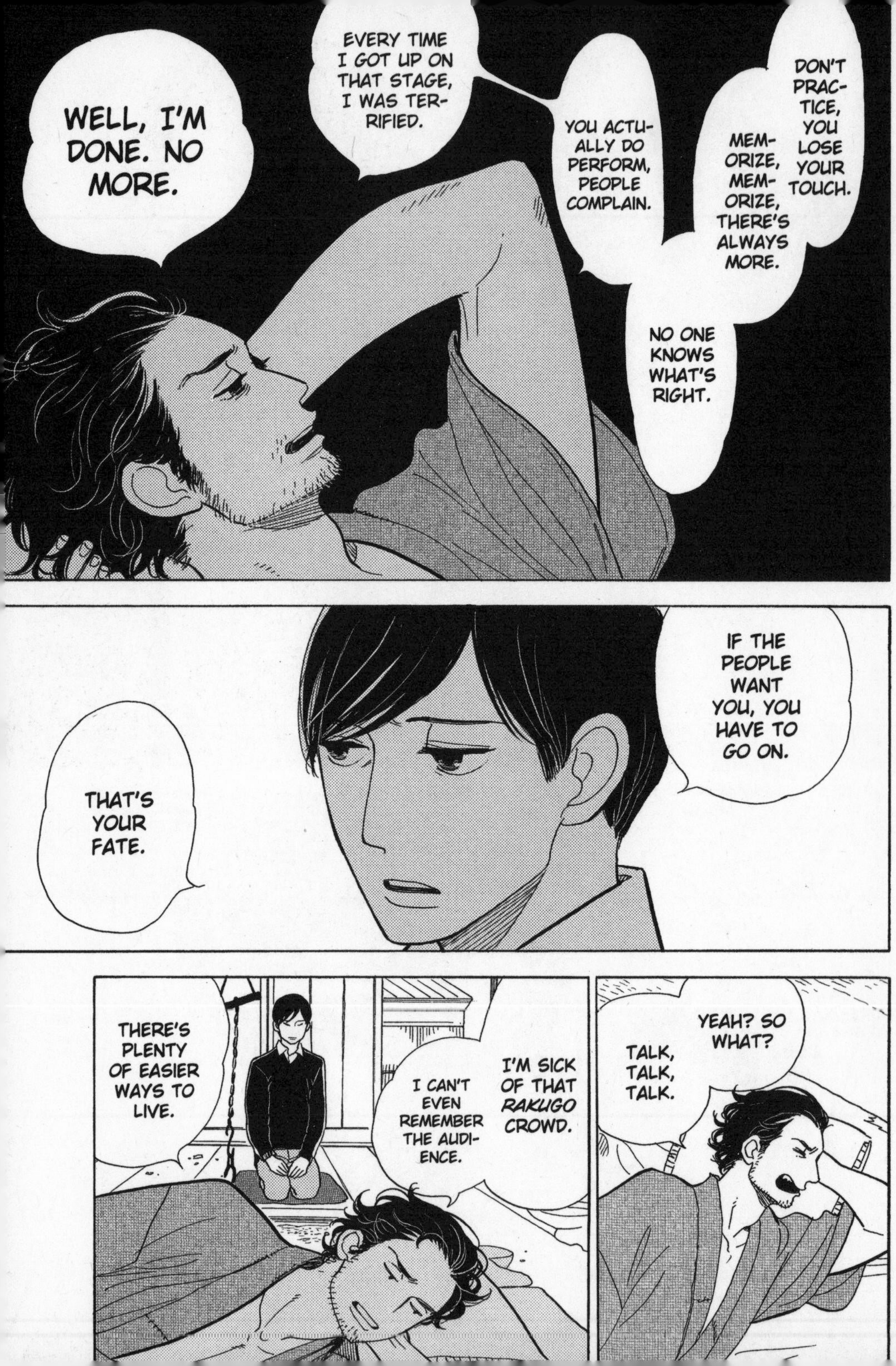
DON'T PRACTICE, YOU LOSE YOUR TOUCH.
MEMORIZE, MEMORIZE, THERE'S ALWAYS MORE.
YOU ACTUALLY DO PERFORM, PEOPLE COMPLAIN.
NO ONE KNOWS WHAT'S RIGHT.
EVERY TIME I GOT UP ON THAT STAGE, I WAS TERRIFIED.
WELL, I'M DONE. NO MORE.
IF THE PEOPLE WANT YOU, YOU HAVE TO GO ON.
THAT'S YOUR FATE.
YEAH? SO WHAT?
TALK, TALK, TALK.
I'M SICK OF THAT *RAKUGO* CROWD.
I CAN'T EVEN REMEMBER THE AUDIENCE.
THERE'S PLENTY OF EASIER WAYS TO LIVE.

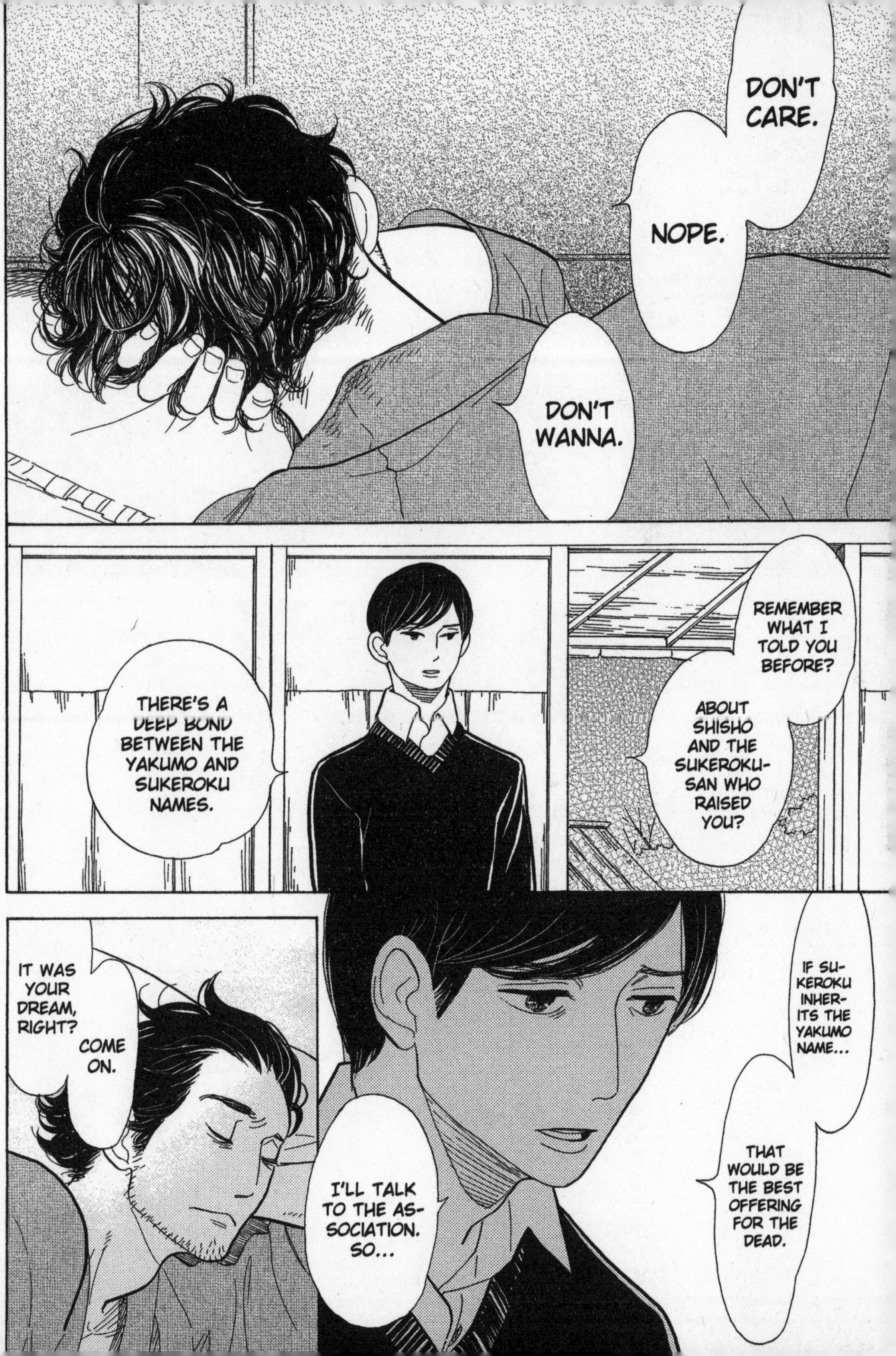
DON'T CARE.
NOPE.
DON'T WANNA.
REMEMBER WHAT I TOLD YOU BEFORE?
ABOUT SHISHO AND THE SUKEROKU-SAN WHO RAISED YOU?
THERE'S A DEEP BOND BETWEEN THE YAKUMO AND SUKEROKU NAMES.
IF SUKEROKU INHERITS THE YAKUMO NAME...
THAT WOULD BE THE BEST OFFERING FOR THE DEAD.
I'LL TALK TO THE ASSOCIATION. SO...
IT WAS YOUR DREAM, RIGHT?
COME ON.

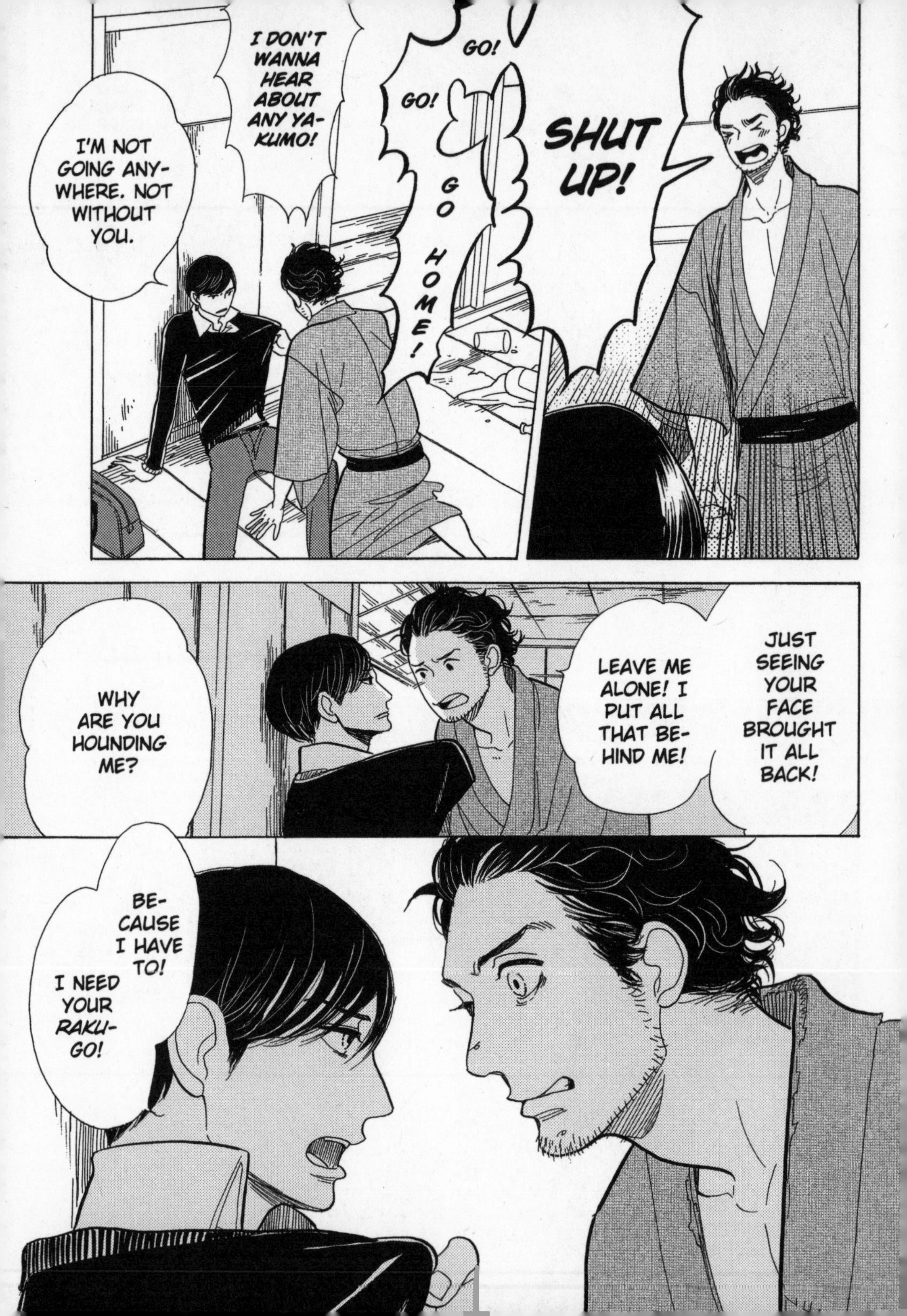
SHUT UP!
GO!
GO!
GO HOME!
I DON'T WANNA HEAR ABOUT ANY YAKUMO!
I'M NOT GOING ANYWHERE. NOT WITHOUT YOU.
JUST SEEING YOUR FACE BROUGHT IT ALL BACK!
LEAVE ME ALONE! I PUT ALL THAT BEHIND ME!
WHY ARE YOU HOUNDING ME?
BECAUSE I HAVE TO!
I NEED YOUR RAKUGO!

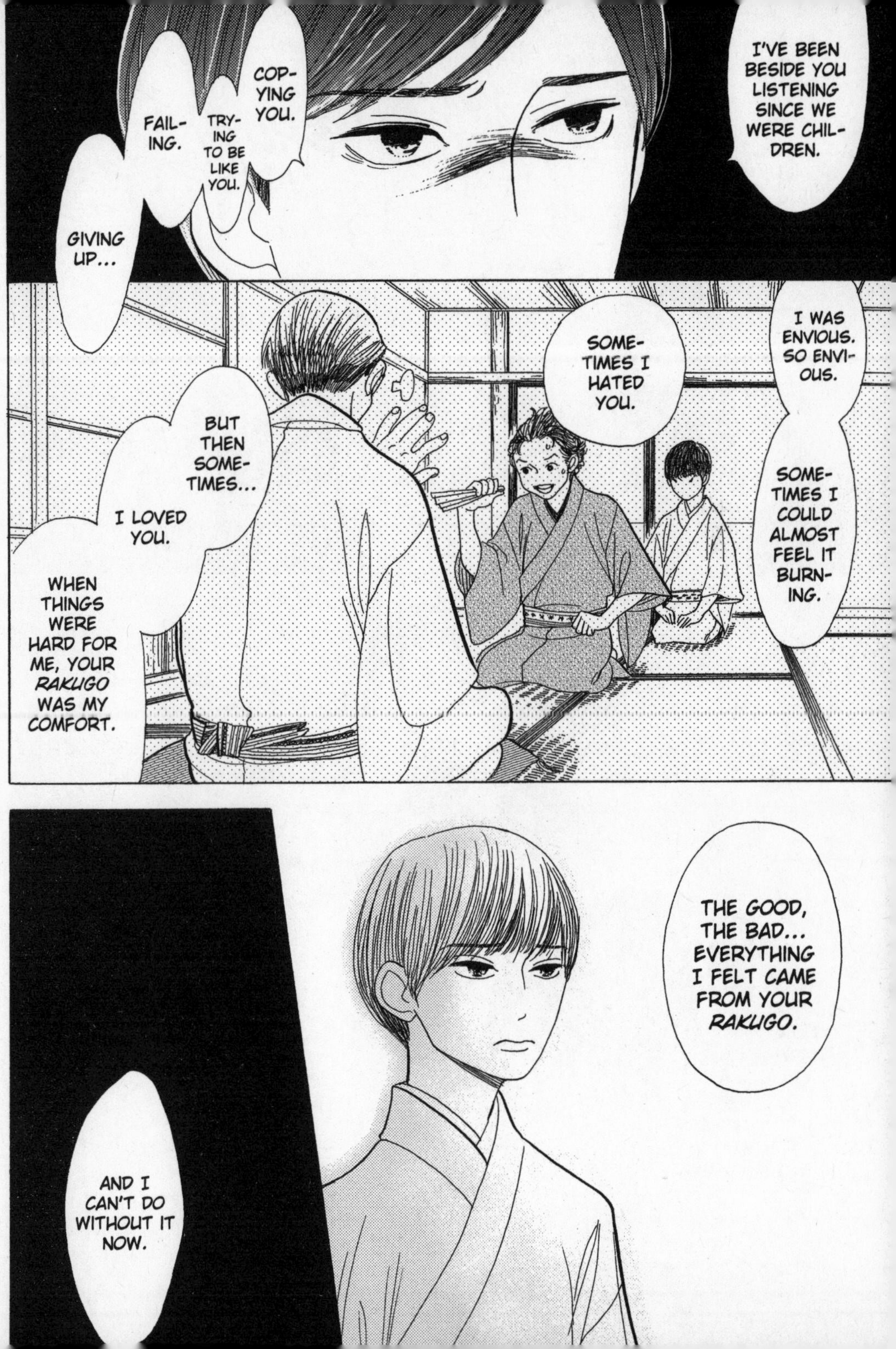
I'VE BEEN BESIDE YOU LISTENING SINCE WE WERE CHILDREN.
COPYING YOU.
TRYING TO BE LIKE YOU.
FAILING.
GIVING UP...
I WAS ENVIOUS. SO ENVIOUS.
SOMETIMES I COULD ALMOST FEEL IT BURNING.
SOMETIMES I HATED YOU.
BUT THEN SOMETIMES...
I LOVED YOU.
WHEN THINGS WERE HARD FOR ME, YOUR *RAKUGO* WAS MY COMFORT.
THE GOOD, THE BAD... EVERYTHING I FELT CAME FROM YOUR *RAKUGO*.
AND I CAN'T DO WITHOUT IT NOW.

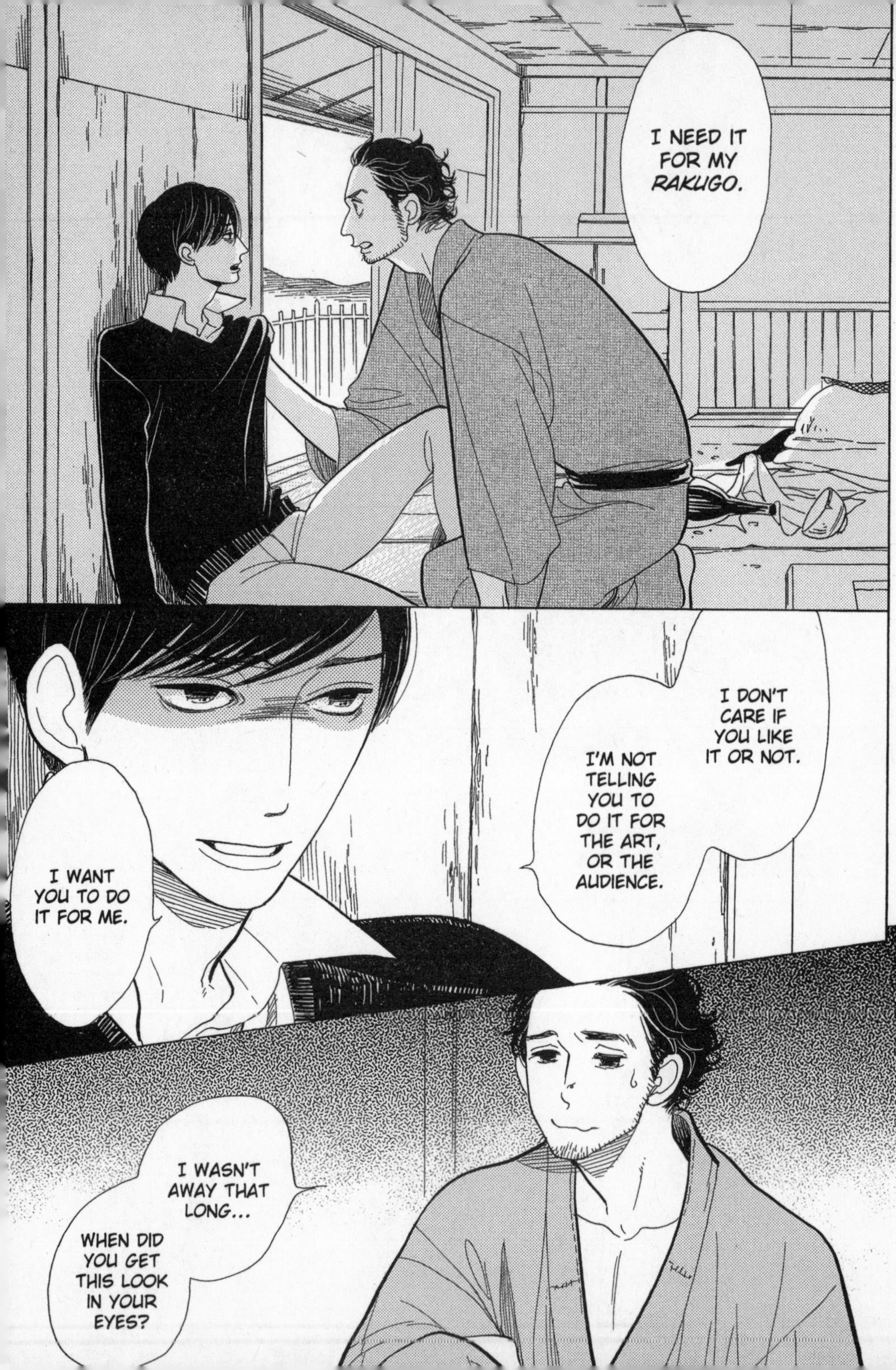
I NEED IT FOR MY RAKUGO.
I DON'T CARE IF YOU LIKE IT OR NOT.
I'M NOT TELLING YOU TO DO IT FOR THE ART, OR THE AUDIENCE.
I WANT YOU TO DO IT FOR ME.
I WASN'T AWAY THAT LONG...
WHEN DID YOU GET THIS LOOK IN YOUR EYES?

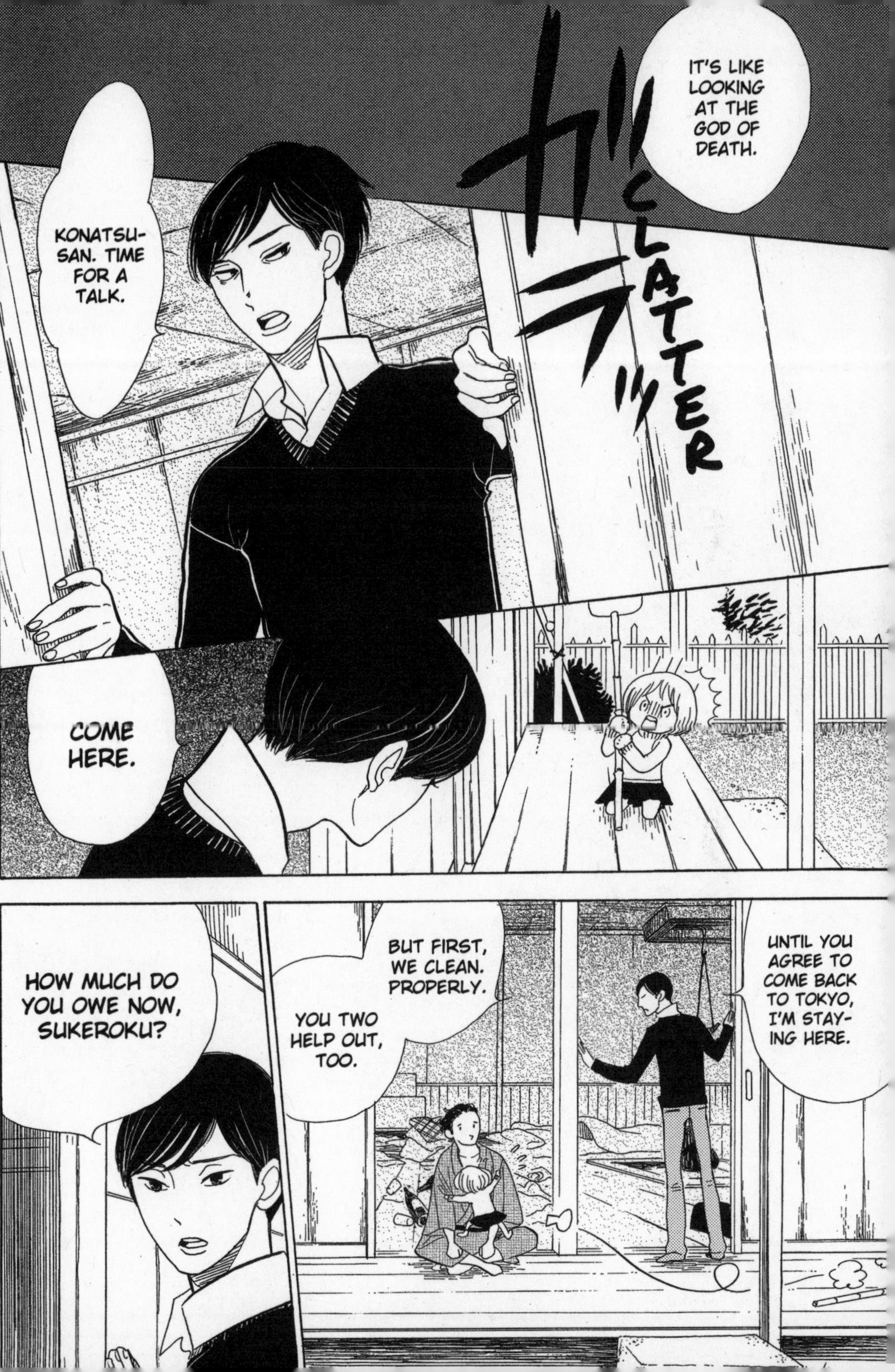
IT'S LIKE LOOKING AT THE GOD OF DEATH.
カラッ
CLATTER
KONATSU-SAN. TIME FOR A TALK.
COME HERE.
UNTIL YOU AGREE TO COME BACK TO TOKYO, I'M STAYING HERE.
BUT FIRST, WE CLEAN. PROPERLY.
YOU TWO HELP OUT, TOO.
HOW MUCH DO YOU OWE NOW, SUKEROKU?

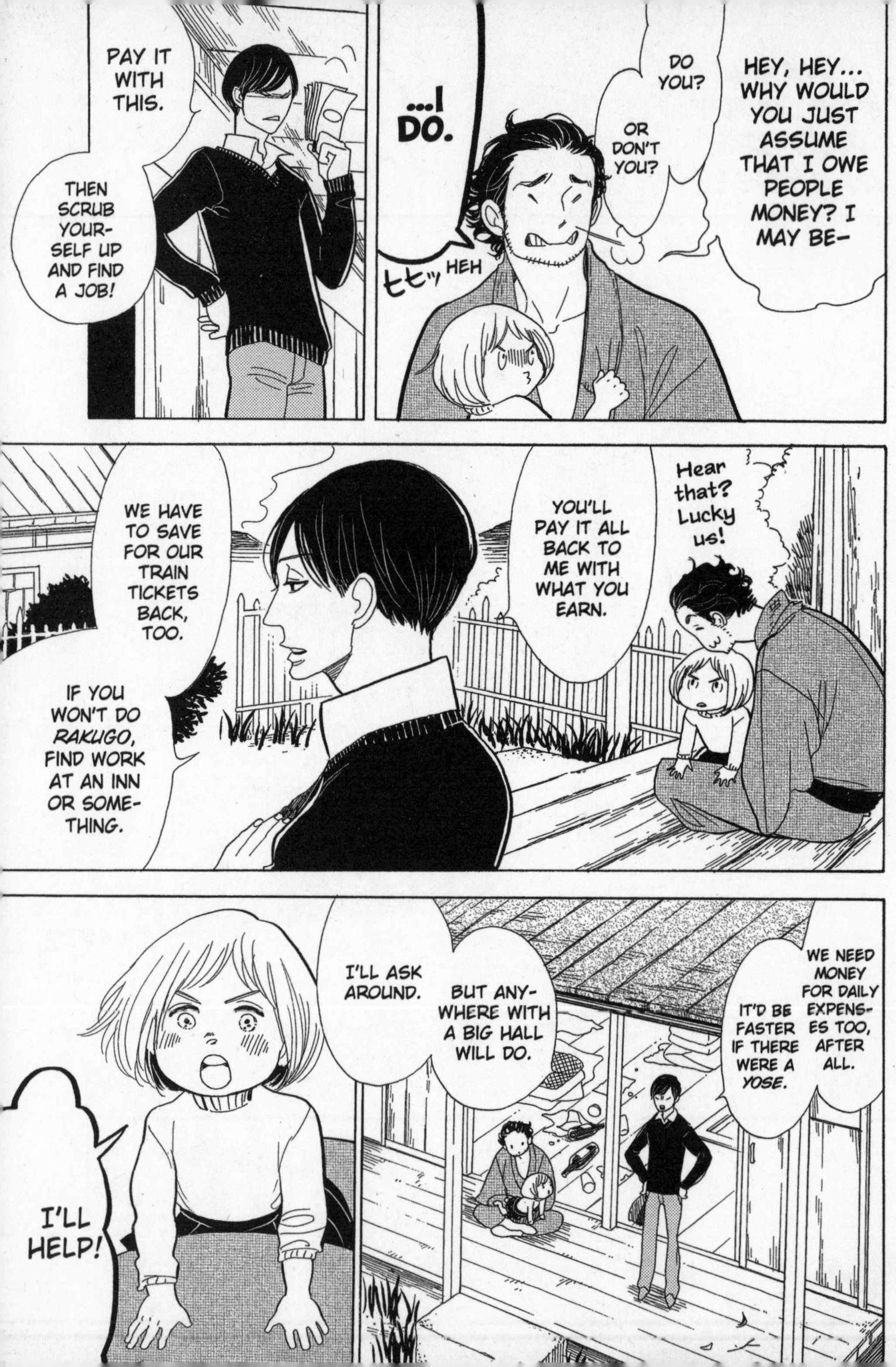
HEY, HEY... WHY WOULD YOU JUST ASSUME THAT I OWE PEOPLE MONEY? I MAY BE-
DO YOU?
OR DON'T YOU?
...I DO.
ヒヒッ HEH
PAY IT WITH THIS.
THEN SCRUB YOURSELF UP AND FIND A JOB!
Hear that? Lucky us!
YOU'LL PAY IT ALL BACK TO ME WITH WHAT YOU EARN.
WE HAVE TO SAVE FOR OUR TRAIN TICKETS BACK, TOO.
IF YOU WON'T DO *RAKUGO*, FIND WORK AT AN INN OR SOMETHING.
WE NEED MONEY FOR DAILY EXPENSES TOO, AFTER ALL.
IT'D BE FASTER IF THERE WERE A *YOSE*.
I'LL ASK AROUND.
BUT ANYWHERE WITH A BIG HALL WILL DO.
I'LL HELP!

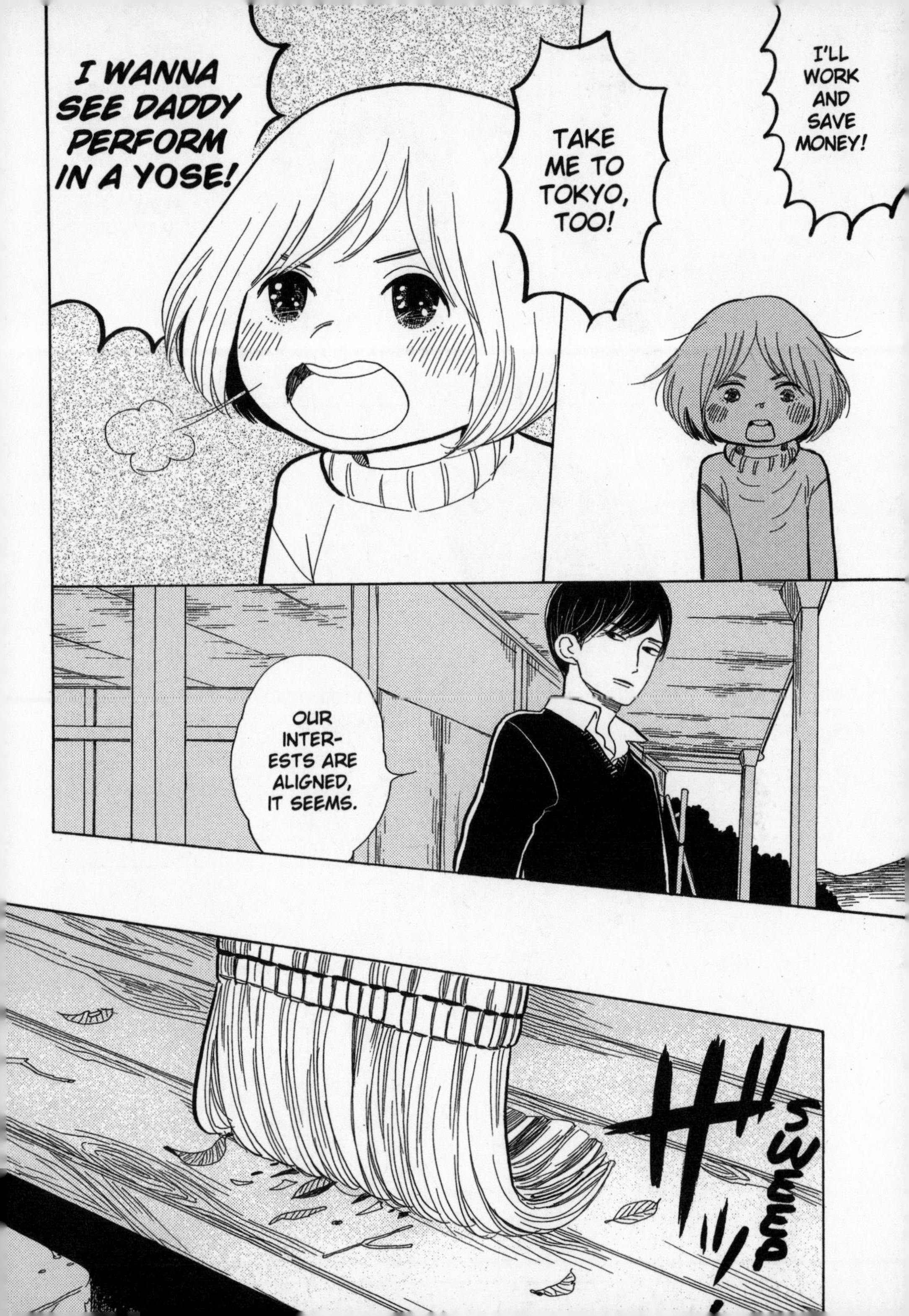
I'LL WORK AND SAVE MONEY!
TAKE ME TO TOKYO, TOO!
I WANNA SEE DADDY PERFORM IN A YOSE!
OUR INTER-ESTS ARE ALIGNED, IT SEEMS.
SWEEP

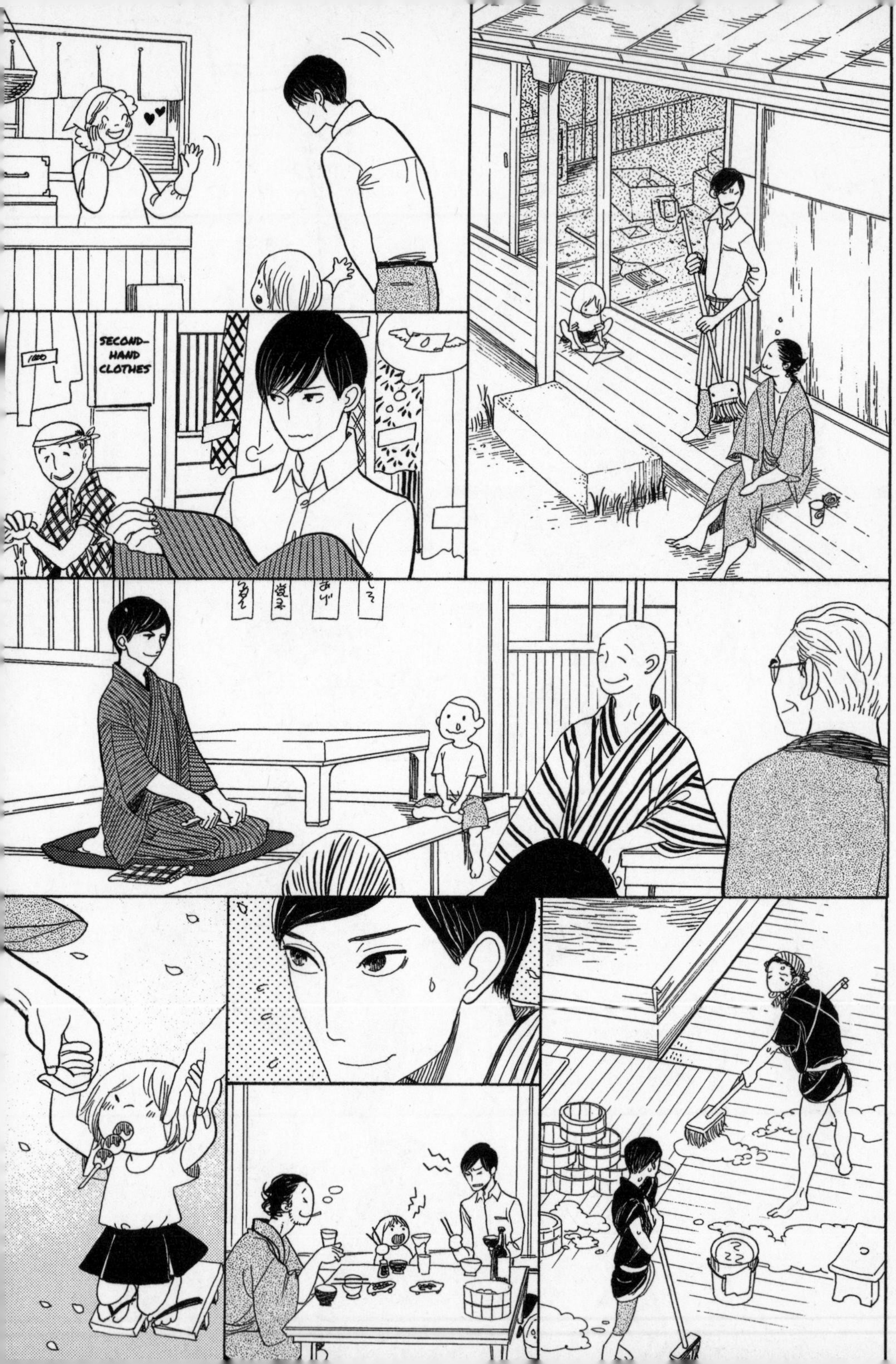
SECOND-HAND CLOTHES
1000
しる
あげ

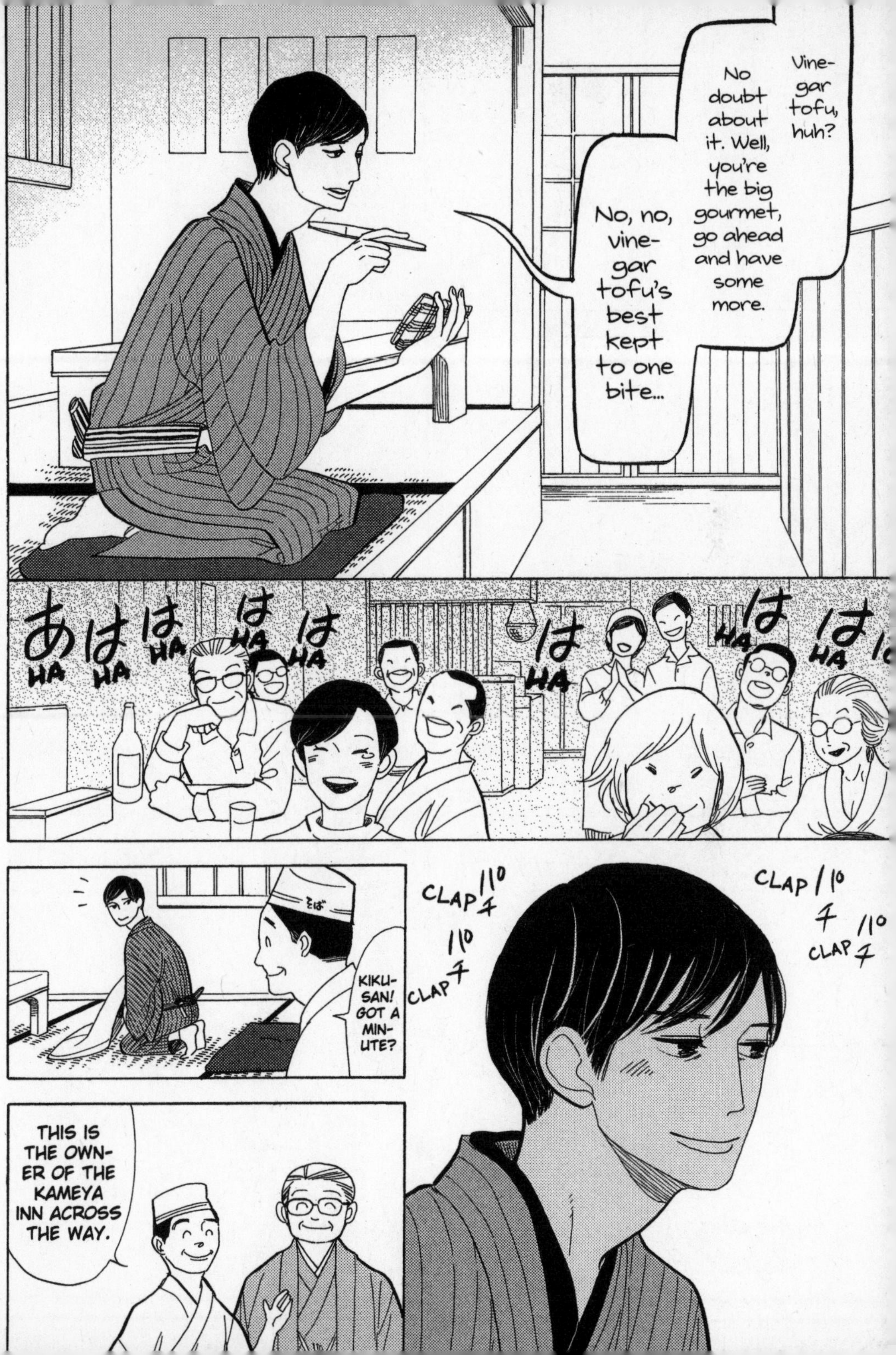

Vinegar tofu, huh?
No doubt about it. Well, you're the big gourmet, go ahead and have some more.
No, no, vinegar tofu's best kept to one bite...
あははははははは
HA HA HA HA HA HA HA HA
CLAP パチ CLAP パチ CLAP パチ
CLAP パチ CLAP パチ
KIKU-SAN! GOT A MINUTE?
THIS IS THE OWNER OF THE KAMEYA INN ACROSS THE WAY.

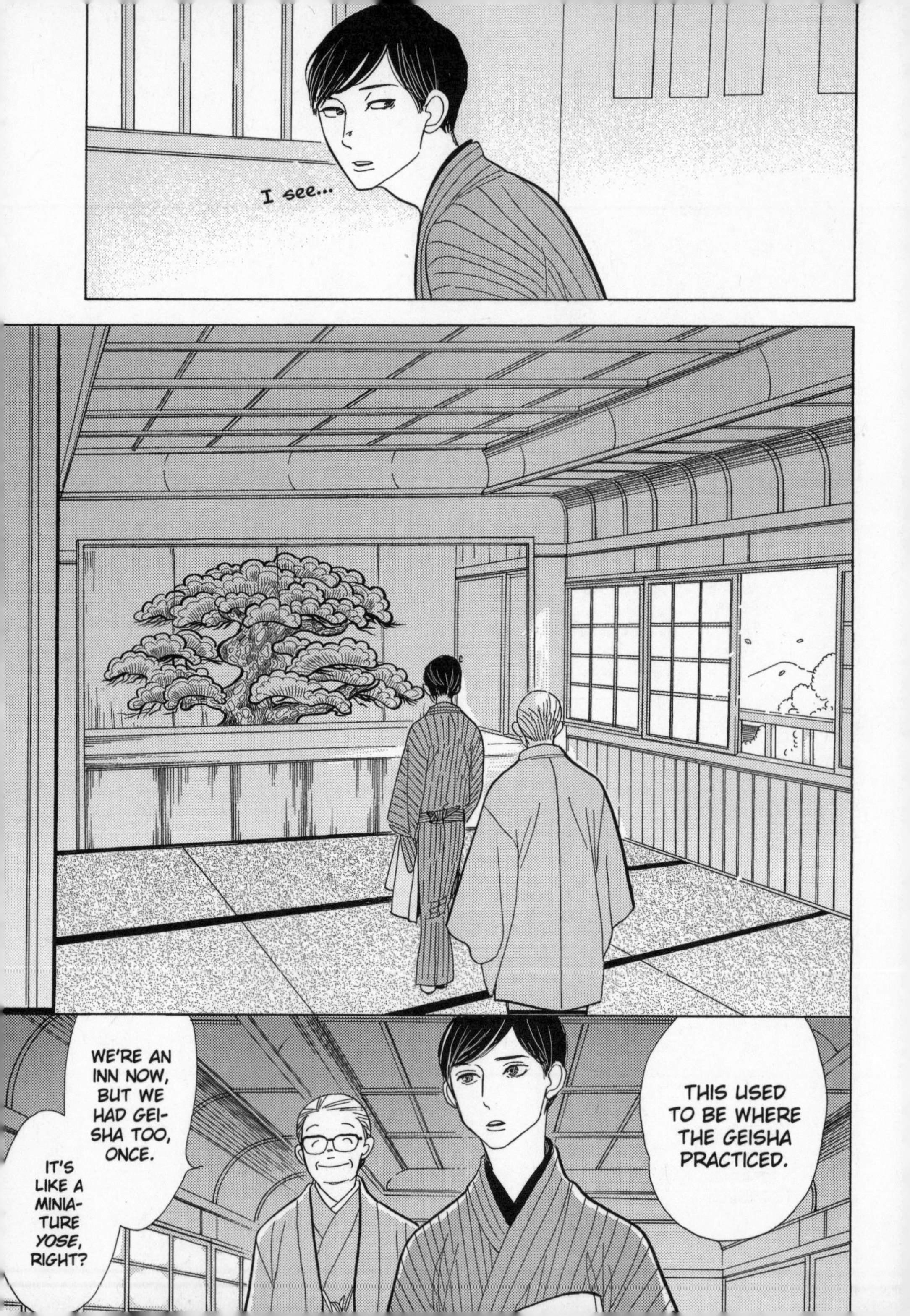
I see...
THIS USED TO BE WHERE THE GEISHA PRACTICED.
WE'RE AN INN NOW, BUT WE HAD GEISHA TOO, ONCE.
IT'S LIKE A MINIATURE *YOSE*, RIGHT?

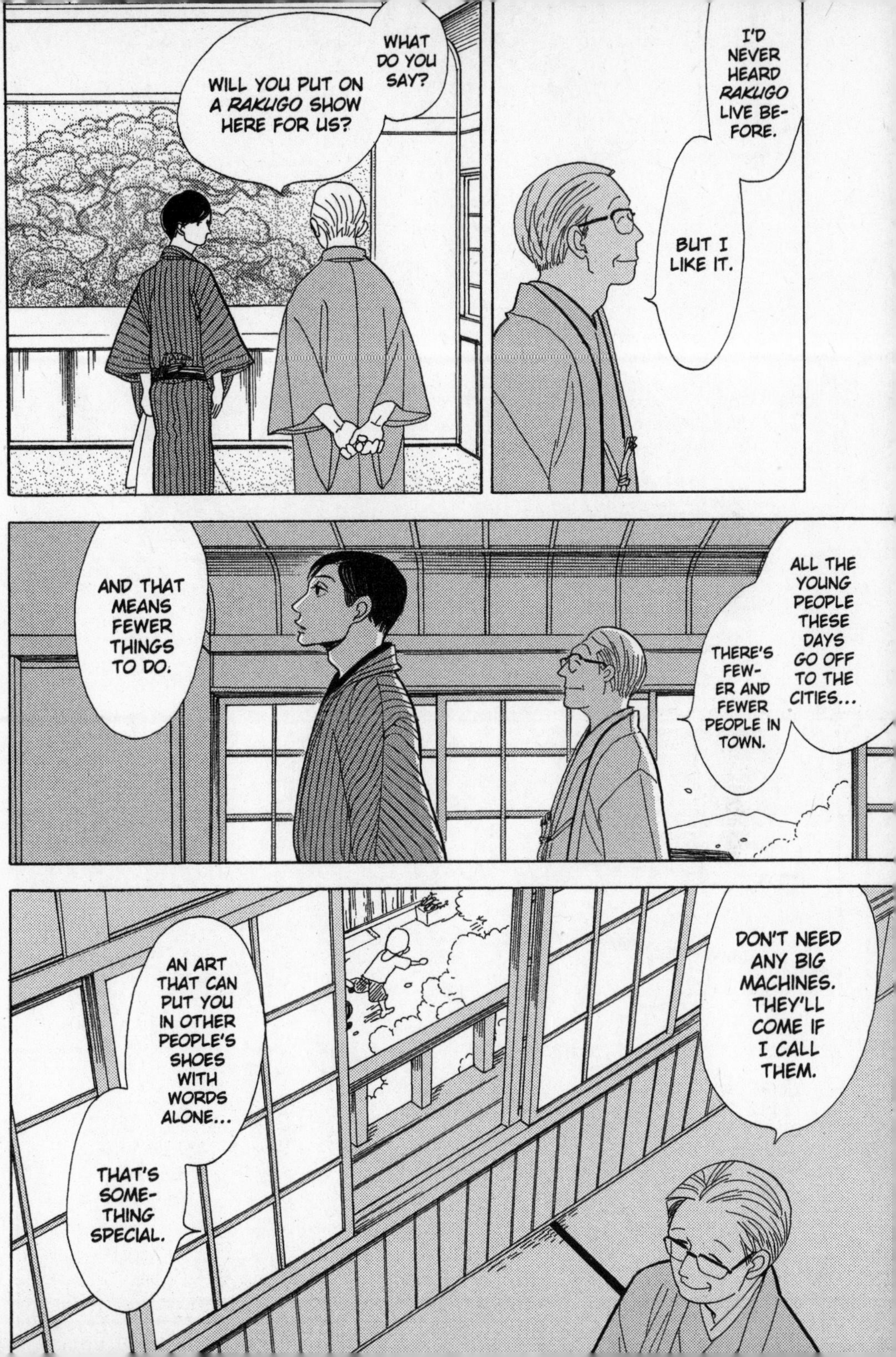
I'D NEVER HEARD *RAKUGO* LIVE BEFORE.
BUT I LIKE IT.
WHAT DO YOU SAY?
WILL YOU PUT ON A *RAKUGO* SHOW HERE FOR US?
ALL THE YOUNG PEOPLE THESE DAYS GO OFF TO THE CITIES...
THERE'S FEWER AND FEWER PEOPLE IN TOWN.
AND THAT MEANS FEWER THINGS TO DO.
DON'T NEED ANY BIG MACHINES. THEY'LL COME IF I CALL THEM.
AN ART THAT CAN PUT YOU IN OTHER PEOPLE'S SHOES WITH WORDS ALONE...
THAT'S SOMETHING SPECIAL.

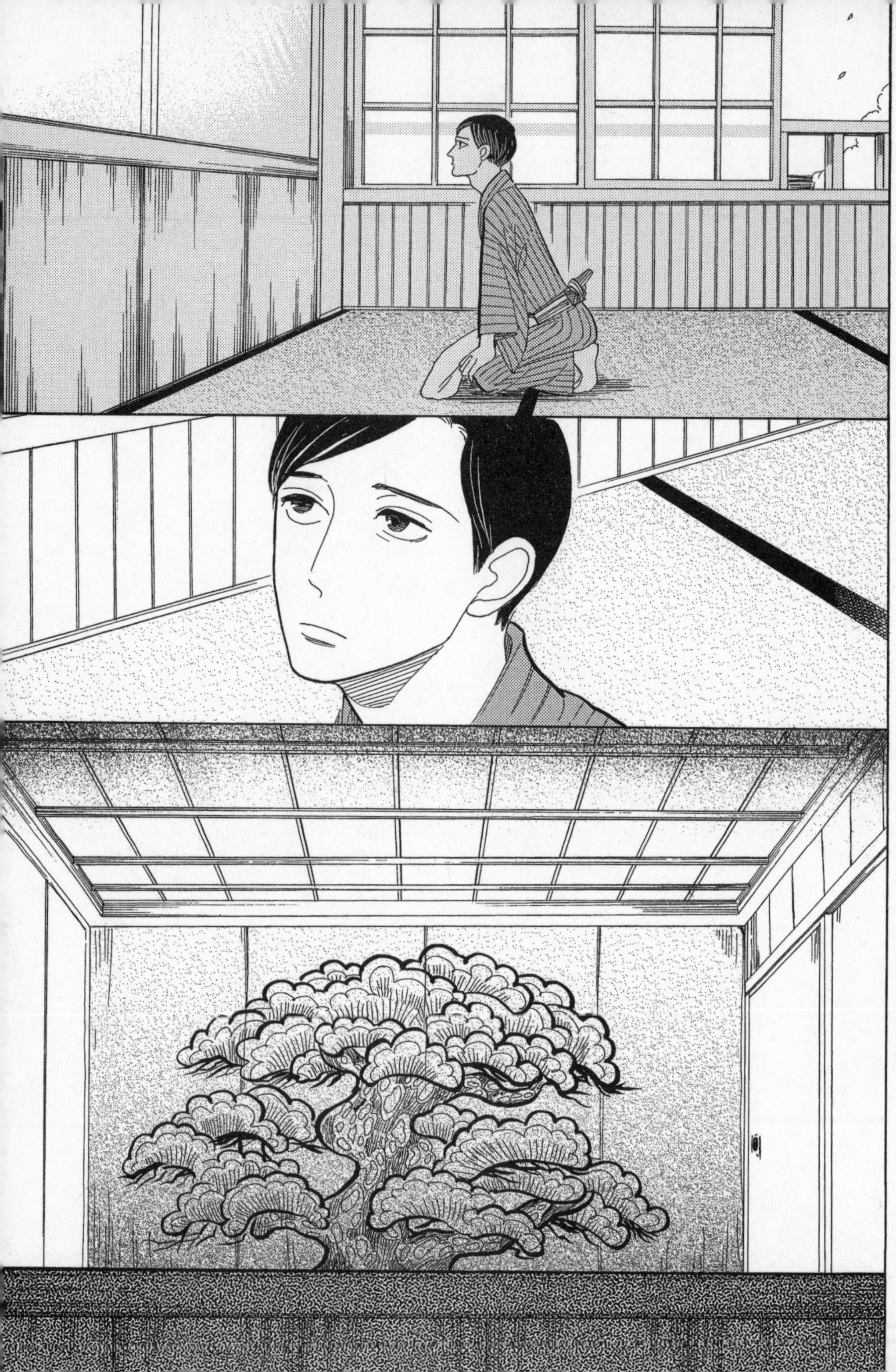

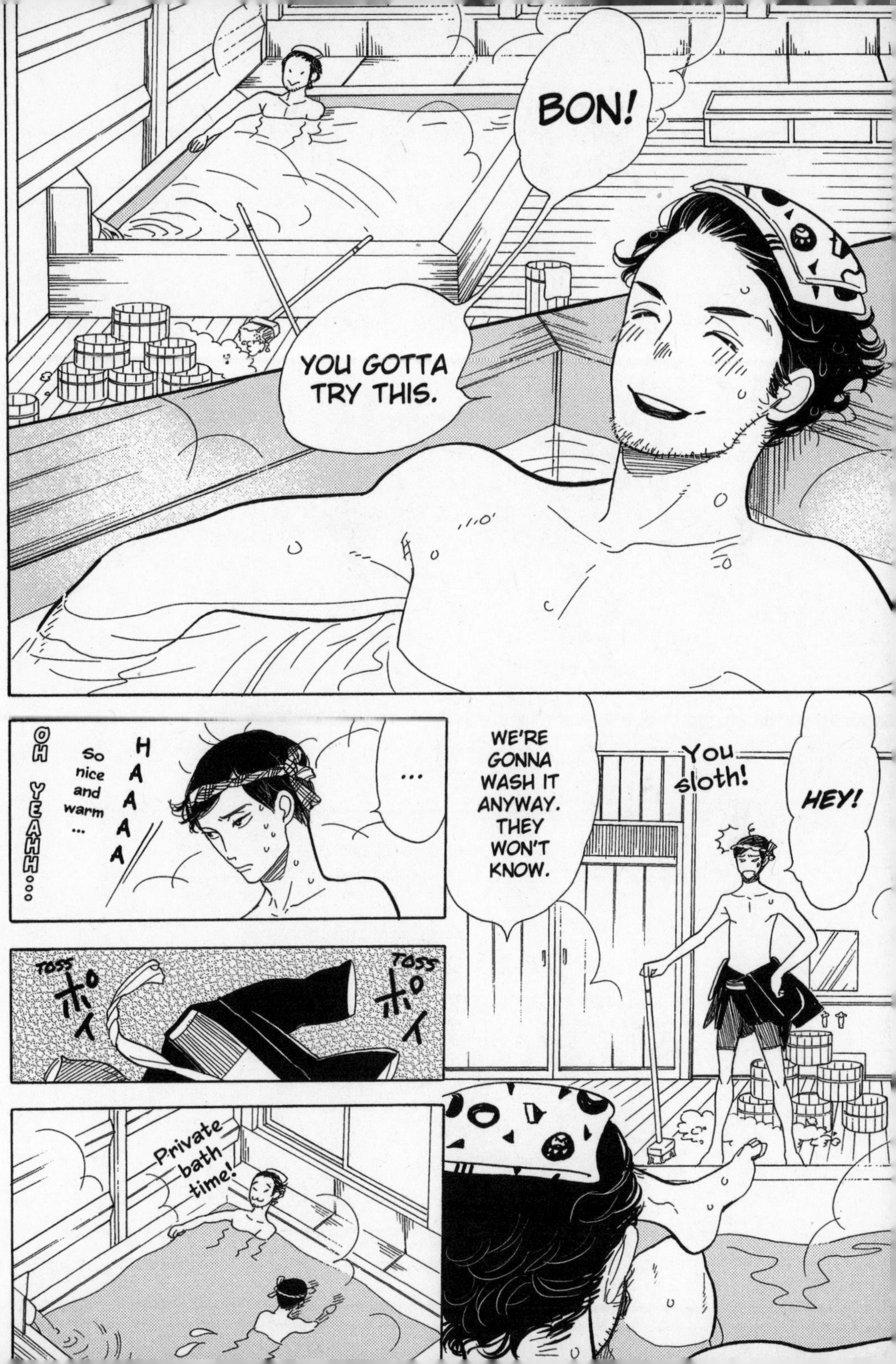
BON!
YOU GOTTA TRY THIS.
HEY!
You sloth!
WE'RE GONNA WASH IT ANYWAY. THEY WON'T KNOW.
...
HAAAA
So nice and warm ...
OH YEAHH...
TOSS ホイ
TOSS ホイ
Private bath time!

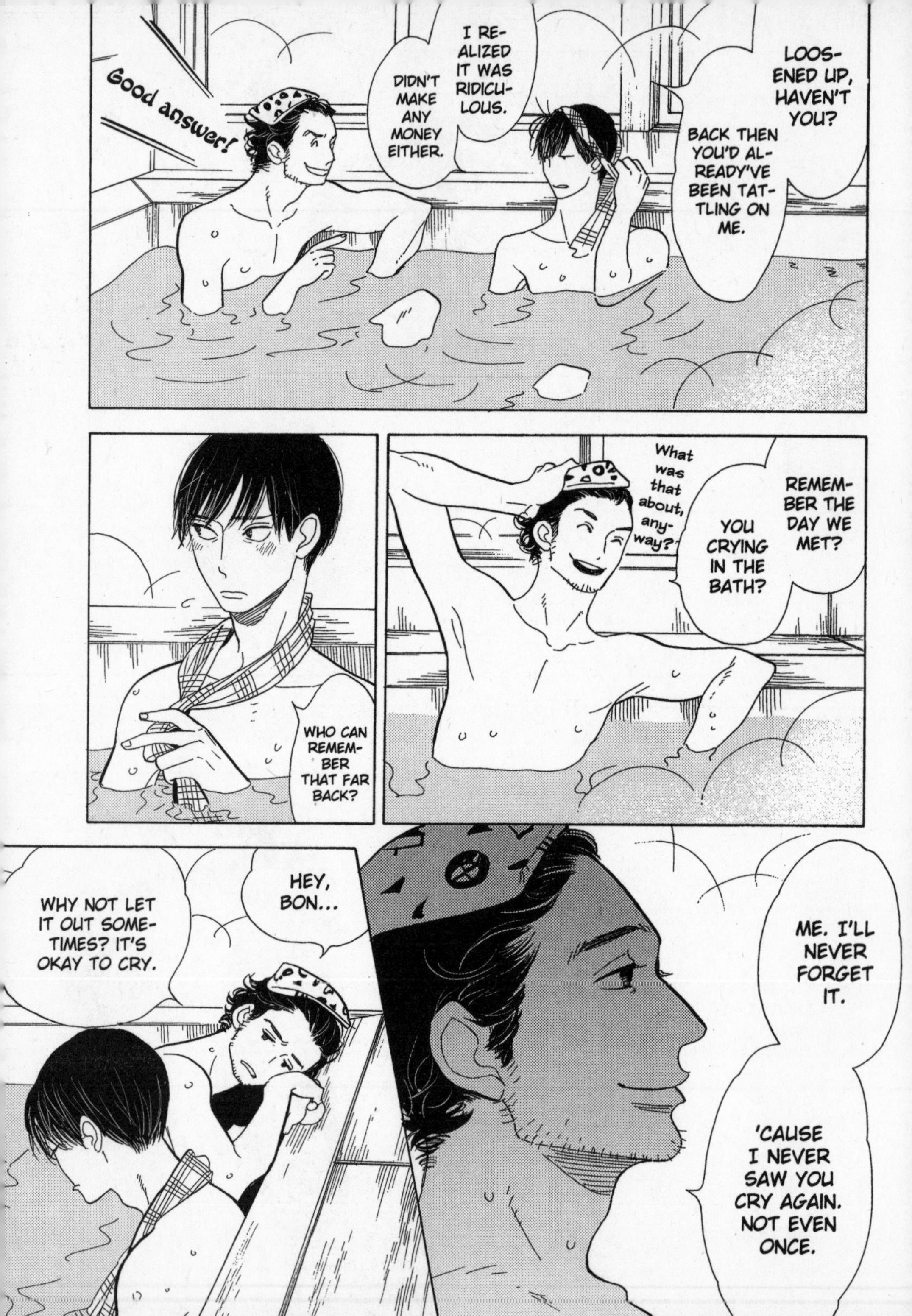

LOOSENED UP, HAVEN'T YOU?
BACK THEN YOU'D ALREADY'VE BEEN TATTLING ON ME.
I REALIZED IT WAS RIDICULOUS.
DIDN'T MAKE ANY MONEY EITHER.
Good answer!
REMEMBER THE DAY WE MET?
YOU CRYING IN THE BATH?
What was that about, anyway?
WHO CAN REMEMBER THAT FAR BACK?
ME. I'LL NEVER FORGET IT.
'CAUSE I NEVER SAW YOU CRY AGAIN. NOT EVEN ONCE.
HEY, BON...
WHY NOT LET IT OUT SOMETIMES? IT'S OKAY TO CRY.

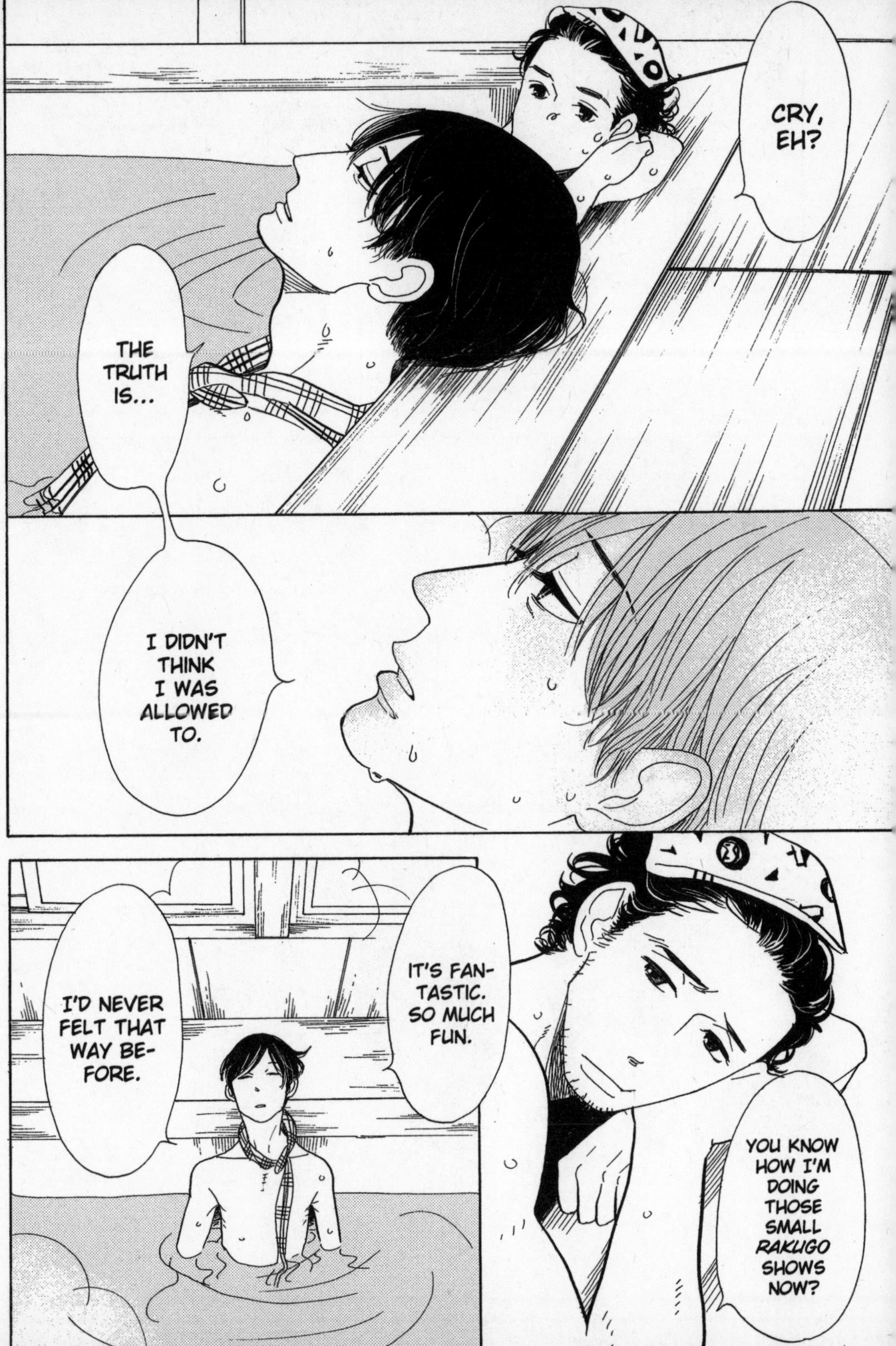
CRY, EH?
THE TRUTH IS...
I DIDN'T THINK I WAS ALLOWED TO.
YOU KNOW HOW I'M DOING THOSE SMALL *RAKUGO* SHOWS NOW?
IT'S FAN-TASTIC. SO MUCH FUN.
I'D NEVER FELT THAT WAY BE-FORE.

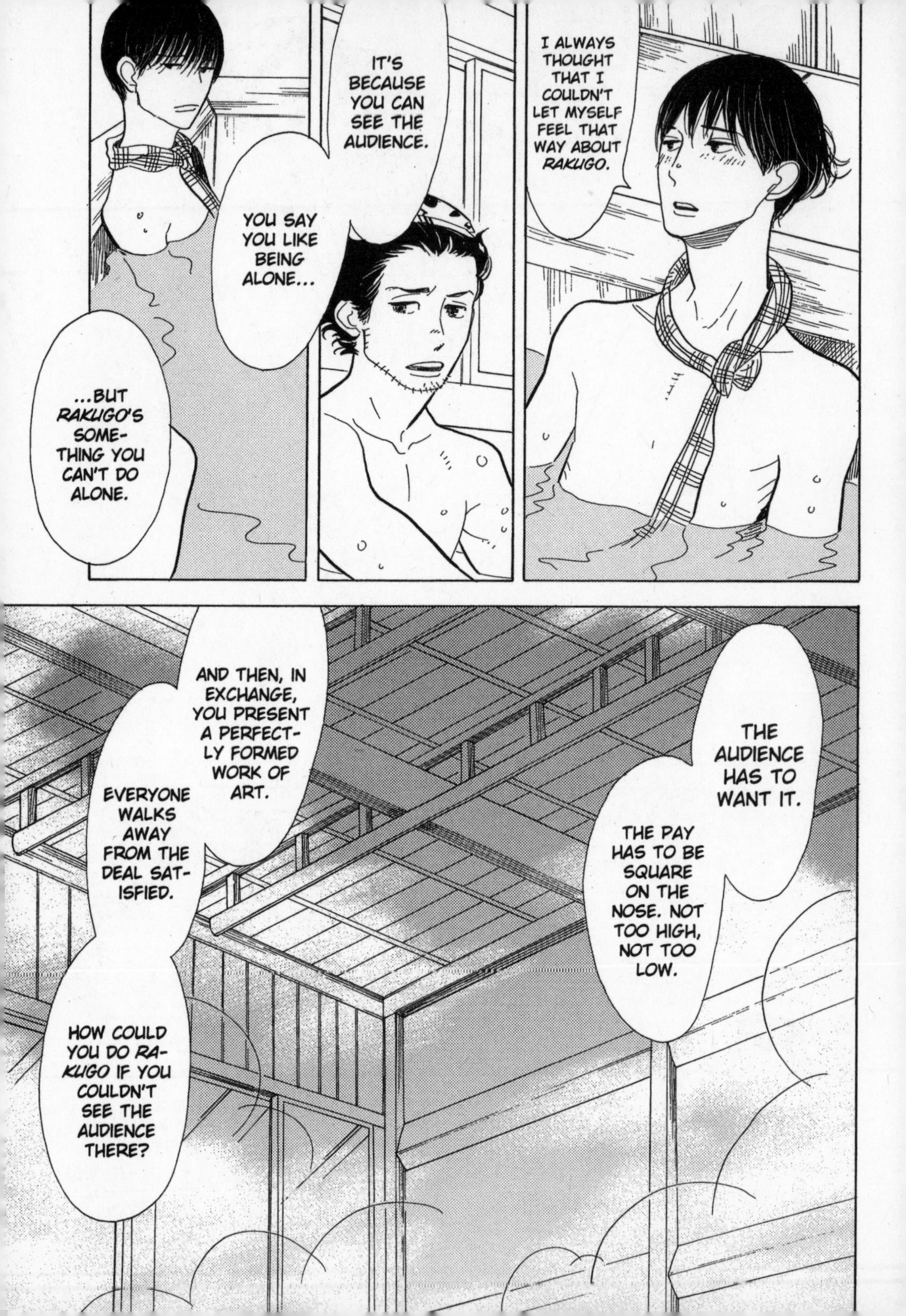
I ALWAYS THOUGHT THAT I COULDN'T LET MYSELF FEEL THAT WAY ABOUT *RAKUGO*.
IT'S BECAUSE YOU CAN SEE THE AUDIENCE.
YOU SAY YOU LIKE BEING ALONE...
...BUT *RAKUGO*'S SOMETHING YOU CAN'T DO ALONE.
THE AUDIENCE HAS TO WANT IT.
THE PAY HAS TO BE SQUARE ON THE NOSE. NOT TOO HIGH, NOT TOO LOW.
AND THEN, IN EXCHANGE, YOU PRESENT A PERFECTLY FORMED WORK OF ART.
EVERYONE WALKS AWAY FROM THE DEAL SATISFIED.
HOW COULD YOU DO *RAKUGO* IF YOU COULDN'T SEE THE AUDIENCE THERE?

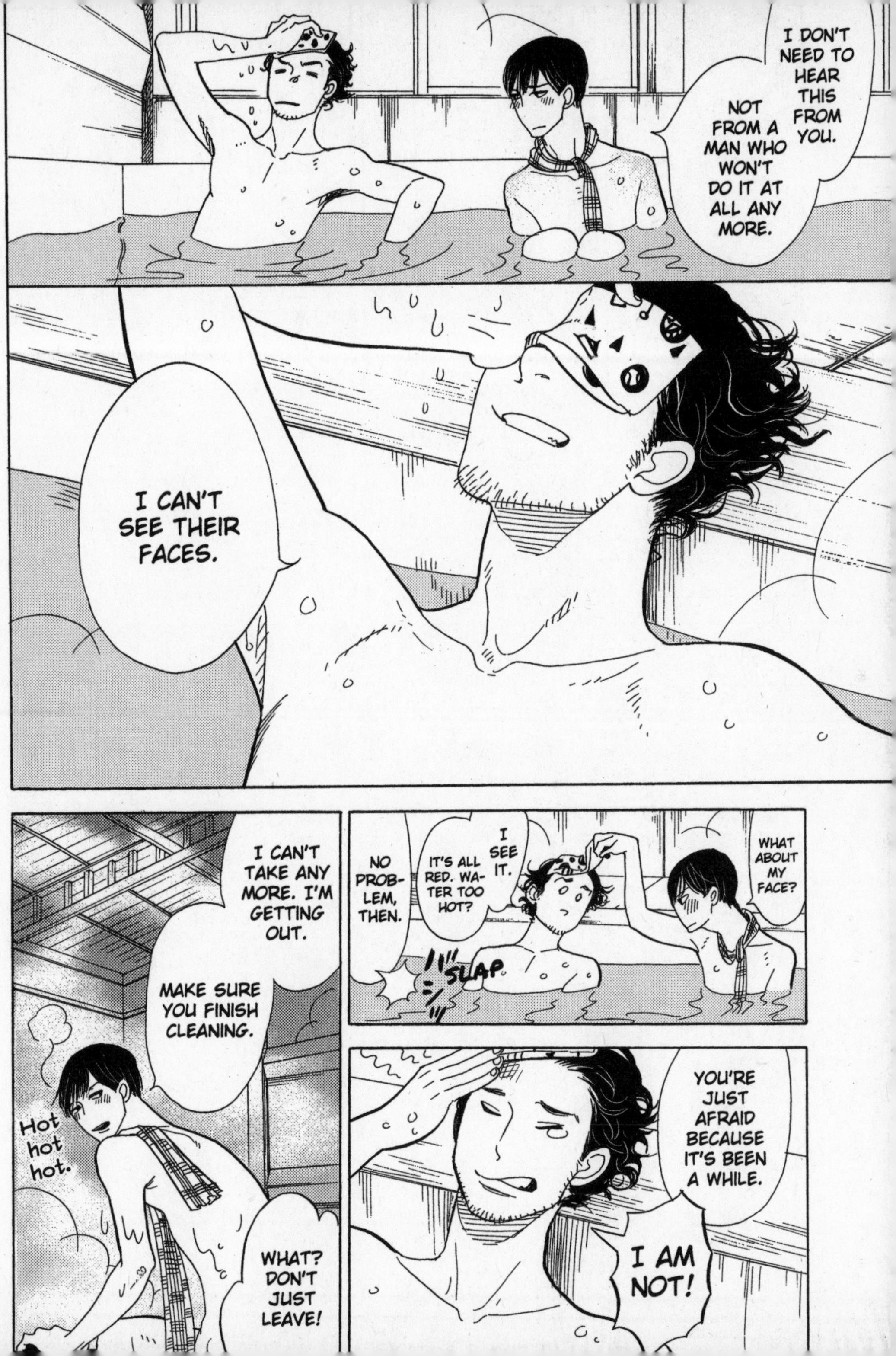
I DON'T NEED TO HEAR THIS FROM YOU.
NOT FROM A MAN WHO WON'T DO IT AT ALL ANY MORE.
I CAN'T SEE THEIR FACES.
WHAT ABOUT MY FACE?
I SEE IT.
IT'S ALL RED. WATER TOO HOT?
NO PROBLEM, THEN.
SLAP
YOU'RE JUST AFRAID BECAUSE IT'S BEEN A WHILE.
I AM NOT!
I CAN'T TAKE ANY MORE. I'M GETTING OUT.
MAKE SURE YOU FINISH CLEANING.
Hot hot hot.
WHAT? DON'T JUST LEAVE!

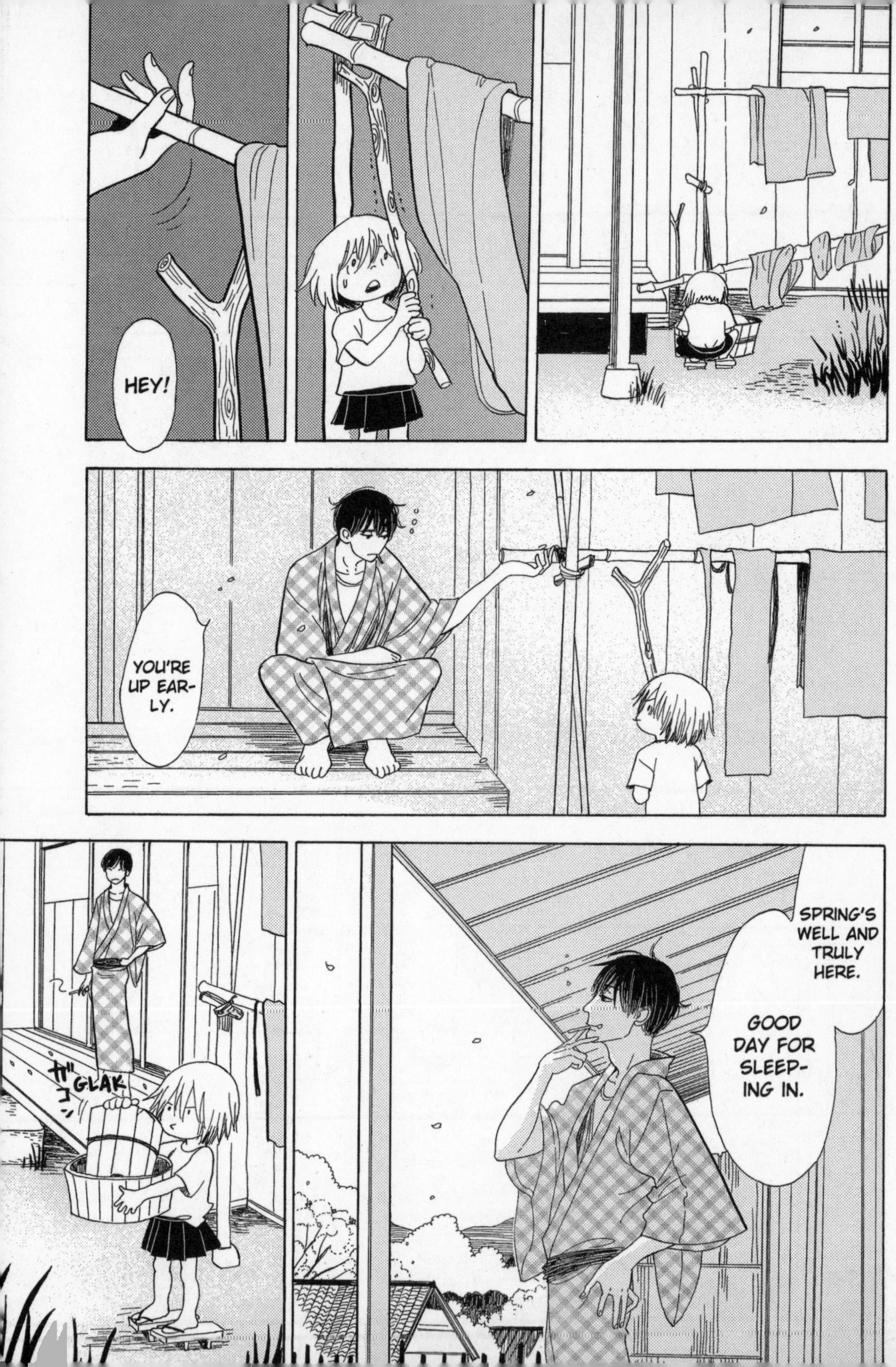
HEY!
YOU'RE UP EAR-LY.
SPRING'S WELL AND TRULY HERE.
GOOD DAY FOR SLEEP-ING IN.
GLAK

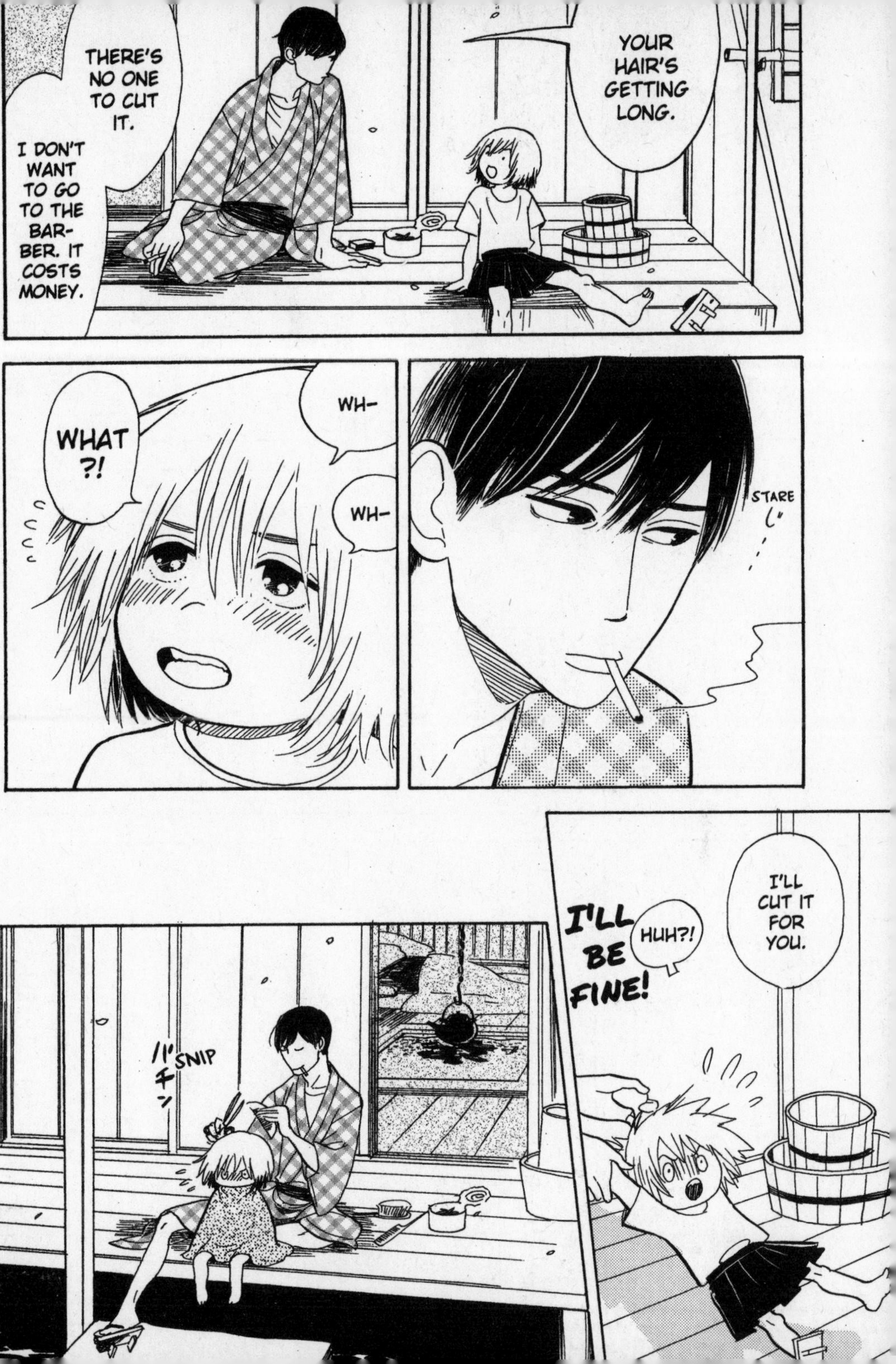
YOUR HAIR'S GETTING LONG.
THERE'S NO ONE TO CUT IT.
I DON'T WANT TO GO TO THE BAR-BER. IT COSTS MONEY.
STARE
WH-
WH-
WHAT?!
I'LL CUT IT FOR YOU.
HUH?!
I'LL BE FINE!
パチン SNIP

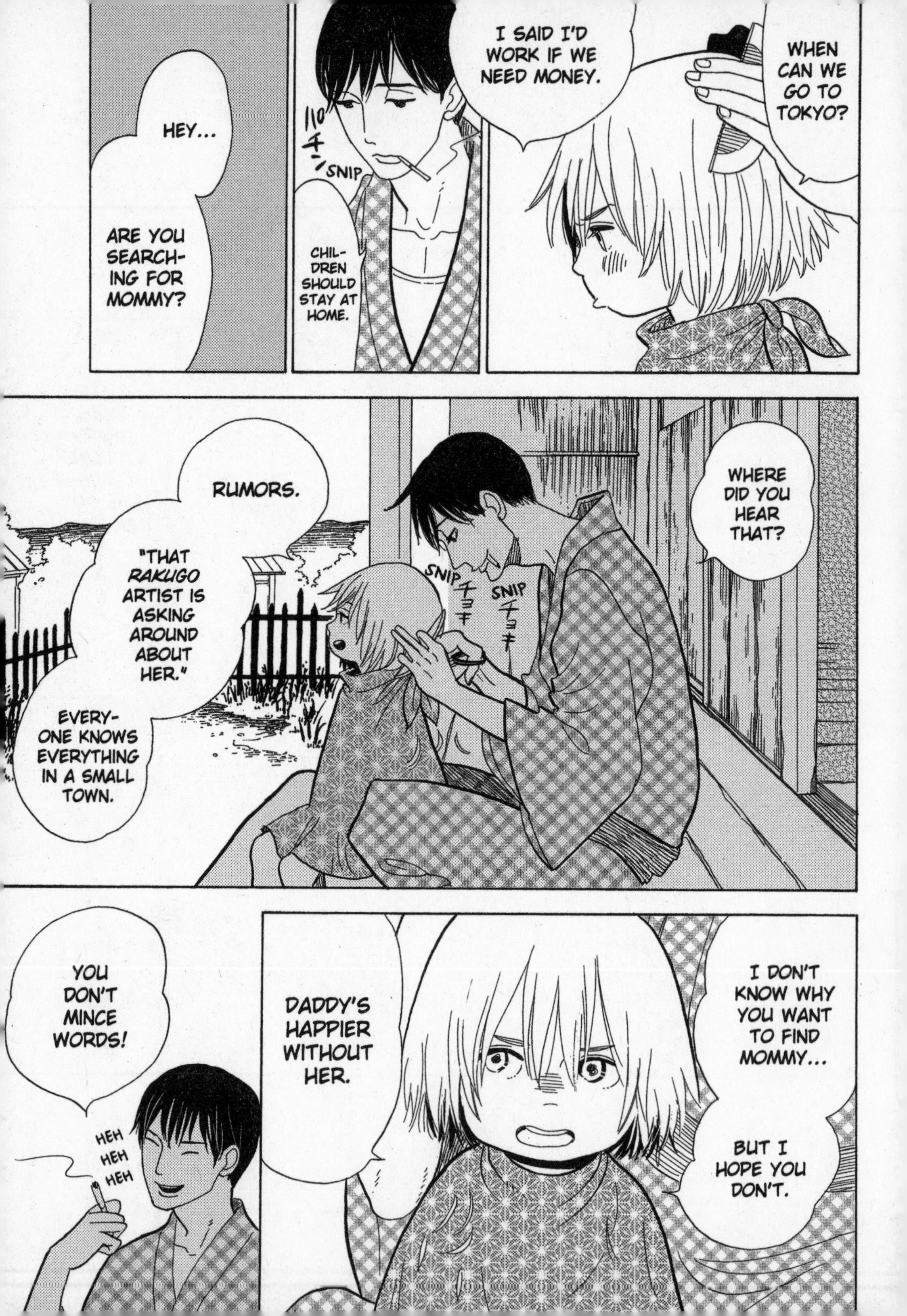
WHEN CAN WE GO TO TOKYO?
I SAID I'D WORK IF WE NEED MONEY.
SNIP
CHILDREN SHOULD STAY AT HOME.
HEY...
ARE YOU SEARCHING FOR MOMMY?
WHERE DID YOU HEAR THAT?
SNIP チョキ
SNIP チョキ
RUMORS.
"THAT *RAKUGO* ARTIST IS ASKING AROUND ABOUT HER."
EVERYONE KNOWS EVERYTHING IN A SMALL TOWN.
I DON'T KNOW WHY YOU WANT TO FIND MOMMY...
BUT I HOPE YOU DON'T.
DADDY'S HAPPIER WITHOUT HER.
YOU DON'T MINCE WORDS!
HEH HEH HEH

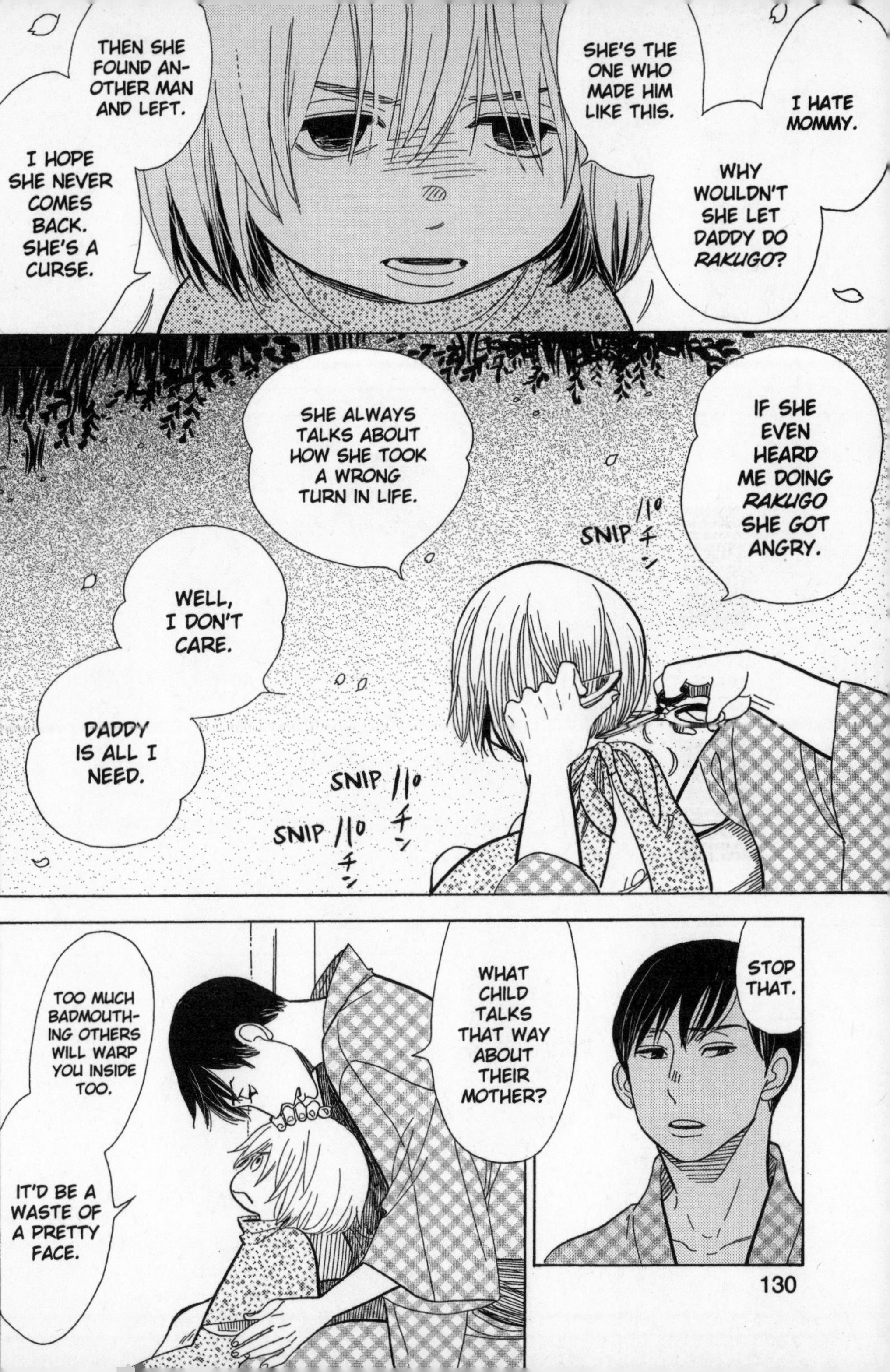
I HATE MOMMY.
WHY WOULDN'T SHE LET DADDY DO *RAKUGO*?
SHE'S THE ONE WHO MADE HIM LIKE THIS.
THEN SHE FOUND AN-OTHER MAN AND LEFT.
I HOPE SHE NEVER COMES BACK. SHE'S A CURSE.
IF SHE EVEN HEARD ME DOING *RAKUGO* SHE GOT ANGRY.
SNIP パチン
SHE ALWAYS TALKS ABOUT HOW SHE TOOK A WRONG TURN IN LIFE.
WELL, I DON'T CARE.
DADDY IS ALL I NEED.
SNIP パチン
SNIP パチン
STOP THAT.
WHAT CHILD TALKS THAT WAY ABOUT THEIR MOTHER?
TOO MUCH BADMOUTH-ING OTHERS WILL WARP YOU INSIDE TOO.
IT'D BE A WASTE OF A PRETTY FACE.

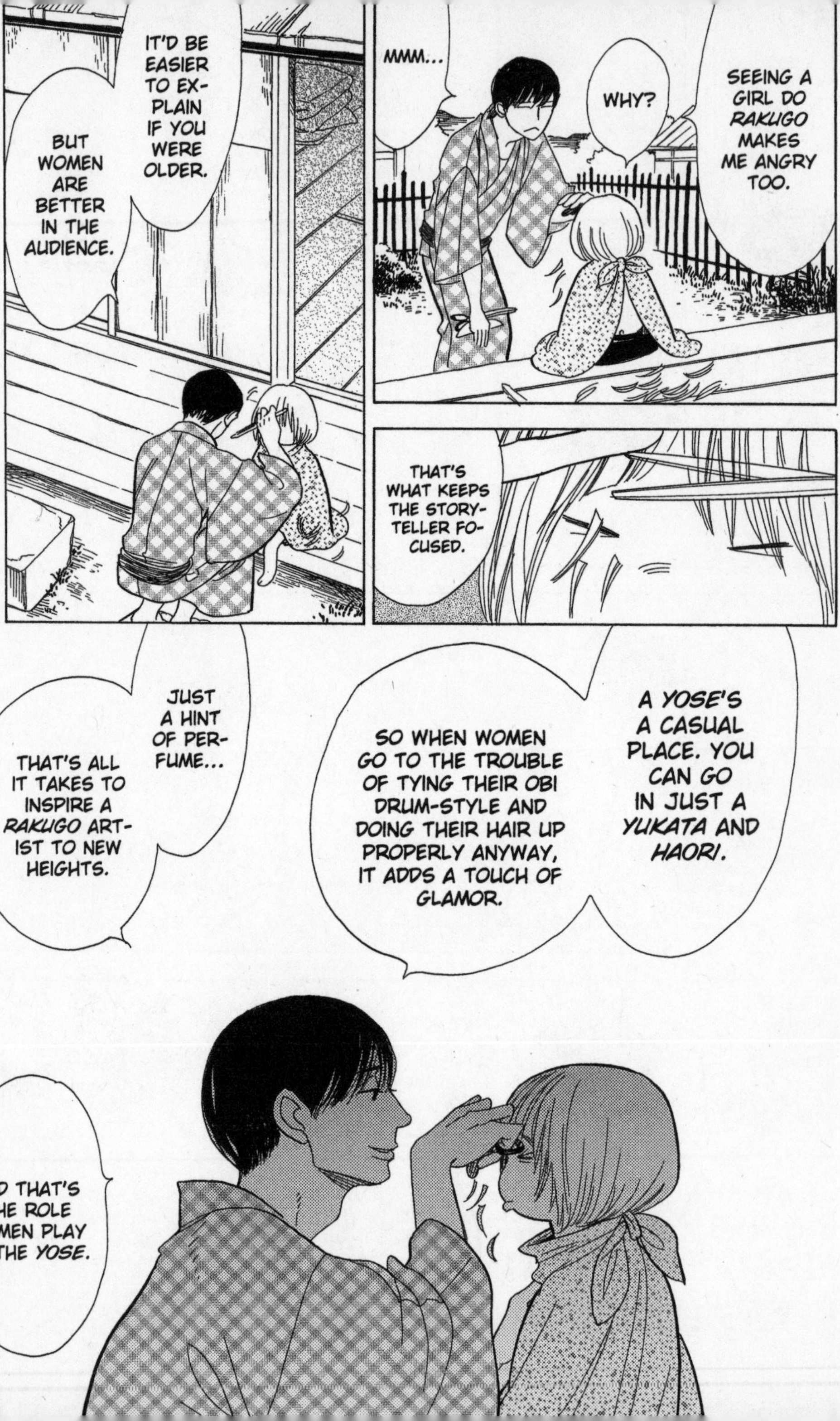
SEEING A GIRL DO RAKUGO MAKES ME ANGRY TOO.
WHY?
MMM...
THAT'S WHAT KEEPS THE STORY-TELLER FOCUSED.
IT'D BE EASIER TO EXPLAIN IF YOU WERE OLDER.
BUT WOMEN ARE BETTER IN THE AUDIENCE.
A YOSE'S A CASUAL PLACE. YOU CAN GO IN JUST A YUKATA AND HAORI.
SO WHEN WOMEN GO TO THE TROUBLE OF TYING THEIR OBI DRUM-STYLE AND DOING THEIR HAIR UP PROPERLY ANYWAY, IT ADDS A TOUCH OF GLAMOR.
JUST A HINT OF PERFUME...
THAT'S ALL IT TAKES TO INSPIRE A RAKUGO ARTIST TO NEW HEIGHTS.
AND THAT'S THE ROLE WOMEN PLAY AT THE YOSE.

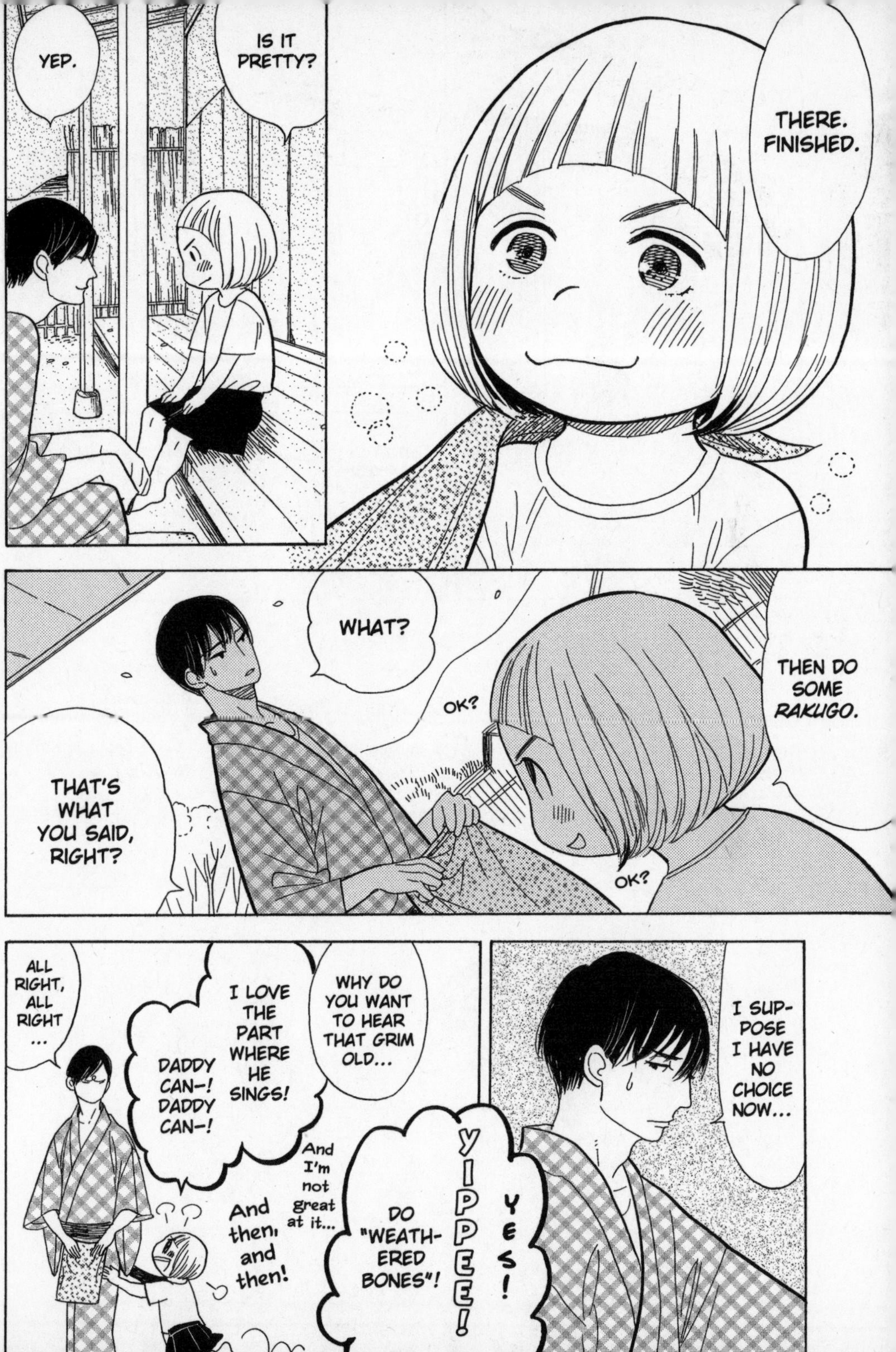
THERE. FINISHED.
IS IT PRETTY?
YEP.
THEN DO SOME *RAKUGO*.
OK?
OK?
WHAT?
THAT'S WHAT YOU SAID, RIGHT?
I SUP-POSE I HAVE NO CHOICE NOW...
YES!
YIPPEE!
DO "WEATH-ERED BONES"!
WHY DO YOU WANT TO HEAR THAT GRIM OLD...
I LOVE THE PART WHERE HE SINGS!
And I'm not great at it...
DADDY CAN-! DADDY CAN-!
And then, and then!
ALL RIGHT, ALL RIGHT...

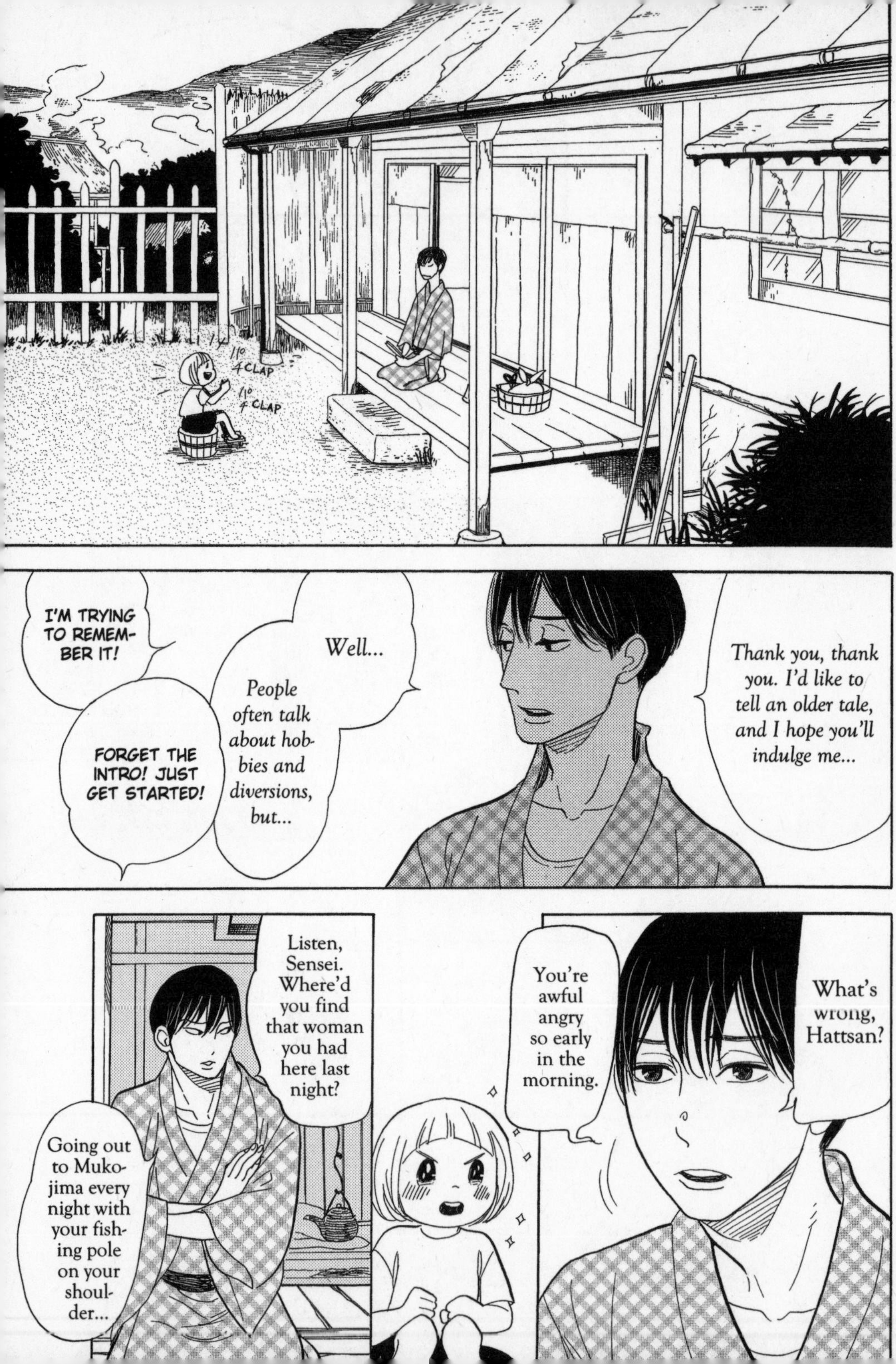
CLAP
CLAP
Thank you, thank you. I'd like to tell an older tale, and I hope you'll indulge me...
Well...
People often talk about hobbies and diversions, but...
I'M TRYING TO REMEMBER IT!
FORGET THE INTRO! JUST GET STARTED!
What's wrong, Hattsan?
You're awful angry so early in the morning.
Listen, Sensei. Where'd you find that woman you had here last night?
Going out to Mukojima every night with your fishing pole on your shoulder...

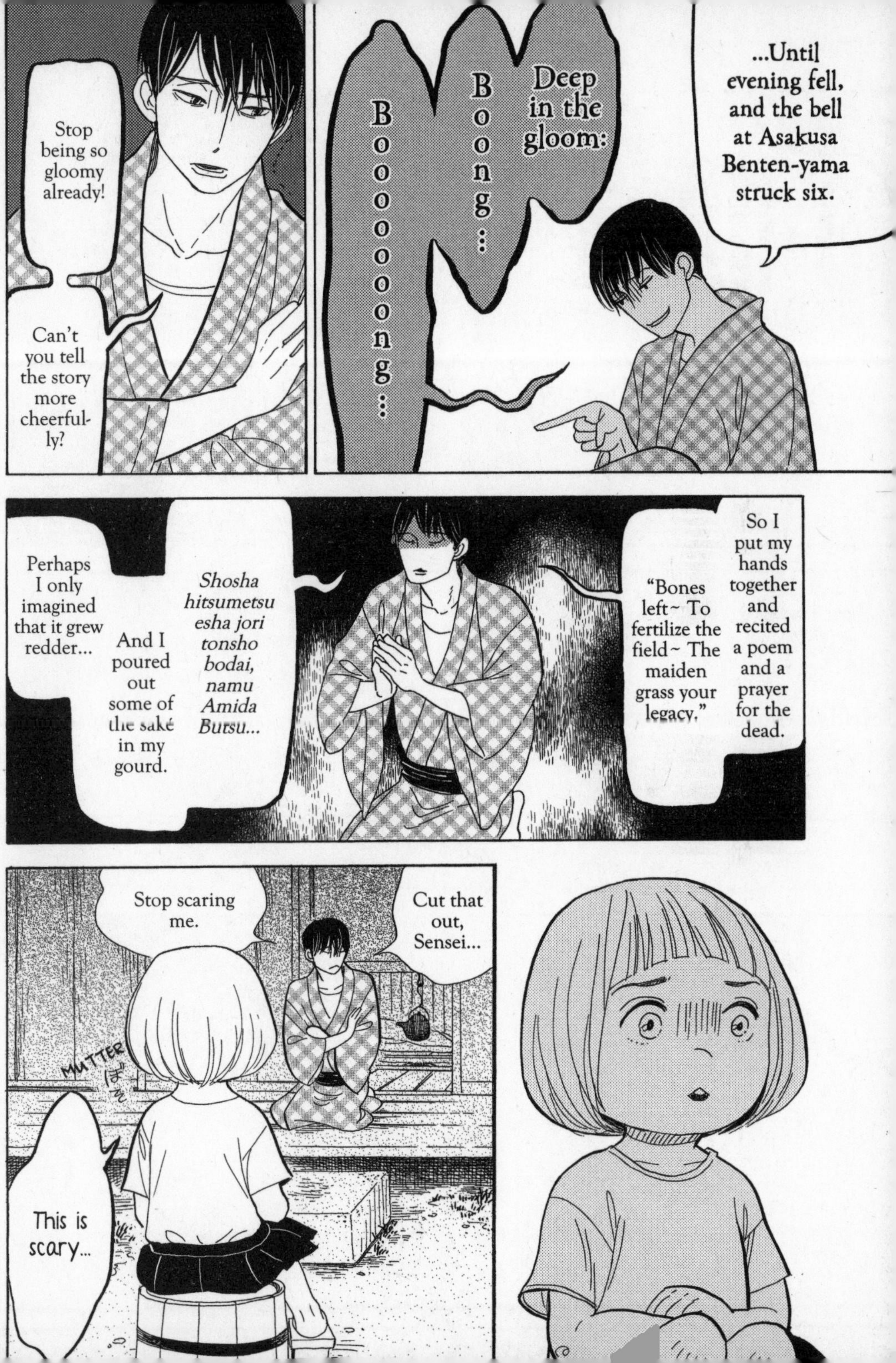
...Until evening fell, and the bell at Asakusa Benten-yama struck six.
Deep in the gloom:
Boong...
Booooooooong...
Stop being so gloomy already!
Can't you tell the story more cheerful-ly?
So I put my hands together and recited a poem and a prayer for the dead.
“Bones left~ To fertilize the field~ The maiden grass your legacy.”
Shosha hitsumetsu esha jori tonsho bodai, namu Amida Butsu...
And I poured out some of the saké in my gourd.
Perhaps I only imagined that it grew redder...
Cut that out, Sensei...
Stop scaring me.
MUTTER
This is scary...

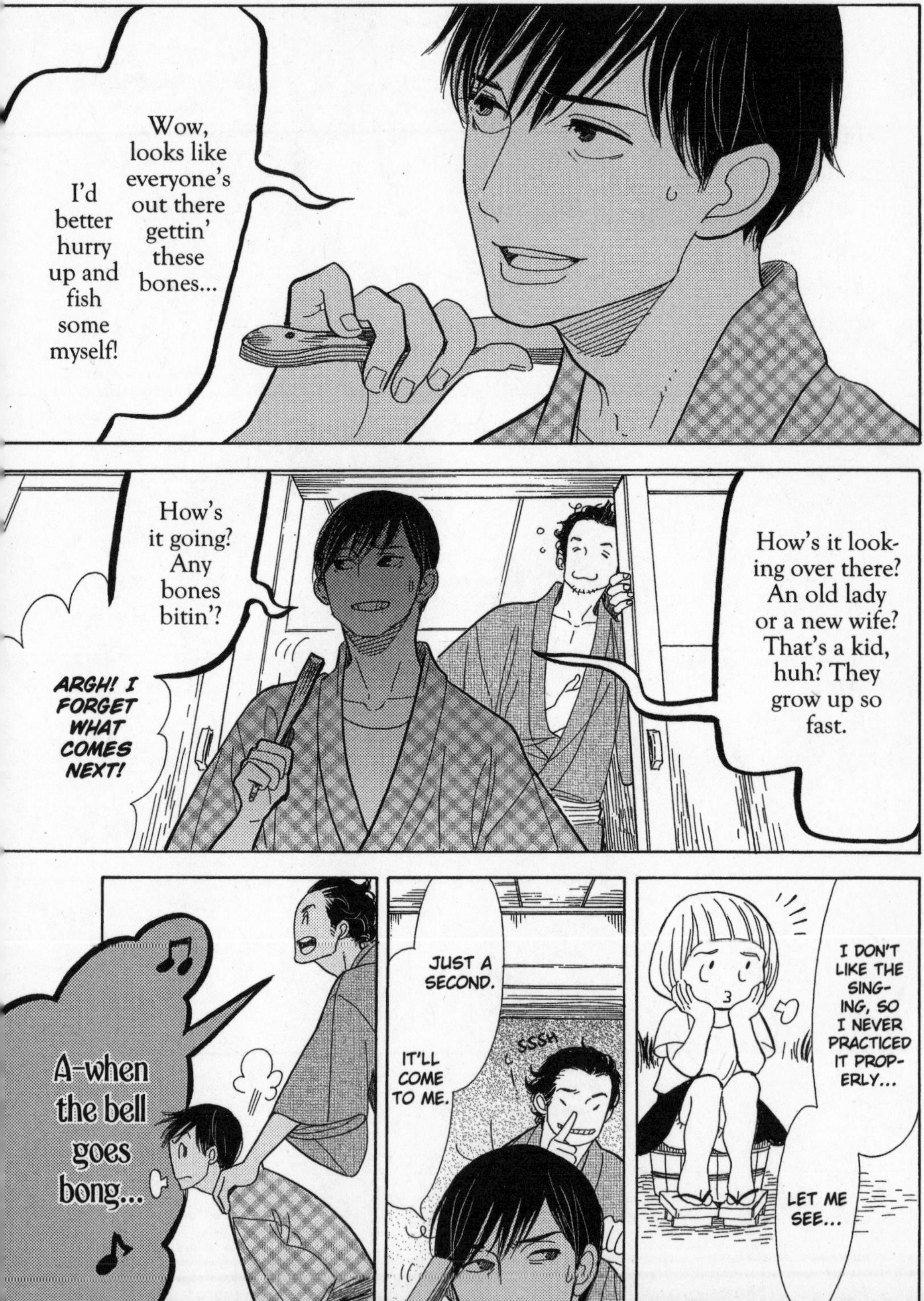
Wow, looks like everyone's out there gettin' these bones...
I'd better hurry up and fish some myself!
How's it looking over there? An old lady or a new wife? That's a kid, huh? They grow up so fast.
How's it going? Any bones bitin'?
ARGH! I FORGET WHAT COMES NEXT!
I DON'T LIKE THE SING-ING, SO I NEVER PRACTICED IT PROP-ERLY...
LET ME SEE...
JUST A SECOND.
SSSH
IT'LL COME TO ME.
A-when the bell goes bong...

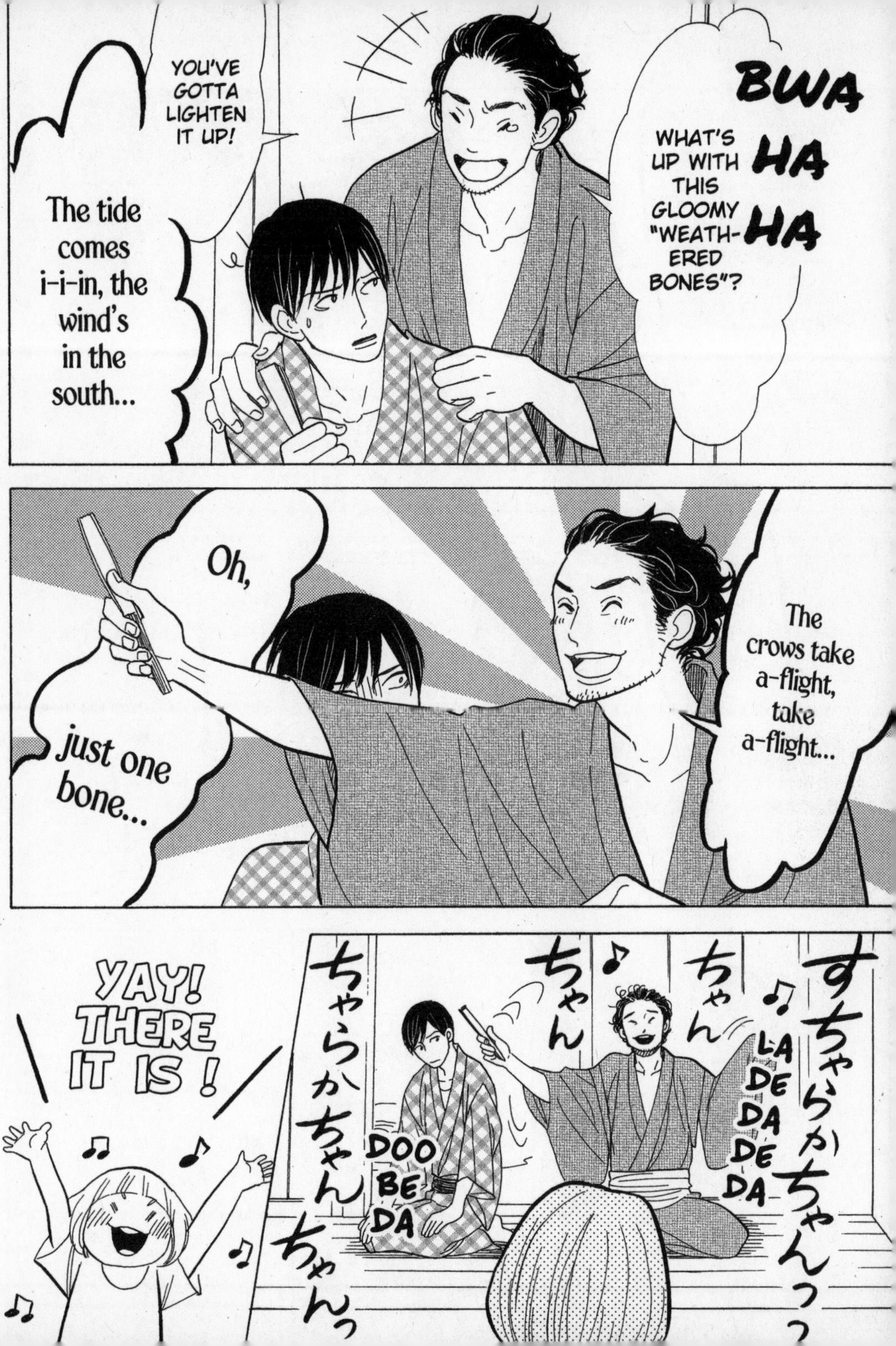
BWA HA HA
WHAT'S UP WITH THIS GLOOMY "WEATHERED BONES"?
YOU'VE GOTTA LIGHTEN IT UP!
The tide comes i-i-in, the wind's in the south...
The crows take a-flight, take a-flight...
Oh,
just one bone...
すちゃらかちゃんっっ
LA DE DA DE DA
ちゃん
ちゃん
ちゃらかちゃんちゃんっ
DOO BE DA
YAY! THERE IT IS!

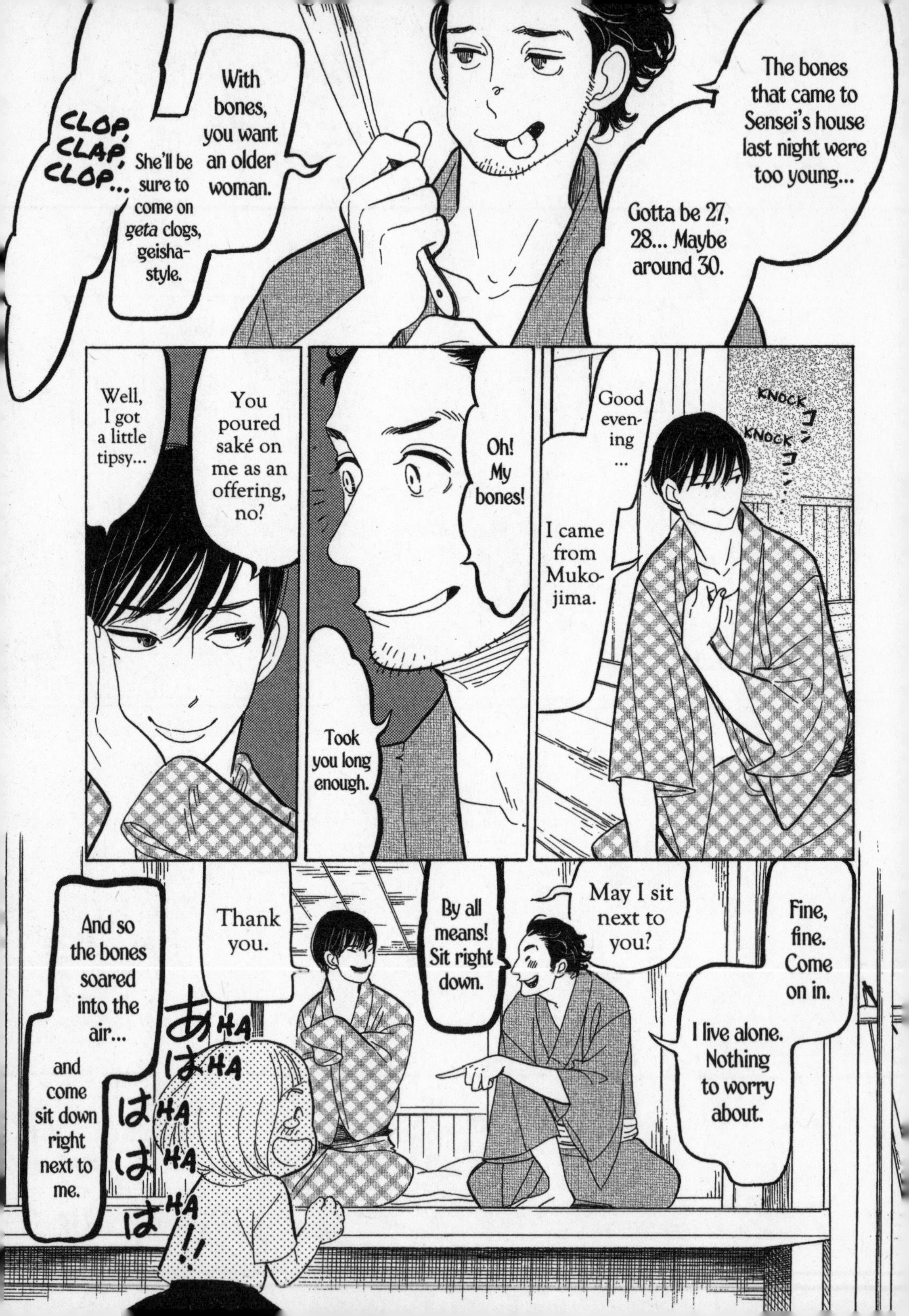
The bones that came to Sensei's house last night were too young...
Gotta be 27, 28... Maybe around 30.
With bones, you want an older woman.
She'll be sure to come on *geta* clogs, geisha-style.
CLOP, CLAP, CLOP...
KNOCK コン KNOCK コン...
Good evening...
I came from Mukojima.
Oh! My bones!
Took you long enough.
You poured saké on me as an offering, no?
Well, I got a little tipsy...
Fine, fine. Come on in.
I live alone. Nothing to worry about.
May I sit next to you?
By all means! Sit right down.
Thank you.
And so the bones soared into the air...
and come sit down right next to me.
あHA はHA はHA はHA!!

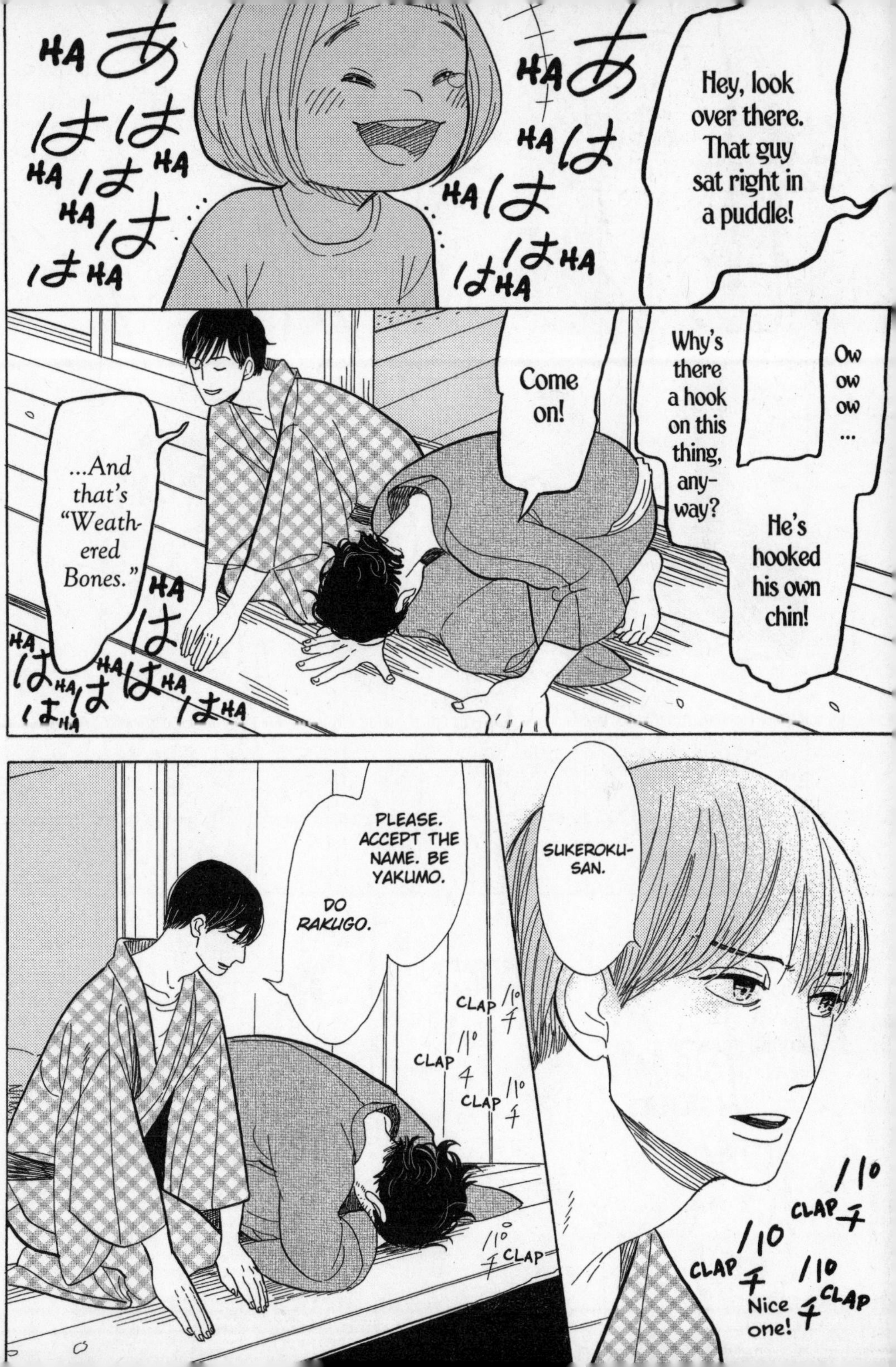
Hey, look over there. That guy sat right in a puddle!
あははははは HA HA HA HA HA HA
あはははは HA HA HA HA HA HA
Ow ow ow ...
He's hooked his own chin!
Why's there a hook on this thing, anyway?
Come on!
...And that's "Weathered Bones."
はははははは HA HA HA HA HA HA HA
SUKEROKU-SAN.
CLAP CLAP CLAP
Nice one!
PLEASE. ACCEPT THE NAME. BE YAKUMO.
DO RAKUGO.
CLAP CLAP CLAP CLAP

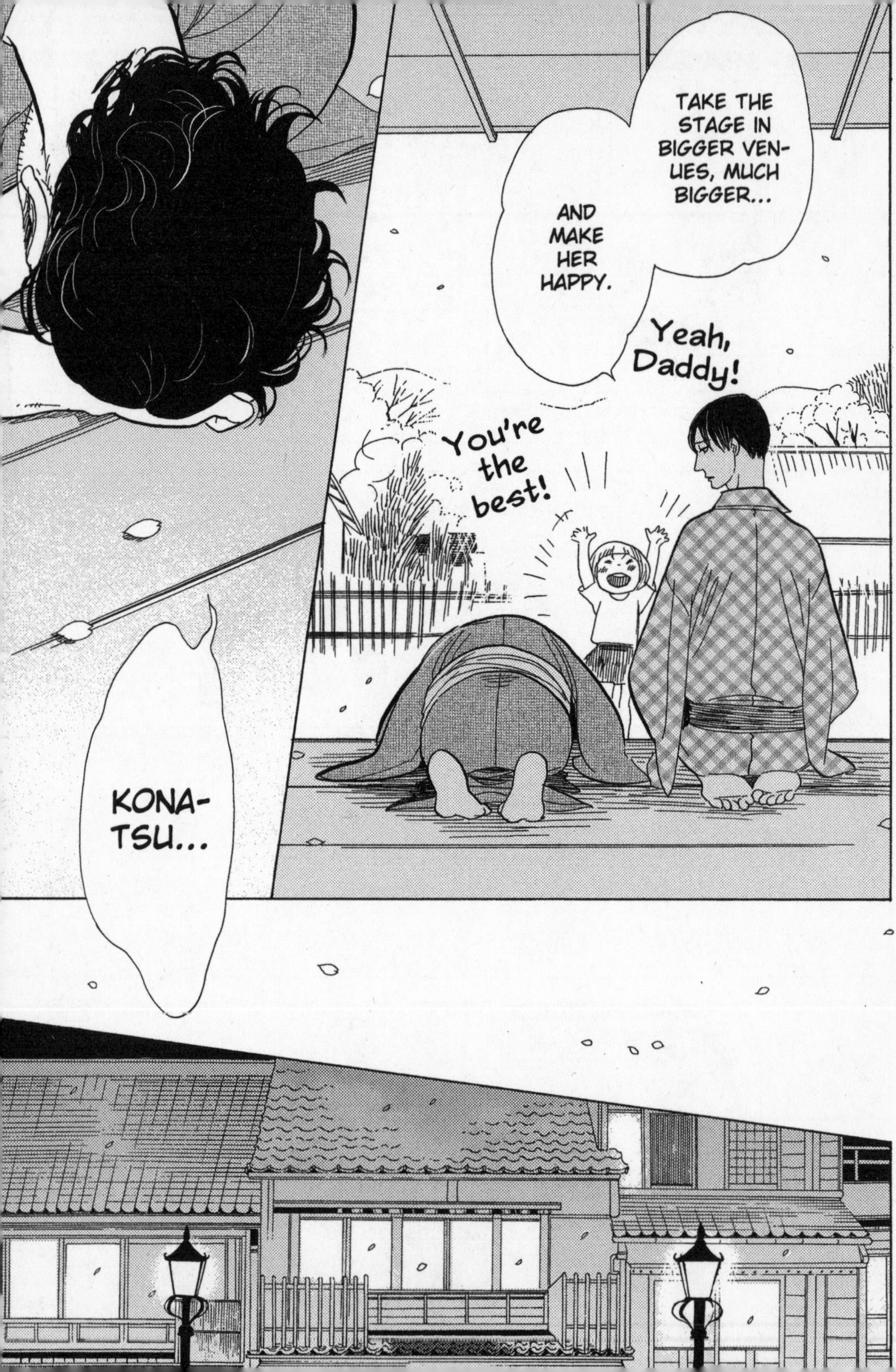
TAKE THE STAGE IN BIGGER VEN-UES, MUCH BIGGER...
AND MAKE HER HAPPY.
Yeah, Daddy!
You're the best!
KONA-TSU...

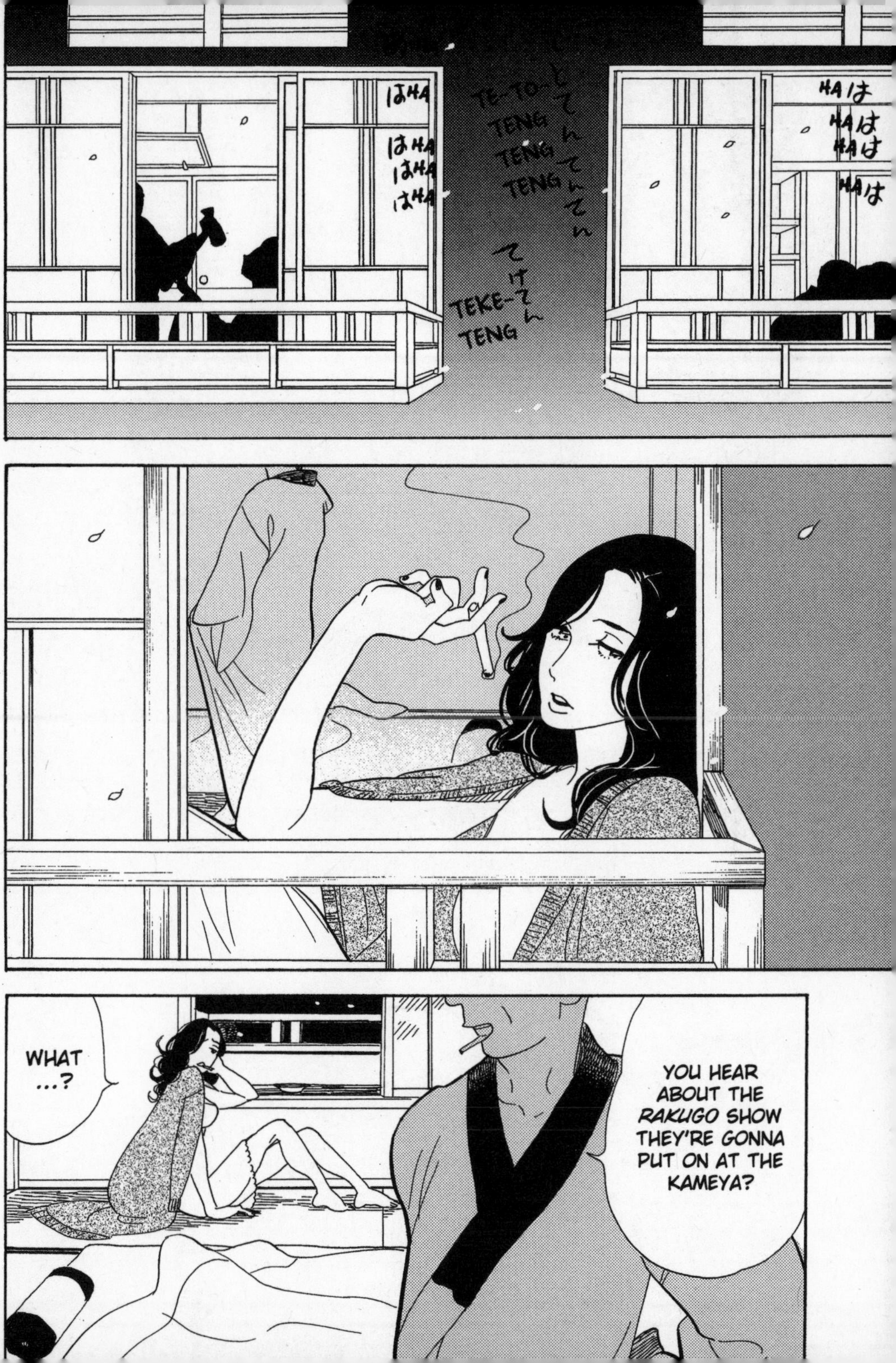
HA は
HA は
HA は
HA は
TE-TO-TENG TENG TENG
てとてんてんてん
TEKE-TENG
てけてん
は HA
は HA
は HA
は HA
YOU HEAR ABOUT THE *RAKUGO* SHOW THEY'RE GONNA PUT ON AT THE KAMEYA?
WHAT ...?

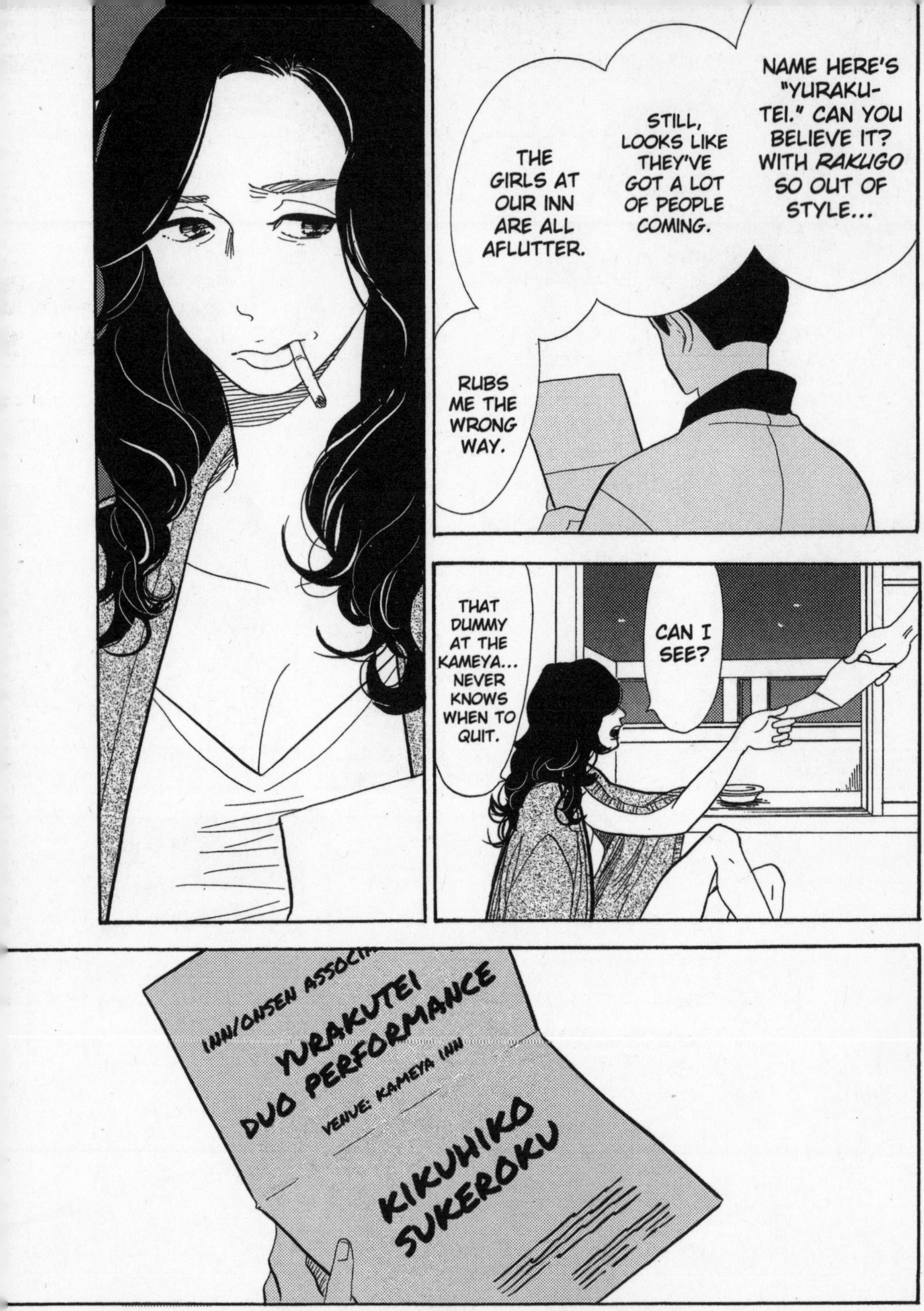
NAME HERE'S "YURAKU-TEI." CAN YOU BELIEVE IT? WITH *RAKUGO* SO OUT OF STYLE...
STILL, LOOKS LIKE THEY'VE GOT A LOT OF PEOPLE COMING.
THE GIRLS AT OUR INN ARE ALL AFLUTTER.
RUBS ME THE WRONG WAY.
CAN I SEE?
THAT DUMMY AT THE KAMEYA... NEVER KNOWS WHEN TO QUIT.
INN/ONSEN ASSOCI
YURAKUTEI DUO PERFORMANCE
VENUE: KAMEYA INN
KIKUHIKO SUKEROKU

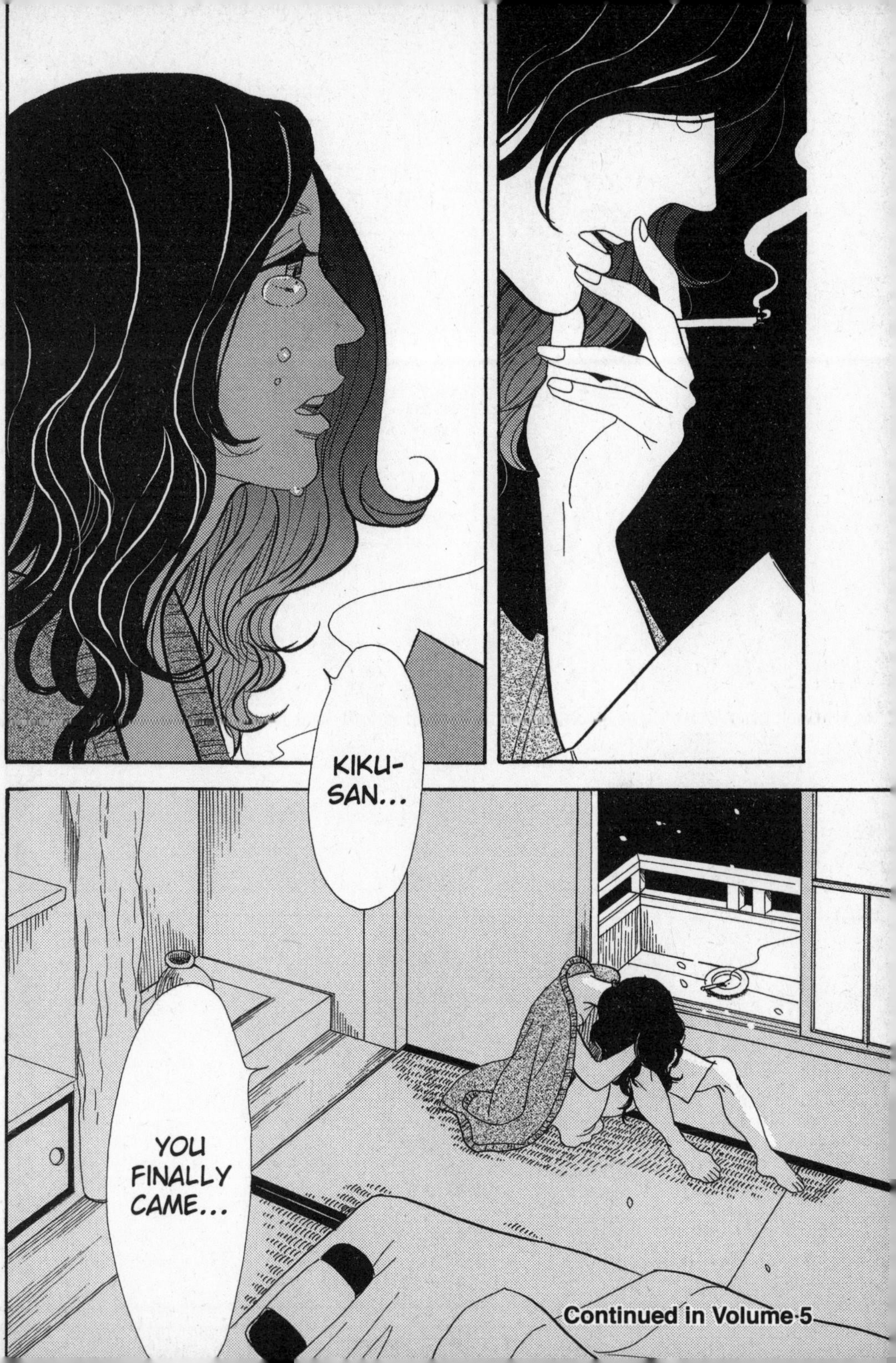
KIKU-SAN...
YOU FINALLY CAME...
Continued in Volume 5

Sources

Rakugo: Showa no Meijin Ankoru 1: Kokintei Shincho
(Rakugo: Showa Masters, Encore, vol. 1: Shincho Kokintei). Shogakukan
Rakugo Tokusen (Special Rakugo Selection), vol. 1/Chikuma BunKonatsu. Chikuma Shobo
Rakugo Hyakusen: Aki (One Hundred Rakugo Selections: Autumn)/
Chikuma BunKonatsu: Chikuma Shobo

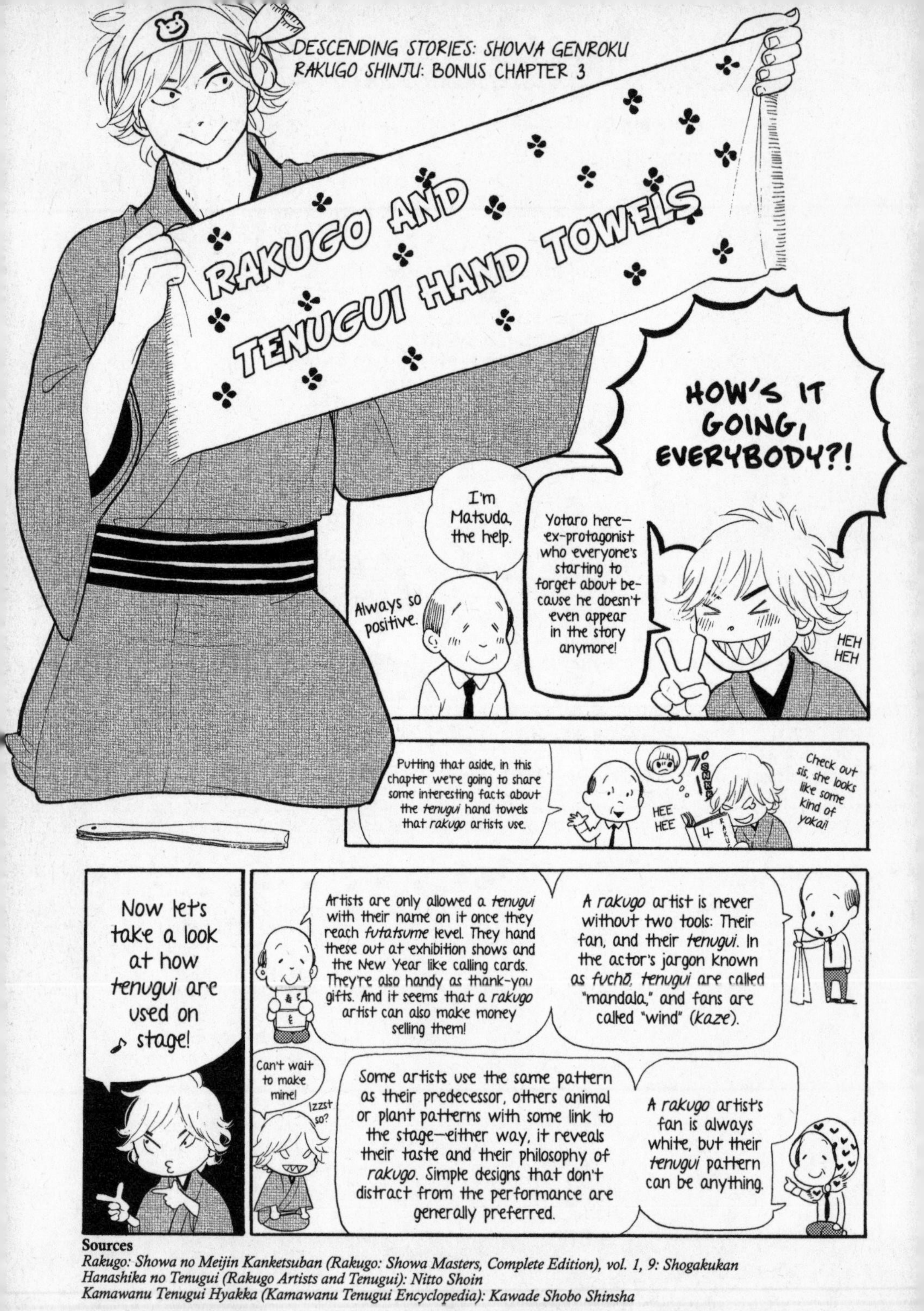
DESCENDING STORIES: SHOWA GENROKU RAKUGO SHINJU: BONUS CHAPTER 3
RAKUGO AND TENUGUI HAND TOWELS
HOW'S IT GOING, EVERYBODY?!
Yotaro here—ex-protagonist who everyone's starting to forget about because he doesn't even appear in the story anymore!
HEH HEH
I'm Matsuda, the help.
Always so positive.
Check out sis, she looks like some kind of yokai!
SNRK
HEE HEE
Putting that aside, in this chapter we're going to share some interesting facts about the *tenugui* hand towels that *rakugo* artists use.
A *rakugo* artist is never without two tools: Their fan, and their *tenugui*. In the actor's jargon known as *fuchō*, *tenugui* are called "mandala," and fans are called "wind" (*kaze*).
Artists are only allowed a *tenugui* with their name on it once they reach *futatsume* level. They hand these out at exhibition shows and the New Year like calling cards. They're also handy as thank-you gifts. And it seems that a *rakugo* artist can also make money selling them!
A *rakugo* artist's fan is always white, but their *tenugui* pattern can be anything.
Some artists use the same pattern as their predecessor, others animal or plant patterns with some link to the stage—either way, it reveals their taste and their philosophy of *rakugo*. Simple designs that don't distract from the performance are generally preferred.
Izzst so?
Can't wait to make mine!
Now let's take a look at how *tenugui* are used on stage!

Sources

Rakugo: Showa no Meijin Kanketsuban (Rakugo: Showa Masters, Complete Edition), vol. 1, 9: Shogakukan
Hanashika no Tenugui (Rakugo Artists and Tenugui): Nitto Shoin
Kamawanu Tenugui Hyakka (Kamawanu Tenugui Encyclopedia): Kawade Shobo Shinsha

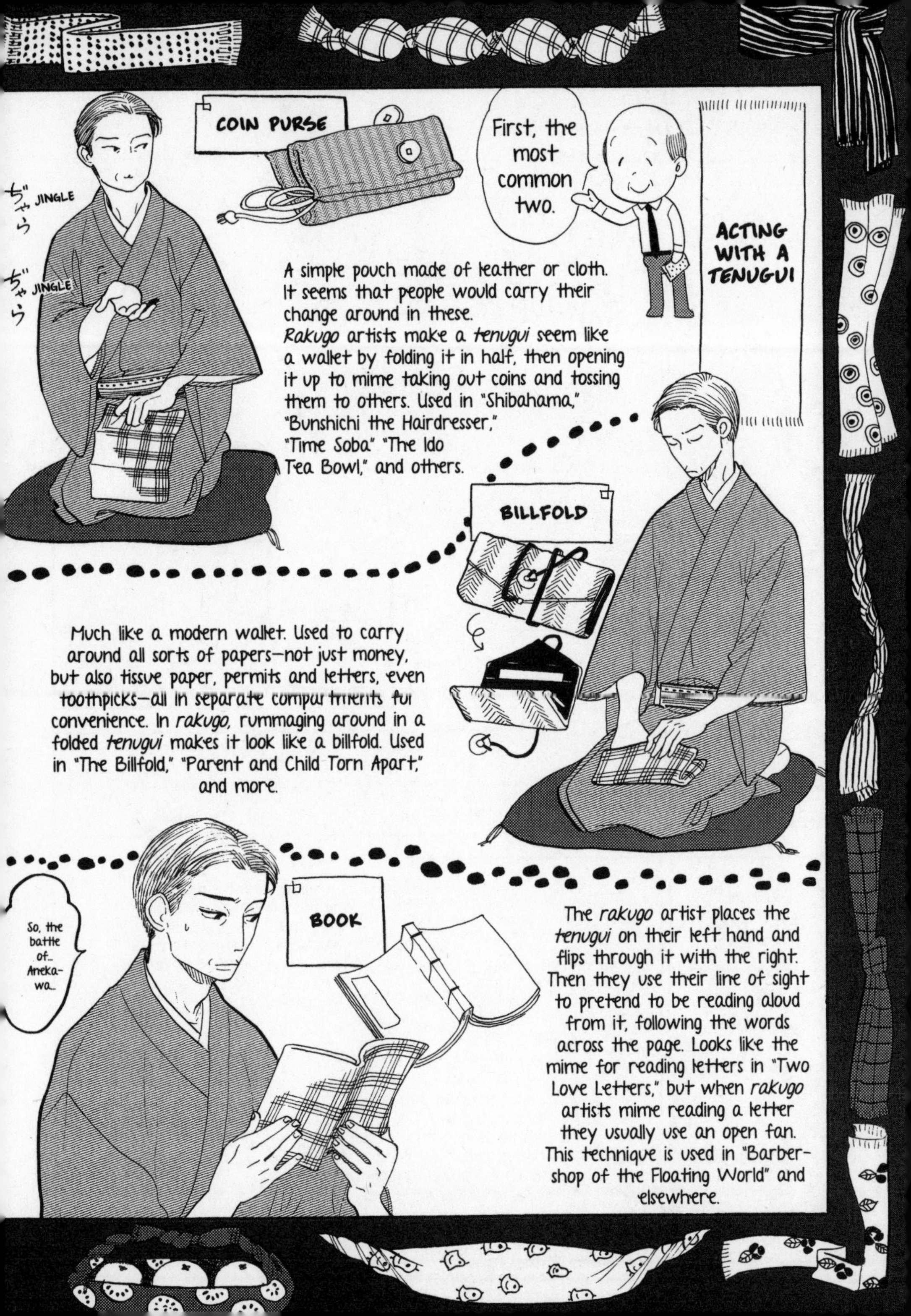
ACTING WITH A TENUGUI
First, the most common two.
COIN PURSE
ちゃら JINGLE
ぢゃら JINGLE
A simple pouch made of leather or cloth. It seems that people would carry their change around in these.
Rakugo artists make a *tenugui* seem like a wallet by folding it in half, then opening it up to mime taking out coins and tossing them to others. Used in "Shibahama," "Bunshichi the Hairdresser," "Time Soba" "The Ido Tea Bowl," and others.
BILLFOLD
Much like a modern wallet. Used to carry around all sorts of papers—not just money, but also tissue paper, permits and letters, even toothpicks—all in separate compartments for convenience. In *rakugo,* rummaging around in a folded *tenugui* makes it look like a billfold. Used in "The Billfold," "Parent and Child Torn Apart," and more.
BOOK
The *rakugo* artist places the *tenugui* on their left hand and flips through it with the right. Then they use their line of sight to pretend to be reading aloud from it, following the words across the page. Looks like the mime for reading letters in "Two Love Letters," but when *rakugo* artists mime reading a letter they usually use an open fan. This technique is used in "Barbershop of the Floating World" and elsewhere.
So, the battle of... Anekawa...

OTHER TENUGUI MIMES

DIG ぐり DIG ぐりぐり

Tobacco case

"Long and Short," "Everyday Hakama," and many more.

GRRR ぐーッ

Stran- gling

"Two Butterflies"

ぐえーっ URKKK

Hang- ing

"Yumehachi"

Sake bottle

♪

"Weathered Bones"

A beautiful mime that includes imitation of a woman's gestures.

Sewing

"Bag of Patience," "Tadanobu the Cat"

SWEATY YOTA-CHAN

I've written quite a lot here, but the truth is that the *tenugui* isn't used as often in *rakugo* as the fan. Making the audience imagine scenes and situations without props is part of the charm of *rakugo*, so not using the *tenugui* much is considered sophisticated.

MOST OF ALL, FOR WIPING SWEAT

More than miming, the *tenugui* is useful for wiping sweat. The stage gets hot easily. It's unsightly to be dripping with sweat, especially during winter. The best *rakugo* artists can wipe their own brow with just the right timing to make it seem like one of their characters are doing it.

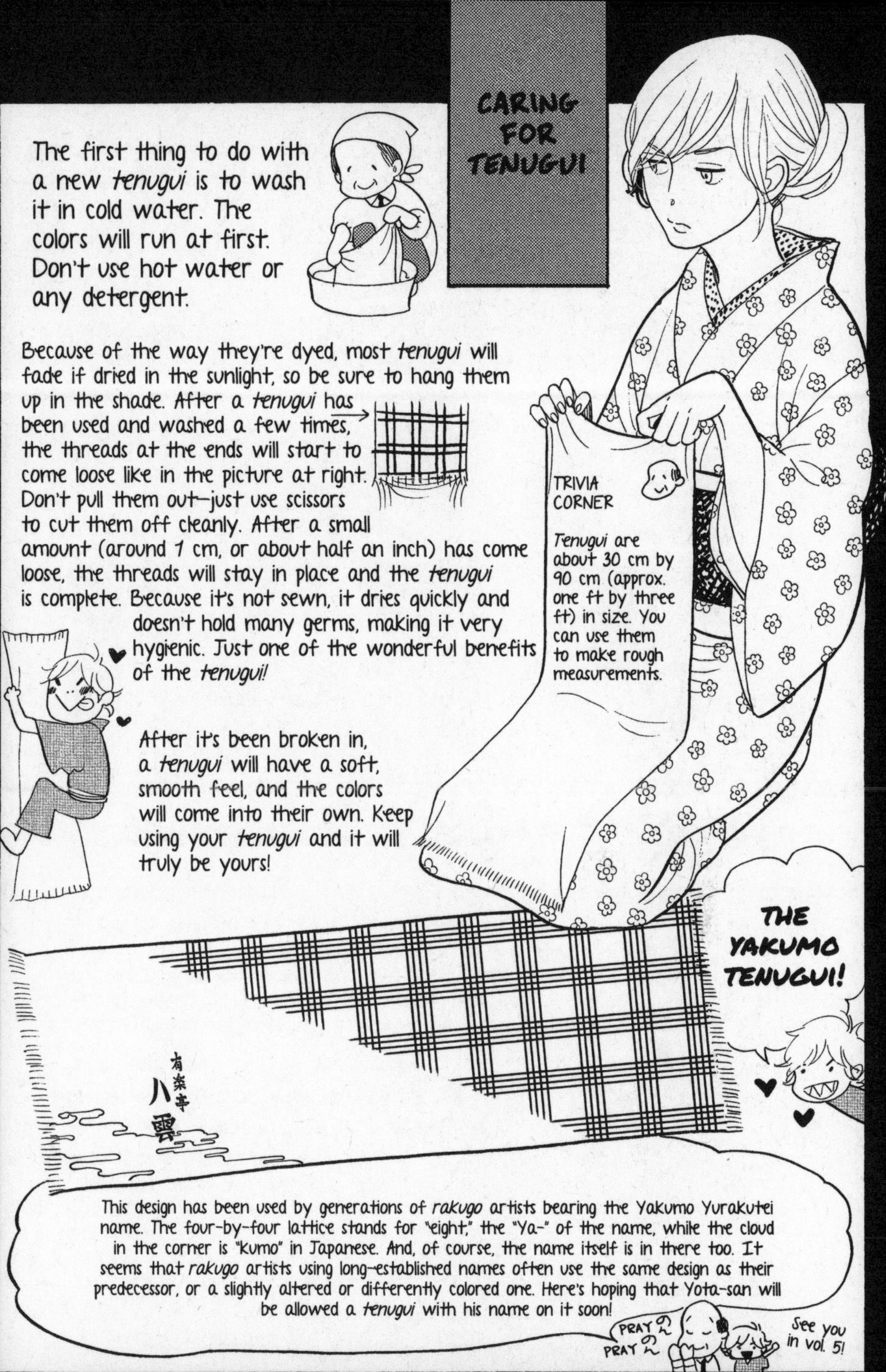
CARING FOR TENUGUI
The first thing to do with a new *tenugui* is to wash it in cold water. The colors will run at first. Don't use hot water or any detergent.
Because of the way they're dyed, most *tenugui* will fade if dried in the sunlight, so be sure to hang them up in the shade. After a *tenugui* has been used and washed a few times, the threads at the ends will start to come loose like in the picture at right. Don't pull them out—just use scissors to cut them off cleanly. After a small amount (around 1 cm, or about half an inch) has come loose, the threads will stay in place and the *tenugui* is complete. Because it's not sewn, it dries quickly and doesn't hold many germs, making it very hygienic. Just one of the wonderful benefits of the *tenugui*!
TRIVIA CORNER
Tenugui are about 30 cm by 90 cm (approx. one ft by three ft) in size. You can use them to make rough measurements.
After it's been broken in, a *tenugui* will have a soft, smooth feel, and the colors will come into their own. Keep using your *tenugui* and it will truly be yours!
THE YAKUMO TENUGUI!
有楽亭
八雲
This design has been used by generations of *rakugo* artists bearing the Yakumo Yurakutei name. The four-by-four lattice stands for "eight," the "Ya-" of the name, while the cloud in the corner is "kumo" in Japanese. And, of course, the name itself is in there too. It seems that *rakugo* artists using long-established names often use the same design as their predecessor, or a slightly altered or differently colored one. Here's hoping that Yota-san will be allowed a *tenugui* with his name on it soon!
PRAY のん
PRAY のん
See you in vol. 5!

THANKS FOR HELP WITH THE TENUGUI
H. and everyone at the dyers
Sawa Sasaraku for advice on the design
Tachibana Umon for yose lettering
Matsumoto, Itan Editing Team
Designers and printers
                              THANK YOU!

And thanks to you, too, for reading!

Haruko Kumota

USE AS A BOOK COVER!

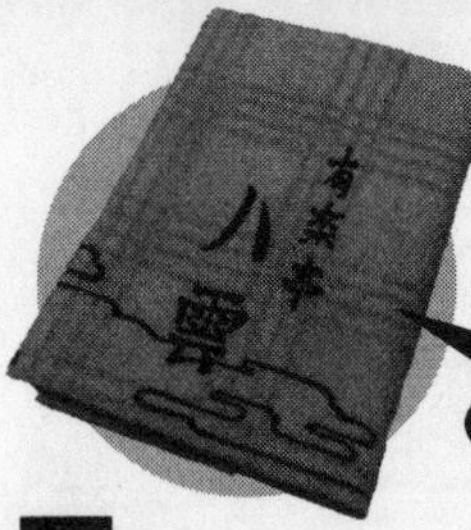

MAKING A CHUSEN-DYED TENUGUI

One of the traditional crafts supporting the world of *rakugo* from the shadows is *chusen*-dyed *tenugui*. *Chusen* dying is an old technique in which the dye is allowed to seep through the material. *Tenugui* made this way are highly absorbent and breathable—simple and unpretentious, but the more you use them, the more attached you become to them. Here's a rundown of the entire process of making the Yakumo Yurakutei *tenugui* we had made for the special (Japanese-only) edition of this book.

CREATING THE DESIGN

Choose pattern, placing, colors, and so on.

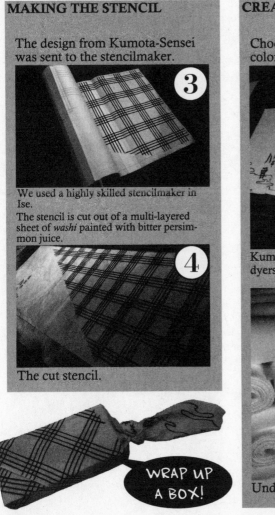

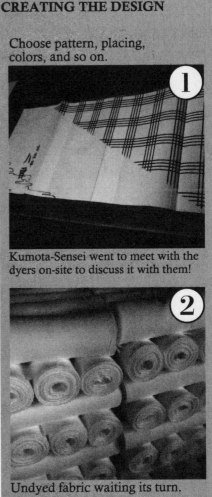

1

Kumota-Sensei went to meet with the dyers on-site to discuss it with them!

2

Undyed fabric waiting its turn.

MAKING THE STENCIL

The design from Kumota-Sensei was sent to the stencilmaker.

3

We used a highly skilled stencilmaker in Ise.
The stencil is cut out of a multi-layered sheet of *washi* painted with bitter persimmon juice.

4

The cut stencil.

WRAP UP A BOX!

WRAP UP TWO CANS OF BEER!

DYEING THE FABRIC

The design from Kumota-Sensei was sent to the stencilmaker.

A sheet of fabric is placed on top and glue applied.

The parts where the glue is will remain undyed.

The sheet of fabric is peeled off and glue is applied. Repeat for every sheet.

Sheets of fabric with glue applied have sawdust sprinkled on their front surface.

This fixes the glue.

It's finally time for the *chusen* dyeing itself!

The fabric is placed in the dyeing bed and dye is added.

A compressor underneath is used to suck the dye through so that it seeps into the fabric.

The fabric is now dyed!

FINISHING UP

The fabric is washed to remove the dye.

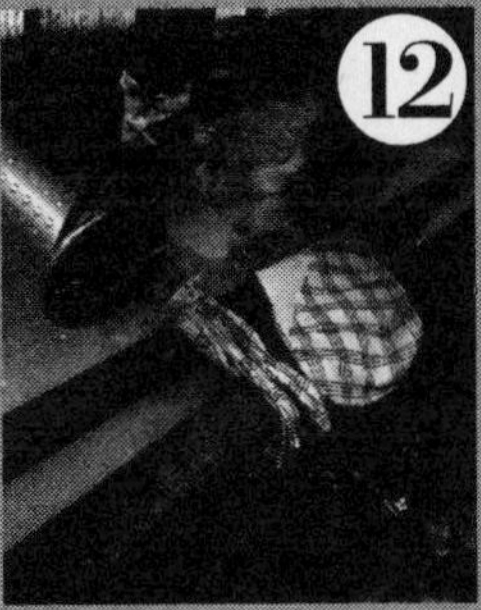

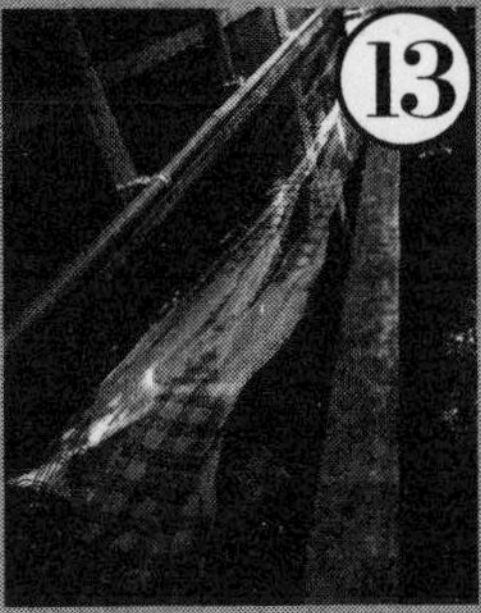

All clean!

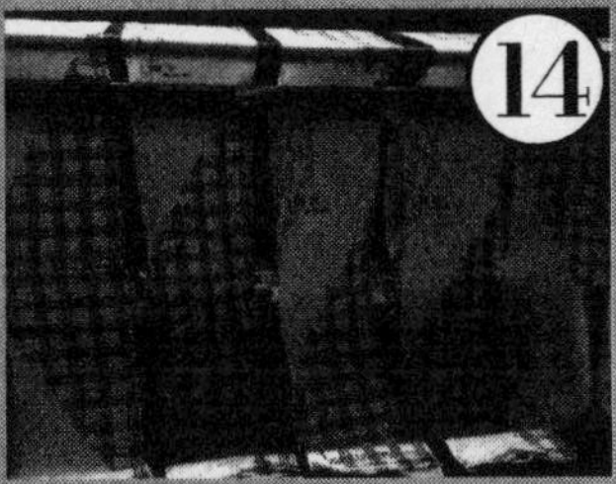

Rollers are used to smooth and dry the sheets of fabric.

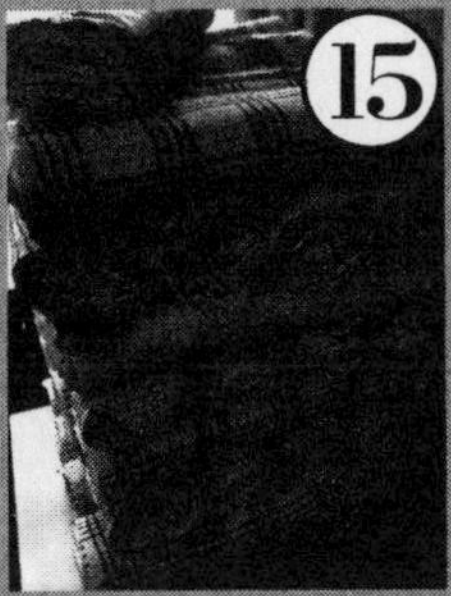

The sheets are rolled up as they dry.

Each sheet is carefully rolled up and prepared for trimming.

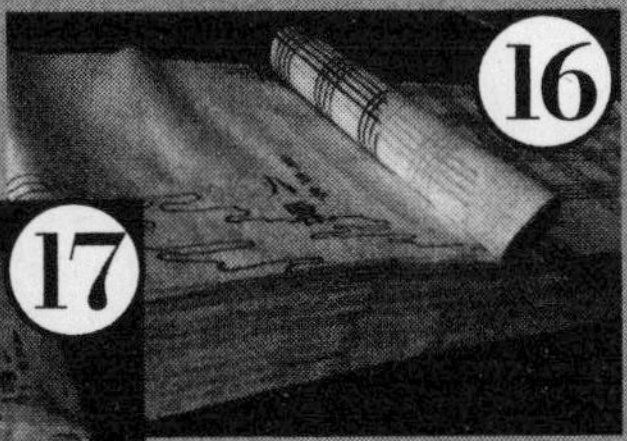

Trimming is now complete.

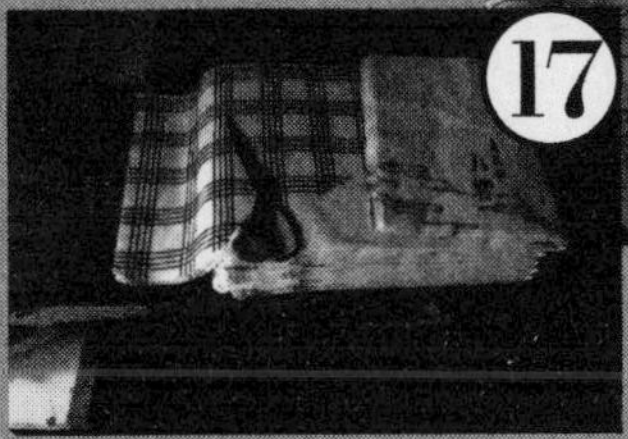

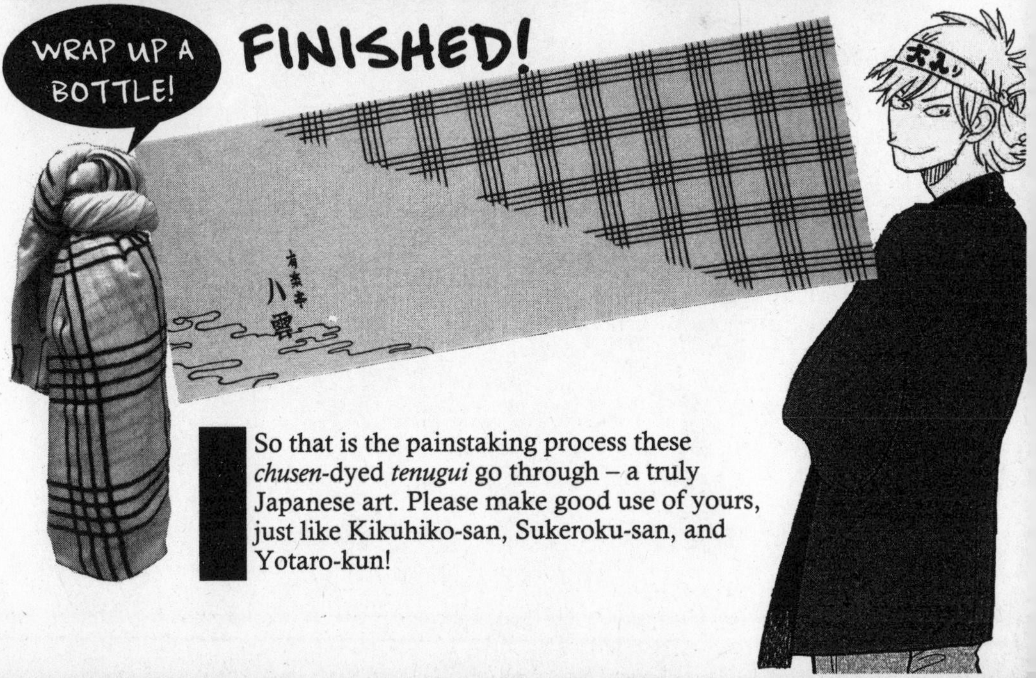
WRAP UP A BOTTLE!
FINISHED!
有楽亭
八雲

So that is the painstaking process these *chusen*-dyed *tenugui* go through – a truly Japanese art. Please make good use of yours, just like Kikuhiko-san, Sukeroku-san, and Yotaro-kun!

DESCENDING STORIES

SHOWA GENROKU RAKUGO SHINJU

Translation Notes

Senryū, page 58
A *senryū* is a satirical or humorous poem with a mora count of 5-7-5—the same form as a haiku. What Yakumo VII recites here would usually be called a *kyōka*, which is similar but in 5-7-5-7-7 form, the same as a *tanka*.

A few years into Taisho, page 65
The Taisho period lasted from 1912 to 1926, corresponding to the reign of Emperor Taisho. It is generally viewed as a brief period of increasing liberalism and democracy between the society-wide upheaval of the preceding Meiji period (1868–1912) and the nationalism and militarism of the early Showa period which followed.

Funeral Service, page 72
Literally "Funeral service (*sōgi*) and farewell ceremony (*kokubetsushiki*)." These are technically considered separate things, although usually held together as in this case.

Head mourner, page 73
The head or chief mourner (*moshu*) is the "host" of the funeral, usually representing the family. Traditionally, a surviving spouse, parent, or sibling acts as head mourner.

I've been crying since the wake, page 73
The wake or vigil (*tsuya*) is held the night before the funeral. Friends and relatives gather around the deceased to stay awake all night sharing stories about them.

"*Itako,*" page 76
Itako-bushi, a folk song dating back to the Edo period. The name evokes the renowned pleasure quarters of Itako in Hitachi Province (modern-day Ibaraki Prefecture).

Vinegar tofu, page 118
Kikuhiko is reciting the end of "Vinegar Tofu." In this story, a group of young men trick the unpopular young master of the Iseya department store into eating rotten tofu by asking if he can identify a mysterious imported delicacy they have obtained. Unwilling to admit that he does not know, he declares that it is "vinegar tofu," and, with great difficulty, forces a piece down. The others urge him to eat more, but he demurs, insisting that vinegar tofu is "best kept to one bite."

Going out to Mukojima, page 133
A picturesque spot on the Sumida River in Edo. Popular among courtesans as a destination for an outing since the Edo period, starting in the Meiji period it became known for its own pleasure quarters.

The bell at Asakusa Benten-yama, page 134
"Benten-yama" refers to the shrine to Benten on a small hill at Senso-ji temple in Asakusa, home to one of Edo's official time-keeping bells.

Shosha hitsumetsu esha jori tonsho bodai, namu Amida Butsu, page 134
A quotation from the Nirvana sutra ("Those who are born must die, those who meet will surely be parted") combined with a prayer for a deceased individual's swift passage to Nirvana and homage to Amida Buddha.

Some kind of *yokai*, page 145
Yokai is a term broadly used to describe demons, ogres, and all sorts of supernatural sorts. Here, Yotaro thinks young Konatsu looks like a *kappa*, a water-dwelling *yokai* often pictured with a similar bowl-cut hairstyle.

RAKUGO STORIES IN THIS VOLUME:

Ko Wakare (子別れ) - Parent and Child Torn Apart (page 58)
Shinigami (死神) - The God of Death (page 81)
Nozarashi (野ざらし) - The Weathered Bones (page 93)
Sudoufu (酢豆腐) - Vinegar Tofu (page 118)

It is said that the roots of the current *Rakugo Kyokai Association* can be traced to the Tokyo *Rakugo Kyokai* formed thanks to the efforts of Ryutei Saraku V following the 1923 Great Kanto Earthquake. Yanagiya Kosan IV was later appointed its chairman and established it anew as the *Rakugo Kyokai Association*. It received permission to become an incorporated association with the Agency for Cultural Affairs acting as its competent authority in 1977, and its stated goal was to "advance the spread of popular performing arts with a focus on classical *rakugo*, contributing to the cultural development of our country in the process." It later became the general incorporated association it is today in 2012. It conducts performances in four theatres (*yose*) in Tokyo, as well as in halls, assembly spaces, schools, and more around the country.

For an overview of the *Rakugo Kyokai* Association, please visit: http://rakugo-kyokai.jp/summary/

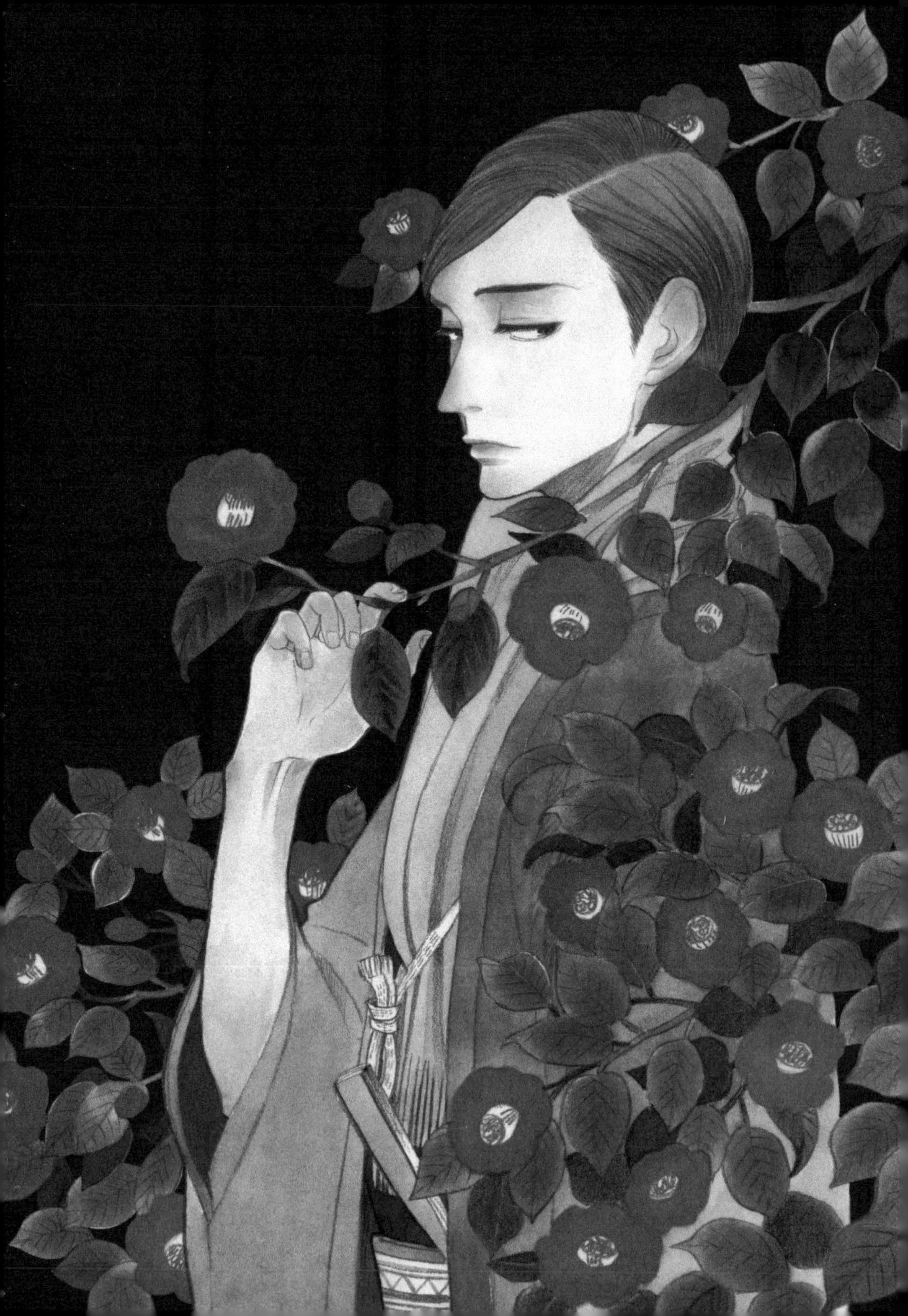

The Black Museum The Ghost and the Lady

By Kazuhiro Fujita

Deep in Scotland Yard in London sits an evidence room dedicated to the greatest mysteries of British history. In this "Black Museum" sits a misshapen hunk of lead—two bullets fused together—the key to a wartime encounter between Florence Nightingale, the mother of modern nursing, and a supernatural Man in Grey. This story is unknown to most scholars of history, but a special guest of the museum will tell the tale of The Ghost and the Lady...

Praise for Kazuhiro Fujita's *Ushio and Tora*

"A charming revival that combines a classic look with modern depth and pacing... **Essential viewing both for curmudgeons and new fans alike.**" — Anime News Network

"**GREAT!** The first episode of Ushio and Tora captures the essence of '90s anime." — IGN

THE STORY SO FAR

YOTARO'S ODYSSEY

Yotaro falls in love with Yakumo Yurakutei's *rakugo* when he hears it in prison. Once free, he becomes Yakumo's apprentice and is soon made a *zenza*. As his appreciation for *rakugo* grows, the incredible *rakugo* of the late Sukeroku takes hold of him and he commits an unthinkable faux pas at a solo recital by his teacher. Facing expulsion, Yotaro begs forgiveness. Yakumo relents, but extracts three promises from his student. Then, he begins to tell the tale of his own promise with Sukeroku...

YAKUMO AND SUKEROKU

Yakumo Yurakutei VII takes two apprentices on the same day: Kikuhiko and Hatsutaro. Complete opposites in personality, they grow together under the tutelage of their shisho (master).

CAST OF CHARACTERS

Yakumo and Sukeroku

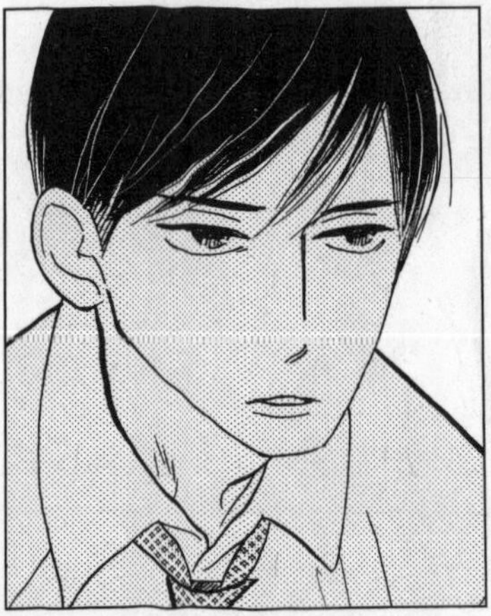

Kikuhiko
Yakumo Yurakutei VIII's stage name during his *futatsume* days. Frustrated by the artistic plateau he feels himself to be on.

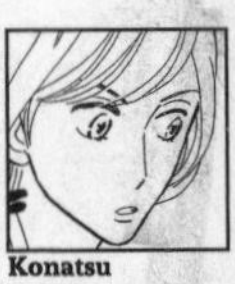

Konatsu
Sukeroku's only daughter, taken in by Yakumo.

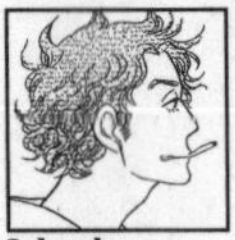

Sukeroku Yurakutei
Legendary *rakugo* artist hailed as a genius before his untimely death.

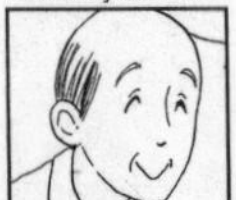

Matsuda-san
Faithful servant and driver of Yakumo VIII and Yakumo VII before him.

Yotaro's Odyssey

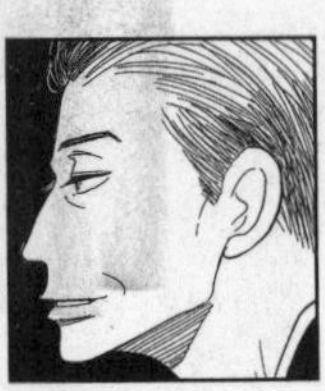

Yakumo Yurakutei VIII
Renowned as the Showa period's last great master of *rakugo*.

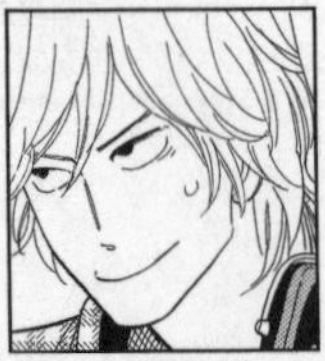

Yotaro (Kyoji)
Reformed street tough who became Yakumo's apprentice.

DESCENDING STORIES

SHOWA
GENROKU
RAKUGO
SHINJU

Haruko Kumota